STUDIES IN HISTORY, ECONOMICS AND PUBLIC LAW

EDITED BY THE FACULTY OF POLITICAL SCIENCE
OF COLUMBIA UNIVERSITY

Volume CXI]   [Number 2

Whole Number 249

LABOR DISPUTES AND THE PRESIDENT
OF THE UNITED STATES

BY

EDWARD BERMAN

AMS PRESS
NEW YORK

COLUMBIA UNIVERSITY
STUDIES IN THE
SOCIAL SCIENCES

249

The Series was formerly known as
Studies in History, Economics and Public Law.

Reprinted with the permission of Columbia University Press
From the edition of 1924, New York
First AMS EDITION published 1968
Manufactured in the United States of America

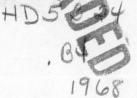
AMS PRESS, INC.
NEW YORK, N. Y. 10003

To

MY PARENTS

TO WHOSE KINDNESS, SYMPATHY AND GENEROSITY
I OWE MORE THAN I CAN EVER REPAY
THIS BOOK IS DEDICATED

INTRODUCTION

THE industrial unrest of the greater part of the nineteenth century manifested itself in occasional strikes, but these usually involved the workers in a single craft, situated in a single locality. Trade unions were largely localized and labor struggles were fought over limited areas. But, as the second half of the century progressed, national unions became more and more common, and with them came an enlargement of the scale of strikes, affecting, for example, many of the employees of a large railroad system, or the miners in a whole district. Thus the problem of strikes, which had hitherto been for the most part local, became district and even national.

With the coming of the twentieth century the struggles of labor became still more inclusive in the number of their participants and in the number of people whom they affected. Strikes of railroad workers or of miners on a district or a nation-wide scale now threatened hardship and inconvenience to great numbers of people, who were likely to find themselves without fuel or the other necessaries of life. Furthermore, they sometimes occasioned violence and disorder which could not be ignored. The problem, having thus become to a large extent a national one, required treatment by an agency having national influence and nation-wide powers.

Accordingly, toward the end of the last century and more and more frequently in the present one, the President of the United States is found using his influence and powers to prevent the suffering and discomfort which are caused by great strikes, and to suppress the disturbances which sometimes come in their wake. The great prestige of his office and the freedom and scope of its powers, have caused him to be especially well qualified for the difficult task of bringing industrial contestants to a peaceful settlement of the issues between them.

It is the purpose of this study to describe the activities of the President in connection with labor disputes, particularly those activities having to do with averting or ending strikes; to estimate their effectiveness and fairness; and, finally, to suggest the presidential program best suited to the prompt, effective, and just treatment of the problems which arise in connection with nation-wide strikes.

To this end the activities of each executive, in whose administration the problems here treated have arisen, are discussed chronologically, commencing with President Cleveland and the Pullman Strike of 1894. Though the principal purpose is to consider those activities by means of which the executive has attempted to avert or to end a particular strike, it will be necessary, for the sake of thoroughness and in order to trace the development of method, to consider some instances in which the part played by the President had another motive. For example, the use of troops, though generally having little to do with preventing or ending a strike, must be briefly considered because it has sometimes had that effect, and because it is one of the important activities of the executive in connection with labor disputes.

It should also be noted that there is no intention of discussing the part played by the President in connection with the broader problem of industrial unrest. The purpose here is to deal with his activities at the time of particular strikes, rather than with his efforts to promote industrial peace in general by aiding in the passage of mediation and arbitration laws or by calling industrial conferences, etc.

The information on which the present study is based has to a large extent come from official government documents. Wherever possible the reports of boards of arbitration or investigation have been relied upon as the most dependable and impartial authorities. When no such boards were appointed, information has been obtained from the reports of congressional committees investigating strikes, or from published testimony given before such committees. Reports of administrative officials, such as the Secretary of Labor and the Secretary of War, those of the U. S. Board of Mediation and Conciliation, and the publications of the U. S. Bureau of Labor Statistics, particularly the Monthly Labor Review, have also been consulted. Much information concerning specific demands of strikers and occurrences during strikes has come from journals published by labor unions, or by employers' associations. Finally newspapers, especially the New York Times, have been of inestimable value for the purpose of obtaining evidence as to dates, events, speeches of the President, and other matters not always available from official sources.

TABLE OF CONTENTS

PAGE

INTRODUCTION 7

CHAPTER I

PRESIDENT CLEVELAND, 1893–1897

1. The Pullman strike of 1894 13

CHAPTER II

PRESIDENT MCKINLEY, 1897–1901

1. The Coeur d'Alene Disturbance, 1899 36

CHAPTER III

PRESIDENT ROOSEVELT, 1901–1909

1. The Anthracite Strike of 1902 46
2. The Miners' Strike in Arizona, 1903 59
3. The Colorado Strike of 1903–1904 60
4. The Coal Strikes of 1906 62
5. The Goldfield Miners' Strike, 1907 64
6. The Threatened Wage Reduction on the Louisville and Nashville Railroad, 1908 70

CHAPTER IV

PRESIDENT WILSON, 1913–1917

1. The Threatened Strike of Conductors and Trainmen on the
   Eastern Railways, 1913 73
2. The Colorado Strike of 1913–1914 76
3. The Threatened Strike of Engineers and Firemen on the Western Railways, 1914 100
4. The Eastern Ohio Coal Strike, 1914–1915 105
5. The Threatened Railway Strike of 1916 and the Adamson Act. 106

PAGE

CHAPTER V

PRESIDENT WILSON, WAR-TIME ACTIVITIES

1. The President's Mediation Commission. 126
2. Miners' Wages and Strike Penalties 129
3. Railway Labor Disputes 130
4. The Shipbuilding Labor Adjustment Board 132
5. The National War Labor Board 137
   a. The Western Union Case 142
   b. The Bridgeport Case 146
   c. The Smith & Wesson Case 148
   d. The New York Harbor Strike, January, 1919 150
6. Conclusion 151

CHAPTER VI

PRESIDENT WILSON, 1919–1921

1. The Shopmen's Strike of 1919 154
2. The Sympathetic Railway Strike in the Southwest, 1919 . . . 164
3. The Steel Strike of 1919 166
4. The Bituminous Coal Strike of 1919 177
5. The Railway Labor Troubles of 1920 193
6. The Anthracite Wage Dispute of 1920 199
7. The Illinois Bituminous Strike of 1920 204
   Appendix: Use of Federal Troops in Labor Disputes, 1917–1921 207

CHAPTER VII

PRESIDENT HARDING, 1921–1923

1. The West Virginia Mine Disturbances of 1921 210
2. The Threatened Railway Strike of 1921 213
3. The Coal Strikes of 1922 214
4. The Railway Shopmen's Strike of 1922 226

CHAPTER VIII

CONCLUSION 248

BIBLIOGRAPHY 275

INDEX 281

CHAPTER I

PRESIDENT CLEVELAND, 1893-1897

I. THE PULLMAN STRIKE OF 1894

THE significance of the Pullman Strike lies not alone in the fact that it tied up the operation of the railways in more than half of the country, since strikes in the two decades preceding had had a similar effect. Its chief significance lies in the fact that the President, by obtaining an injunction to end the strike, inaugurated a precedent which was of serious import to labor, and the effects of which have made themselves more and more apparent ever since.

The cause of this industrial disturbance was comparatively unimportant. Pleading the decline in business due to the depression of 1893, the Pullman Palace Car Company put into effect a cut in wages in the fall of that year. The company, at its plant in Pullman, a suburb of Chicago, not only manufactured cars, but also kept in repair those cars which it leased to the railroads. The latter work was done according to contracts with the roads, prices for the work having been fixed in advance of 1893. In the manufacturing department, however, the company's business decreased considerably. But it based its wage reduction on conditions in this department and applied it to the contracting department as well. This action, added to the feeling on the part of the employees that their wages were too low to enable them to live decently, was the most important cause for dissatisfaction. Moreover, though the company had reduced the wages of its employees, it had not reduced the rents which they had to pay to the company for the use of its houses. Employees complained further that there were numerous unfair and oppressive shop conditions.[1]

In March, 1894, being dissatisfied with the situation described, large numbers of the employees of the company sought organization, and joined the American Railway Union. This body had been organized as an industrial union in Chicago in June, 1893, with the purpose of including all the workers connected with the railways, and had grown at the expense of the older railway brotherhoods, to the conservative trade-union methods of which it was opposed.[2] On May 7 and May 9 a committee of Pullman employees from all departments waited upon the management and urged that wages be restored to the level of the previous year. The company refused to grant any concession, claiming that business conditions did not justify a change. The committee was promised that none of its members would be discharged for coming to the management. On the next day, however, three of the committeemen were discharged for alleged lack of work.[3] That evening the local unions met and voted to strike at once.[4] On May 11 2500 men quit, leaving only about 600 at work. This number being insufficient to operate the plant, the company closed it down and did not reopen it until nearly three months later.[5]

From June 9 to June 26 the American Railway Union held its regular convention in Chicago. The strike at Pullman was frequently discussed and the delegates heard re-

[1] *Report of the U. S. Strike Commission*, Senate Executive Document No. 7, 3rd Sess., 53rd Cong., pp. xxxiii-xxxvi.

[2] *Ibid.*, pp. xxiii, xxv.

[3] The manager of the company, T. H. Wickes, asserted that they were not laid off because they were committeemen. *Ibid.*, p. 587.

[4] *Ibid.*, pp. xxxvii-xxxviii.

[5] *Ibid.*, p. 586.

ports from the strikers themselves. On June 15 the Union proposed to the Pullman Company, which had already refused arbitration on the ground that there was nothing to arbitrate, that the question of arbitration itself be submitted to a commission to decide if the issues were or were not arbitrable. The company, however, declined to receive any communication from the Union. On June 21 the convention, under instructions from the local unions, voted unanimously that members of the American Railway Union should stop handling Pullman cars on the railroads on June 26 unless the Pullman Company would consent to arbitration by that time. On the 22nd it sent another proposal for arbitration to the company, which again refused to receive it.[1]

On the same day the General Managers Association, an organization representing 24 railroads entering Chicago, whose purpose it was to handle managerial and labor problems as a unit, adopted the following resolution:

That we hereby declare it to be the lawful right and duty of said railway companies to protest against said boycotts; to resist the same in the interests of their existing contracts, and for the benefit of the travelling public, and that we will unitedly act to that end.[2]

The Association, beginning June 26, when the boycott started, directed and controlled the contest for the railways.

The readiness of the American Railway Union to act was perhaps due not only to its sympathy for the fellow unionists in Pullman, but also to the disturbed and apprehensive condition of the railroad employees because of wage reductions on the different lines, the practice of blacklisting, and the growth of the General Managers Association, which they

[1] *Report of the U. S. Strike Commission, op. cit.,* p. xxxix.
[2] *Ibid.,* p. xlii.

considered a menace to labor.[1] The boycott in a few days spread all over the central and western United States, and when it became apparent that the railways would refuse to detach Pullman cars, it developed into a strike, the employees refusing to work unless the trains were made up without the Pullmans.

On June 28, two days after the strike began, information came to the Postoffice Department at Washington that at several points on the Southern Pacific system the mails were completely obstructed, and that strikers refused to permit trains to which Pullman cars were attached to move over the lines. On receiving this information Attorney General Olney sent the following telegram to the United States district attorneys in California:

See that the passage of regular trains, carrying U. S. mails in the usual and ordinary way, as contemplated by the act of Congress and directed by the Postmaster General, is not obstructed. Procure warrants or any other available process from U. S. courts against any and all persons engaged in such obstruction, and direct the marshal to execute the same by such number of deputies or such posse as may be necessary.

On the same day and on the following days similar complaints came to Washington from all parts of the West, sometimes accompanied by charges of the forcible seizure of trains and other violence. In all cases where it appeared that there was interference with the passage of the mails the Attorney General sent messages similar to the above to the U. S. district attorneys. On June 30 the district attorney at Chicago reported that mail trains had been stopped the night before in the suburbs of that city by a band of strikers, that an engine had been cut off and disabled, that it was

---

[1] *Report of the U. S. Strike Commission, op. cit.,* p. xxxix.

growing more and more likely that all trains would have to be stopped, and he recommended that the U. S. Marshal at Chicago be empowered to employ special deputies who should be placed on the trains to protect the mails. Mr. Olney at once authorized the marshal to employ all the additional deputies necessary.[1]

At the same time the Attorney General appointed Edwin Walker, well known as a railroad attorney and, at the time, counsel for the Chicago, Milwaukee and St. Paul,[2] to be special attorney in charge of conducting the government's case against the strikers in the courts. In a letter to Mr. Walker, the Attorney General wrote, " It has seemed to me that if the rights of the United States were vigorously asserted in Chicago, the origin and center of the demonstration, the result would be to make it a failure everywhere else and to prevent its spread over the entire country." He also recommended that Mr. Walker and U. S. Attorney Milchrist obtain an injunction against the strikers in the federal courts, pointing out that instead of relying entirely on warrants for arrest issued under the criminal statutes, an injunction based on the general principles of law and on the Anti-trust Act of 1890 would be more effective in ending the strike.[3]

It should be noted that the lawless elements in the city were augmented at this time by many criminals and adventurers attracted to it by the Columbian Exposition. The strike gave these elements a chance to burn, plunder, and commit all sorts of crimes. Although the railway managers and some of the government officials prosecuting the strikers

---

[1] Cleveland, *The Government in the Chicago Strike of 1894*, Princeton, 1913, pp. 10, 11, 14.

[2] *Book of Chicagoans*, 1905, p. 590.

[3] Appendix to the Report of the Attorney general, 1896, *Correspondence in the Chicago Strike*, pp. 59, 60, 61; Cleveland, *op. cit.*, p. 15.

maintained that the violence and obstruction to traffic was the fault of the latter, it has been conceded by more impartial authorities that the strikers were but a very small part of the mobs, and that a comparatively small number of those on strike were involved in lawless acts. The mobs were composed generally of hoodlums and recruits from the criminal classes.[1]

The U. S. Marshal at Chicago, who on July 1 reported that he had sworn in 400 deputies and that many more would be required to protect mail trains, made numerous arrests of strikers and others on warrants charging criminal obstruction to the passage of the mails. But the government attorneys at Chicago, agreeing with the Attorney General as to the insufficiency of this procedure, determined to obtain an injunction. In conference with several attorneys for the railroads, they drew up a bill in equity,[2] based on the law prohibiting obstruction to the mails and on the Sherman Act, empowering U. S. Attorneys to seek an injunction in the circuit courts to restrain violation of the act, and declaring illegal all conspiracies in restraint of interstate trade and commerce.[3]

On July 2 Judges Wood and Grosscup answered the request of Attorneys Walker and Milchrist by issuing the most sweeping injunction order ever handed down by a federal court up to that time. Eugene V. Debs, the president of the American Railway Union, the other officers of the Union, and "all other persons whomsoever" were ordered absolutely to desist and refrain " from in any way or manner interfering with, hindering, obstructing, or stopping" any of the business of the railroads entering Chicago,

[1] *Rep. of the Strike Com.* pp. xliii, xliv, xlv.

[2] Appendix to Rep. of Att'y Gen., 1896, *op. cit.,* Letter from Walker to Olney, p. 63.

[3] *U. S. Compiled Statutes,* 1918, sec. 8563 (9), sec. 8820, 8823.

or any trains carrying U. S. mails or engaged in interstate commerce, or from interfering with or injuring the property of said railroads, or from trespassing on such property for the purpose of said obstruction, or from injuring signals, switches, etc., or " from compelling or inducing or attempting to compel or induce, by threats, intimidation, persuasion, force or violence, any of the employees of any of the said railways to refuse or fail to perform any of their duties as employees " in carrying mail or in interstate commerce, or " from compelling or inducing or attempting to compel or induce, by threats, intimidation, force, or violence any of the employees " to leave the service of the railroads or from entering their service, or " from doing any act whatever in furtherance of any conspiracy or combination to restrain either of said railway companies or receivers in the free and unhindered control and handling of interstate commerce over the lines of said railroads, and of transportation of persons and freight between or among the states; and from ordering, directing, aiding, assisting, or abetting in any manner whatever any person or persons to commit any or either of the acts aforesaid." [1]

Thereafter, when he thought it necessary, the Attorney General had his attorneys obtain similar injunctions in many districts throughout the West and the Central West.[2] In most cases the injunctions were granted on the same grounds as at Chicago, but in some of the western states the fact that the railroads were by law military and post roads of the United States, and that some were also in the hands of receivers appointed by federal courts gave further bases for the injunctions.

---

[1] *In re Debs*, 64 Fed. Rep. 724.

[2] See Appendix, 1896, *op. cit., passim*; also the *Report of the Att'y Gen.*, 1894, p. xxxiv.

Needless to say, if the injunctions could be enforced, the strike, and all violence arising out of it, as well as the obstruction of the mails and interstate commerce, would at once come to an end. A reading of the injunction shows that it could be interpreted to prevent any act whatever, peaceful or otherwise, done in connection with the strike. But to grant an injunction has always proved easier than to enforce one. At the time that the Chicago injunction was issued on July 2, Attorney Walker informed the government that he thought it would require troops to enforce it and to protect the mails. On the same day U. S. Marshal Arnold attempted to read the injunction to a mob at Blue Island, a suburb of Chicago, but was hooted down and was not permitted to continue. He reported to the Attorney General, described the violence of the mobs, and said he believed only U. S. troops could handle the situation. Attorneys Walker and Milchrist, and Judge Grosscup, who had granted the injunction, concurred in his request for troops.[1]

On July 3, after consultation between the President, members of the cabinet, and General Miles, who had been called from his headquarters near Chicago, the following message was sent to the officer in charge of federal troops stationed near that city:

It having become impracticable, in the judgment of the President, to enforce by ordinary course of judicial proceedings the laws of the United States, you will direct Colonel Crofton to move his entire command at once to the city of Chicago, leaving the necessary guard at Fort Sheridan, there to execute the orders and processes of the U. S. courts, to prevent the obstruction of the U. S. mails, and generally to enforce the faithful execution of the laws of the United States. He will

[1] Appendix, 1896, *op. cit.,* pp. 62, 63.

confer with the U. S. marshal, the U. S. district attorney, and
Edwin Walker, special counsel. Acknowledge receipt and report action promptly.

By order of the President.

J. M. Schofield, Major General.[1]

The troops arrived in Chicago on July 4 and for the next
few days were kept busy putting down the violence of the
mobs and aiding the marshals in serving injunction writs
and other court processes.[2] Orders similar to the above
were sent to many commanders in the West, and federal
troops were used in numerous instances for the same purposes as in the neighborhood of Chicago. In some cases
they were sent at the request of state governors; in other
cases because a particular railroad on which the strike had
taken effect, was in the hands of a federal court acting as
receiver, and troops were called to enforce the orders of the
court. Elsewhere the roads had been designated by law as
roads for military and naval service. The extension of the
strike to such roads and the consequent absence of communication between military posts was considered sufficient
reason for using troops to see that the trains were run.
After the first week of July violence became less common,
and by the middle of the month peace had been restored to
practically all of the disturbed areas. Troops were finally
withdrawn from Chicago on July 20.[3]

There occurred, shortly after the troops arrived in
Chicago, an interesting but acrimonious controversy be-
tween Governor Altgeld, of Illinois, and President Cleveland.
The Governor, who did not send the state militia into
Chicago until July 6, protested against the President's action

[1] *Rep. of the Strike Com.*, p. 340; *N. Y. Tribune*, July 4, 1894.

[2] Cleveland, *The Government in the Chicago Strike of 1894*, pp. 27-30.

[3] Wilson, *Federal Aid in Domestic Disturbances.*, Sen. Doc., vol. xix,
2nd Sess., 67th Cong., pp. 195-202.

in sending in federal troops, denying both the necessity for them, and the President's right to send them in unless the Governor or the state legislature applied for them. Several messages were exchanged by the two executives, and the correspondence ended when the President sent the following on July 6:

While I am still persuaded that I have neither transcended my authority nor duty in the emergency that confronts us, it seems to me in this hour of danger and public distress, discussion may well give way to active efforts on the part of all in authority to restore obedience to law, and to protect life and property.[1]

It seems probable from available reports of events in Chicago during the first week of July, that troops were needed at the time the President sent them. Under the statutes the President's technical right to send them does not seem open to question. It is true that an act of Feb. 28, 1795 (*Revised Statutes,* Section 5297), gives the President power to send troops in case of an insurrection against a state government only when the state legislature, or, if it cannot be convened, the governor requests that they be sent. But Section 5298 (Act of July 29, 1861) empowers the President to use troops whenever it is impracticable to enforce, by the ordinary course of judicial proceedings, the laws of the United States. Other statutes, (*R. S.* 1989, *R. S.* 5299) give him the right to use troops to enforce the processes of the federal courts, to enforce the execution of all laws guaranteeing civil rights, and to prevent conspiracies which deprive anyone of rights guaranteed by the Constitution and the laws. On the assumption that the strike ob-

---

[1] Cleveland, *The Government in the Chicago Strike of 1894,* p. 44. For the correspondence between Cleveland and Altgeld, see the book here cited and Governor Altgeld's annual message of 1895.

structed the mail, prevented communication on military roads, and involved violence restricting civil rights, the use of troops to enforce the laws regarding these subjects was justified. Furthermore, once injunctions were issued, troops could be used under the law to enforce them.

Criticism of the government's use of troops in the Pullman Strike must be made, if at all, on other grounds. The federal authorities should, as a matter of courtesy, have asked Governor Altgeld for state troops as soon as they thought some military force was needed. This was never done. Secondly, the underlying assumption of the administration was that the strike as such violated the law, an assumption which does not seem justified by the facts. The use of troops was partly based on this assumption and their use, therefore, from that point of view, does not seem to have been entirely warranted. Furthermore, the troops about Chicago were practically under the control of Edwin Walker, a railway attorney. The injustice of their use does not arise from their own activities, for no serious complaint of their methods arose, but it does come from the government's basic assumption, and from the appointment of Mr. Walker as the legal representative of the administration.

The Chicago injunction was served on President Debs and other union officers a few days after it was issued. Its use, and the presence of troops to enforce it, as well as to help the marshal and his deputies in enforcing the laws, was not, however, considered sufficient action on the part of the government to end the strike. On July 2 Attorney Walker, in a letter to the Attorney General, recommended that indictments against Mr. Debs and others be sought from the Federal Grand Jury. "The result of a trial under the indictments," he wrote, "will be of little importance, and there may be no necessity of such trial. The very fact, however, that the government has called a grand jury for the

purpose of investigating these offences, and the return of
the indictments which in my opinion are sure to follow, will
have a greater restraining effect on Debs and his followers
than our proceeding by injunction." [1]   This method of procedure received the approval of the Attorney General, and
on July 10 the Federal Grand Jury at Chicago returned
indictments against the officers of the American Railway
Union charging complicity in obstructing the mails and interstate commerce. [2]

In his charge to the Grand Jury Judge Grosscup referred
to the law of conspiracy, and declared that if the jury should
find that a body of men had combined together for the purpose of hindering or obstructing the mails or restraining
interstate commerce, whether temporarily or permanently,
by forcible methods, or by quitting employment, and preventing others, by threats, intimidation, or violence, from
taking their places, it would constitute a criminal conspiracy. [3]

On the same day Mr. Debs and other officers were arrested by the U. S. Marshal, and were released on bail of
$10,000. [4]   A week later, on July 17, the government at-
torneys filed information with the federal court against them
for contempt of court because of disobedience of the injunction of July 2.   The strike leader and three others volun-
tarily appeared before the court, which set a hearing on the
contempt charges for the following week and fixed bail at
$3000.   They refused, however, to give bail, and were com-
mitted to jail. [5]   On July 19 the Federal Grand Jury returned over twenty indictments again charging Mr. Debs and

---

[1] Appendix to the Rep. of the Att'y Gen., 1896., p. 64.
[2] Cleveland, *op. cit.*, p. 34.
[3] *In re Grand Jury*, 62 Fed. Rep., 828, 831.
[4] *N. Y. Tribune*, July 11, 1894.
[5] Appendix, *op. cit.*, p. 87.

others with conspiracy against the mails and interstate commerce. Seven days later the U. S. Circuit Court charged with hearing the contempt cases postponed them until later in the year.[1]

Meanwhile the strike had been completely defeated. On July 13 the government's counsel reported that it was practically broken. Attempts were made throughout the first half of July to get the Pullman Company and the General Managers Association to make a settlement of some kind. On July 6 the Chicago Board of Aldermen asked the Association to talk the strike over, but the latter refused. A few days later they made an attempt to get Mr. Pullman to submit to arbitration the question as to whether or not there was anything to arbitrate, but met with the same refusal. About July 12 Mayor Pingree of Detroit and Mayor Hopkins of Chicago made similar unsuccessful attempts.[2]

On the 13th the American Railway Union, through Mayor Hopkins, sent a proposal for settlement to the General Managers Association. " Let it be stated," the letter said, " that they do not impose any condition of settlement except that they be returned to their former positions. They do not ask the recognition of their organization or of any organization." This proposal the managers refused even to receive.[3] It is not difficult to understand the position of the employers. As soon as they saw that the government was using all its powers to fight the strikers, victory for them was assured. To agree to a settlement of any kind short of absolute defeat of the strikers was entirely unnecessary. Furthermore, by the 10th or 11th of July there really was " nothing to arbitrate." One doesn't arbitrate with a thoroughly beaten opponent.

---

[1] Appendix, *op. cit.*, pp. 90-93.

[2] *Rep. of the Strike Com.*, pp. 350-351.

[3] *Ibid.*, p. 58.

On July 12 a committee representing organized labor saw
President Cleveland and asked him to appoint a commission
under the law of 1888 to investigate the railroad strike.
The President replied that he would do so, but that all
strikes must first be called off and all violence cease. The
next day he assured callers that the commission would have
nothing to do with arbitration.[1] Evidently the President
also saw " nothing to arbitrate."

The Act of October 1, 1888,[2] provided for the arbitration
of labor disputes in the field of transportation. Each side
was to agree to arbitration and was to appoint one member
of a board. The two thus chosen were to name a third
member. This board had the right to subpoena witnesses
and its award was to be published, but otherwise the procedure was of a voluntary nature throughout. The provisions just described were never put to use. But the act
also provided that the President of the United States, in
case of railway labor disputes, might appoint a commission
of inquiry which was to have full powers of investigation
into the causes and conditions of the controversy and the
means of adjusting it, and was to make its report to the
President. In accordance with his promise such a commission was appointed by Mr. Cleveland on July 26. Its
members were Carroll D. Wright, Commissioner of Labor,
John D. Kernan of New York, and N. E. Worthington of
Illinois.[3] It held hearings in August and September. It
was, of course, appointed too late to have a hand in settling
the strike, but it made a report on November 14, 1894,[4]

[1] *N. Y. Tribune,* July 13 and 14.

[2] 25 Stat. 501.

[3] The act required that the Commissioner of Labor should head the
commission and that one of its other two members should be a resident
of the state in which the dispute occurred.

[4] *Rep. of the Strike Commission,* pp. xv-xvii.

which, together with the testimony taken by it, is perhaps the most valuable source of information in regard to the strike.

In the meantime, on August 2, the same day on which the Pullman plant reopened, a convention of the American Railway Union voted to recommend to the local unions that the strike be called off at once. This was done when the delegates returned to their homes, and the strike formally ended on all the roads.[1]

On the 14th of December the federal court found Mr. Debs and a number of his associates guilty of contempt for disobeying the injunction and sentenced them to jail for terms varying from three to six months. Judge Wood found that the defendants, by continuing to direct the strike after July 2, were engaged in a conspiracy to hinder and obstruct interstate commerce and the passage of the mails in a way to constitute a public nuisance, thus violating the restraining order.[2] Some time afterwards the trial of the leaders on the indictments returned by the Grand Jury was begun, but the government attorneys had the case dismissed.[3]

On January 14, 1895, the strike leaders in jail for contempt of court appealed to the U. S. Supreme Court for writs of error and of habeas corpus. The first writ was denied, but the Supreme Court heard arguments on the writ of habeas corpus. In a decision handed down on May 27, 1895, Justice Brewer rendering the opinion, the petition was denied.[4] The direct question was one as to whether the lower court had jurisdiction, but the opinion contained a lengthy discussion, *obiter dicta,* defending the action of the

[1] *Rep. of the Strike Commission,* p. 151.

[2] *In re Debs,* 64 Fed. Rep. 724, 739.

[3] *Report of the Commission on Industrial Relations,* vol. xi, Washington, 1916. p, 10771.

[4] 15 Sup. Ct. Rep. 900.

government in its suit for the injunction, of the court in granting it, and upholding vigorously the injunction process and the right of the court to punish for contempt when its order is disobeyed.[1]

The President, during the summer of 1894 and for many years after, received much commendation from citizens all over the country for the decisive and unhesitating part he played in ending the strike. That he ended it no one can doubt who reads the facts. That his action was determined and unhesitating seems equally clear; for in three or four days he had put into effect all the powers necessary to bring an end to the strike. After that the issue was at no time in doubt. The strike was doomed to early defeat. Undoubtedly the principal purpose of the President was to prevent the hardships and inconvenience to the public which the strike certainly involved, and to put down the violence which it brought in its wake. His purpose seems most commendable. But it may be questioned whether the methods used in accomplishing his purpose were fair.

The strike was probably unjustified, and considered from the point of view of the railway employees, foolish. It was doomed to failure from the first, because it necessarily antagonized public opinion. This does not refer to the original strike at Pullman. The evidence shows conclusively that that strike was justifiable. But for the American

---

[1] The court proceedings discussed here were not the only ones involved in the strike. A great many strikers all over the country were arrested and sentenced to prison for varying terms on charges of contempt of court for disobeying the various injunctions, for violations of federal laws concerning the obstruction of the mails, etc. For decisions in the more important of these cases, see *In re Phelan*, 62 Fed. Rep. 803; *In re Grand Jury*, 62 Fed. Rep. 840; *U. S.* v. *Cassidy*, 67 Fed. Rep. 698; *S. Calif. R. R. Co.* v. *Rutherford*, 62 Fed. Rep. 796, in which strikers were directly enjoined from leaving their jobs; *U. S.* v. *Elliott*, 62 Fed. Rep. 801; and *U. S.* v. *Agler*, 62 Fed. Rep. 824.

Railway Union to make the Pullman issue, concerning as it did only about 3000 workers, nation-wide in scope and to inaugurate a great sympathetic strike affecting adversely a large proportion of the people of the United States seems reckless and unthinking in the extreme. Furthermore, with a business depression of great severity and considerable unemployment existing at the same time, it was very unwise from the point of view of tactics.

Despite all this it should be noted that there was no federal law forbidding a sympathetic strike, nor was there one the intent of which was to forbid a railroad strike. The union was within its rights under the law, as it was then understood, in declaring a strike, and in its struggle with the General Managers Association it was entitled to some measure of consideration from a federal government which was supposed to represent the interests of all the people.

Reference has been made to the appointment of Edwin Walker by the Attorney General to take charge of the government's campaign against the strikers. It was perhaps necessary that a good lawyer acquainted with conditions in Chicago be put in charge of affairs. But it should have appeared equally necessary to the administration that the person appointed to such a position should, as far as possible, be one whose appointment could not lay the government open to the charge of interfering in the strike for the purpose of helping the General Managers Association defeat the strikers. The record of Edwin Walker as a lawyer should have prevented the government from appointing him as its representative in Chicago.

From 1865 to 1883 he had been General Solicitor for the Chicago and Great Eastern, which in 1870 was amalgamated with the Pennsylvania system. From 1869 to 1884 he had been General Counsel for the Chicago, Danville and Vincennes. From 1870 to 1896 he was the Illinois counsel for the Chicago, Milwaukee and St. Paul.[1] To appoint a man with such a career, regardless of his ability, at a time when he was still acting as counsel for one of the roads which were fighting the strikers cannot be regarded as other than an act deserving of severe criticism. Furthermore, Edwin Walker took a very active part in disposing of the troops and deputy marshals to the different railroads. When, therefore, the strikers charged that the government permitted itself to wage the battle of the General Managers Association, largely under the direction of that organization, it must be admitted that they had some basis for their charge.

Another basis for the same charge lay in the method of appointing and controlling the deputy marshals. On June 30 the Attorney General had authorized U. S. Marshal Arnold to employ enough deputies to prevent obstruction of the mails.[2] Concerning these men the U. S. Strike Commission reported that, out of about 5000 who were appointed, about 3600 were selected by and appointed at the request of the General Managers Association and of the railroads. Said the commission, "They were armed and paid by the railroad companies, and acted in the double capacity of railroad employees and United States officers. While operating the railroads they assumed and exercised unrestricted United States authority when so ordered by their employers or whenever they regarded it as necessary. They were not under the control of any Government official while exercising authority." As the commission said, "This is placing officers of the Government under the control of a combination of railroads. It is a bad precedent, that might well lead to serious consequences." [3]

---

[1] *Book of Chicagoans*, 1905, p. 590; *Who's Who*, 1910, 1911.

[2] Appendix to the report of the Attorney General, 1896, p. 60.

[3] *Rep. of the Strike Com.*, p. xliv; p. 270, Testimony of J. M. Egan, General Manager for the Managers Association; p. 341, Testimony of J. C. Donnelly, Chief Deputy.

Furthermore, in addition to these men, 1400 or more men were chosen on the streets by the U. S. Marshal and his chief deputy. Many of them were worthless, men who were frequently reported drunk, who often exercised very poor judgment, and who were often arrested while on duty by the Chicago police for indiscriminate shooting, and in several cases for highway robbery.[1] Their appointment was even protested by Attorney Walker, who on July 9 wired to Attorney General Olney, " At risk of being thought meddlesome I suggest that the marshal is appointing a mob of deputies that are worse than useless." The next day Mr. Olney himself protested against their appointment.[2]

But nowhere does one find either Mr. Olney or Mr. Walker protesting against such a miscarriage of the authority of the United States as the selection, arming, and paying of the U. S. deputy marshals by the railroads in Chicago. And it seems strange that a protest from high authority against the employment of such disreputable men as those described in the preceding paragraph should have been delayed until more than a week after the appointment of deputies was authorized, until the strike had been practically defeated and the violence for the most part was at an end. The responsibility for such negligence in supervising the action of subordinates lies squarely on the shoulders of the administration.

The government attorneys secured many indictments against the strikers, and many of them were arrested for violating the Sherman Act, which makes illegal a conspiracy in restraint of interstate trade or commerce. Everyone who knows the history of that act is aware that the sole intent

---

[1] *Rep. of the Com.*, pp. 341, 353, 368, 370.

[2] Appendix, *op. cit.*, pp. 76, 78.

of its framers, and of practically every member of Congress who gave the matter thought, was to find some means of restricting the pernicious activities of the trusts. But the first effective use to which the act was ever put by the Attorney General was to end a strike of railway laborers. The law with equal justice might have been used to end the existence of the General Managers Association, a combination directly concerned with uniting all the Chicago railroads engaged in interstate commerce, so that their labor and managing policies might be made as nearly uniform as possible. The same organization might have been indicted, as the strikers were, for conspiring to obstruct the mails. In the contracts which the government made with the railways concerning the carrying of the mails, it was not provided that mail trains should also carry Pullman cars. It would have been reasonable from the legal point of view, it seems, to have compelled the railroads to carry the mails on trains to which no Pullman cars were attached. For the roads well understood that the railway employees would not object to running such trains.

At a meeting held in Chicago on July 2 the managers decided to withdraw passenger trains and not to accept freight, for the purpose of forcing the government to interfere. They called this adopting " coercive measures " and publicly announced their program.[1] To an impartial student of the strike it would seem that the administration would have been as well justified in proceeding against the railways as it was in proceeding against the strikers on the charges of violating the Sherman Act and conspiring to obstruct the mails.

Of all the government's activities during the strike, its use of the injunction against the leaders of the American Railway Union undoubtedly caused the most discussion

[1] *N. Y. Tribune*, July 3, 1894.

throughout the country, especially in legal circles. It is pertinent at this point to consider the wisdom, the justifiability, and the efficacy of its use in the Chicago troubles. It has already been observed that Congress had never passed a law forbidding railway strikes. The injunctions obtained by Messrs. Milchrist and Walker and by other government attorneys did that very thing. The injunctions were addressed to everyone, the strike leaders "and all other persons," "all other persons whomsoever," etc. It is apparent that the prohibition of one or more acts, a prohibition which can be enforced at law, and which is addressed to all persons whomsoever, is a law. The lawmaking power in our government is not given to the courts, but is supposed to be reserved to the legislature.[1] But in the Pullman case the Attorney General decided that the strike was undesirable and thereupon induced the federal courts to make every act of the strikers, whether peaceable or not, which was connected with the strike, unlawful. It seems reasonable to maintain that such a power ought to be left in the hands of the people, represented in the legislature, and ought not to be exercised by any federal judge, appointed for life, and with practically no responsibility to the people.

To summarize, the use of the injunction in the Pullman strike was undesirable (1) because it violated rights which American citizens have always regarded as guaranteed to them by the Constitution,[2] (2) because it enabled an appointed official to make the law for the people of the United States, (3) because the impossibility of its general enforcement subjected the courts to the likelihood of contempt and ridicule, (4) because it aroused the hostility of labor to-

[1] See C. N. Gregory, 11 *Harvard Law Review* 487; W. H. Dunbar, 13 *Law Quarterly Review* 374; C. C. Allen, 28 *American Law Review*, 828.

[2] *Cf. supra.*, pp. 18, 19.

wards the government, (5) because it gave the stamp of approval by the government to a process which has since become a most important ally of employers in restricting the right of workers to carry on activities ordinarily supposed to be their unquestioned privilege, and (6) because it was obtained in several instances at the request of and after conferences with the railway managers, thus laying the administration open to the charge of being under the direction of the railways.

Was there anything the President might have done, other than those things which have been described, to prevent hardship to the people, which was perhaps what he honestly desired most of all to accomplish? Mr. Cleveland made no move to settle the Pullman strike itself, nor to bring the two parties to an amicable settlement before the general strike began. For nearly three weeks before the boycott was declared the newspapers contained references to the fact that the American Railway Union was seriously considering action. He must have known also that the Pullman Company had refused arbitration and that this refusal was the immediate cause of the difficulty. The President, of course, had no power in law to compel arbitration, but numerous instances in later years are evidence of the power behind the request of the President of the United States that the parties try to reach a settlement before breaking off relations.[1] Under the Act of 1888 the President, however, did have the power to appoint a commission of inquiry for the purpose of investigating railway strikes and suggesting a method of adjustment. But Mr. Cleveland wrote no letter, the existence of which is known, asking any party concerned to

---

[1] Mr. Cleveland, a Democrat, could not have pleaded the strict constructionist excuse that he had no power to ask the parties to arbitrate at the same time that he made use of the injunction for a purpose never dreamed of in earlier times.

arbitrate, to delay, or to concede anything to avoid the strike. And he waited until July 26 to name the commission he was empowered to appoint, and which, had it been appointed five or six weeks earlier, might have been successful in avoiding the strike altogether.

Instead, he delayed action until the strike and all its regrettable effects were upon the nation, and then he proceeded to end it in such a way that not only the wage earners of the country but many other citizens felt that the government had resigned a large share of its authority to the railroads for their unrestricted and arbitrary use in defeating the strikers.

CHAPTER II

President McKinley, 1897-1901

I. THE COEUR D'ALENE DISTURBANCE, 1899

THE single important instance in which President Mc-Kinley used the executive power in a labor dispute was in the case of a strike of lead and silver miners in the Coeur d'Alene district of Idaho in 1899. The district had for a number of years been the scene of struggles between the miners, members of the Western Federation of Miners, and the mining companies. In 1895 the mines in Wardner, Idaho, which had before that time employed both union and non-union men, decided not to employ members of the union thereafter, and also put into effect wages below the customary scale. For the next few years working conditions continued the same, with considerable dissatisfaction among the men, especially among those in the district who belonged to the union.[1]

In April, 1899, attempts made to organize the Bunker Hill mine led to the company's dismissal of a number of union men. On April 23 the Wardner union met and appointed a committee, which waited on the company and demanded an increase in wages and recognition of the union. The committee was informed that the company would not grant recognition. At a second meeting of the union a strike was declared. The entire body of members then

[1] *Report of the Industrial Commission,* vol. xii, Washington, 1901, pp. lxxxv-vi.

285]   *PRESIDENT McKINLEY, 1897-1901*   37

marched to the Bunker Hill mine and urged the non-union
men to join the organization.   The mine superintendent
thereupon announced an increase in wages and declared that
men joining the union would be discharged.   For the next
few days the union members made further efforts to get the
men to join them.   But by the 26th or the 27th it was apparent that the strike had failed, and the company resumed
operation.[1]

On April 28 members of the miners' unions from the
towns of Gem, Burke, and Mullan made preparations to
travel in a body to Wardner, for the purpose of assisting
their fellow unionists.   On the 29th they commandeered a
Northern Pacific train and forced the engineer to run it past
its regular route on to Wardner.   At Gem some of the
miners broke open the powder house of the Helena & Frisco
mine and seized eighty boxes of dynamite.   Witnesses of
what happened believed that the majority of men who went
to Wardner did not expect any violence and did not want it.
But it is quite certain that a small group were bent on destruction, and they had carefully laid their plans.[2]

There were by that time probably 500 or more in the band,
and about 150 of them were masked.   A number of the
masked members took the dynamite from the train and ex-
ploded it on the company's property.   All of the buildings
but one were destroyed, causing a loss of nearly $250,000.
At the same time two men were killed by shots coming from
some individuals in the mob.   After the explosion the men
went back to the train and rode away.[3]

Immediately after hearing of the riot Governor Steunenberg of Idaho, who was then ill, gave State Auditor Sinclair

[1] *Report of the Industrial Commission, op. cit.,* p. lxxxvii.
[2] *Ibid.,* p. lxxxviii.
[3] *Ibid.,* p. xc.

power to proceed to the seat of the trouble and take whatever measures were necessary to convict the parties to the crime.   Mr. Sinclair, finding that the county authorities had not taken any measures to apprehend the guilty, recommended that the Governor declare martial law in the district, on the ground that a state of insurrection prevailed.[1]   On the evening of the 29th the Governor applied to President McKinley for federal troops.   He pointed out that the legislature was not in session, that it was impossible to convene it to ask for troops, and that since all the available Idaho National Guard was in the Philippines, federal troops were necessary to suppress the insurrection in Shoshone County. General Merriam was at once instructed by the War Department to interview the Governor and to call whatever troops were necessary.[2]   Troops were ordered into the district on May 1 and May 2.[3]   On May 3 Governor Steunenberg declared the county to be in a state of insurrection and rebellion, and announced that martial law was in effect.[4]

Immediately on the arrival of the troops the state authorities, with the aid of the soldiers, proceeded to arrest the miners all over the district.   Six or seven hundred men were thus arrested without warrant by state officers, who were protected by federal troops, and the prisoners were turned over to the latter to guard.   Hundreds of these men were held for months in a hastily constructed " bull pen ", with no opportunity for trial and no charges preferred against them.   Many of them were discharged from time

[1] *Report of the Industrial Commission, op. cit.,* p. xci.

[2] *Report of the House Committee on Military Affairs on the Coeur d'Alene Labor Troubles,* 1st Sess., 56th Cong., House Report 1999, pp. 7-8.

[3] *Report of Brigadier General Merriam,* 1st Sess., 56th Cong., Senate Document 24, p. 2.

[4] *Rep. House Com., op. cit.,* p. 9.

to time because no grounds for holding them could be found by the authorities. At the end of July nearly 200 prisoners were still held under guard by federal troops.[1]

On May 8 State Auditor Sinclair, acting as personal representative of the Governor, issued a proclamation to the following effect: that any mine owners in Shoshone County employing members of the criminal organizations (i. e., the miners' unions) which had caused property to be destroyed and murders to be committed, would have their mines closed; that all parties applying for underground work would be required to obtain permits from the state authorities authorizing them to work; that parties applying for such permits must be prepared " first, to deny all participation in the riots of April 29, 1899, in Shoshone County, and second, to deny or renounce membership in any society which has incited, encouraged, or approved of said riots or other violation of public law; " and that mine owners must refuse employment to any miner not having a duly signed permit.[2]

The proclamation ended as follows:

" Examined and approved:

    H. C. Merriam,

        Brigadier General, United States Army."

The permits that each applicant for work had to obtain required that the following statement be signed:

I did not participate, actively or otherwise, in the riots which took place at Wardner on the 29th of April, 1899. Believing that the crimes committed at Wardner on said date were actively incited, encouraged, and perpetrated through and by means of the influence and direction of the miners' unions of the Coeur d'Alenes, I hereby express my unqualified disapproval of said acts, and hereby renounce and forever adjure

---

[1] *Rep. Ind. Com.,, op. cit.,* pp. xciii-xcv., *Rep. Gen. Merriam,* p. 13.
[2] *Rep. Ind. Com., op. cit.,* p. 390.

all allegiance to the said miners' unions . . . . and I solemnly pledge myself to obey the law and not to again seek membership in any society which will encourage, or tolerate any violation of law.[1]

The proclamation and the permit were prepared by Judge Lindley, attorney for the Bunker Hill Company, and State Auditor Sinclair, and were approved by General Merriam.[2] Dr. France, the representative of the state authorities to whom or to whose deputies miners had to make application for permits to work, was at the time employed by the mine owners as company doctor.[3]

The permit system was put into effect despite an Idaho state law, approved March 6, 1893, which made it unlawful for any employer to enter into oral or written agreement requiring the promise of an employee not to become a member of a labor organization.[4] Mr. Sinclair, explaining the permit system before the Industrial Commission in July, 1899, said that the proclamation was submitted to General Merriam " as a matter of courtesy, to give the application dignity, and to receive assurance, in case there was an attempt made to obstruct its enforcement, that [the Auditor] could call on the troops . . . . for protection." [5]

On May 29 the Adjutant General of the Army informed General Merriam that President McKinley had received resolutions from the Western Federation of Miners charging that owners of mines in the Coeur d'Alene might not employ a miner unless he first made an affidavit that he was a non-union man, and that the troops were being used to en-

---

[1] *Rep. Ind. Com., op. cit.,* p. 391.

[2] *Ibid.,* p. 471.

[3] *Ibid.,* p. 391.

[4] *Ibid.,* p. 391.

[5] *House Com. Rep., op. cit.,* p. 113.

force this order. The President desired a statement of the facts. The next day General Merriam replied that no affidavits were required, and described the permit system. On May 31 Secretary of War Alger sent the following order to the general:

You will instruct Major Smith, commanding at Wallace, that he is to use the United States troops to aid the state authority simply to suppress rioting and to maintain peace and order. Those were your original instructions. The Army must have nothing whatever to do with enforcing rules for the government of miners or miners' unions. That is a matter for the local authorities to deal with.[1]

In his annual report made July 31, 1899, General Merriam denied ever having received the " original instructions " referred to in Secretary Alger's telegram. He asked for a copy of them but did not receive it.[2]

From time to time various charges were made concerning the cruel and abusive treatment of the prisoners guarded by the federal troops, the unsanitary condition of the prison in which they were confined, and their continued detention by the troops with no charges preferred against them, no trial, and no opportunity to consult with counsel.[3] There is evidence of severe discipline of practically all the prisoners then held, in September, 1899, when a number of them were found digging a tunnel in order to escape.[4] Aside from this the charges concerning cruel and abusive treatment do not seem to have been justified. It is true that conditions were not altogether sanitary, but the evidence shows that the federal authorities did their best to improve them. It

---

[1] *Rep. Ind. Com., op. cit.,* p. 393.

[2] *Rep. Brig, Gen. Merriam., op. cit.,* p. 13.

[3] See Senate Document 25, 1st Sess., 56th Cong.

[4] *House Com. Rep., op. cit.,* p. 91.

was not true that the prisoners were not permitted to consult with counsel. Complaint on this point was justifiable, however, because only one attorney was permitted to see all the prisoners held.

On September 28 Elihu Root, who had succeeded R. A. Alger as Secretary of War, asked Governor Steunenberg whether the insurrection had been suppressed, so that federal troops might be withdrawn. In case this was not desirable the Secretary was " much disinclined to have the troops of the United States continued longer in the attitude of retaining in custody the citizens of a state who [had] remained so long without being tried, and [he felt] bound to urge that, if it [were] not convenient to bring the prisoners to speedy trial, [the Governor would] substitute civil guards as their custodians and relieve the troops of the United States from further performance of that duty." [1]

The Governor replied on October 10, asserting that the troops were still necessary, that he feared violence if they were withdrawn, and promising that the state authorities would guard the sixty-five remaining prisoners beginning November 1.[2] On October 20 the federal troops ceased guarding the prisoners, but they remained in the district for some months longer before being finally withdrawn.[3]

The activities of the troops in the Coeur d'Alenes gave rise to much criticism of President McKinley. As is usual in such cases, much of it was engendered by political hostility, but there was ground enough for honest criticism of the administration for its part in the affair. The administration is to be criticized for acts of omission rather than for acts of commission. When the President sent troops

[1] House Com. Rep., op. cit., p. 17.

[2] Ibid., pp. 18-25.

[3] Wilson, Federal Aid in Domestic Disturbances, p. 215.

into the district he was entirely responsible for what they did, and he should not have neglected to watch over and regulate their action and withdraw them as soon as the state was able to reassume control.

There was no good excuse for allowing the troops to be so entirely under the control of the state authorities. The Army Regulations of 1895, Paragraph 490, direct that in " the enforcement of the laws troops are employed . . . . and act under the orders of the President as commander-in-chief. They cannot be directed to act under the orders of any civil officer." Nevertheless, State Auditor Sinclair was, in effect, commander-in-chief of the United States troops in the Coeur d'Alenes. The officers in charge of the soldiers seem to have placed themselves entirely under his orders, lent their support to the numerous arrests made, guarded the prisoners, given the prestige of the United States army to the permit system, and in various other ways acted rather as state militia than as part of the regular United States forces. To a certain extent this may have been necessary, but certainly such complete surrender of federal authority was neither wise nor fair, considering the anti-union policies adopted by the state authorities.

Under the federal laws [1] the President is empowered to use the United States forces in case of insurrection in a state, on the application of the legislature of a state, or if the legislature cannot be convened, at the request of the governor. In the present instance Governor Steunenberg pointed out that the Idaho law required notice of several weeks before the legislature could be convened. In the emergency there was no time for this, and troops were accordingly sent at the Governor's request. But the troops remained in the Coeur d'Alenes for many months, and no attempt was made

---

[1] *Revised Statutes,* Section 5297.

either by the Governor or by the President to have the Idaho legislature ask that the troops be retained, or assume control of affairs in the district. It is an open question whether the people of Idaho, as represented in the legislature, wished the troops to continue their stay. It was the duty of the President to find out the desire of the legislature, since that was evidently the purpose of the federal law, but no step in this direction was taken, and the troops remained to carry out the will of those in control of the executive department of the state.

One of the most important grounds for criticism was the continued use of soldiers of the United States for the purpose of aiding in the arrest of hundreds of men without warrant and of holding them as prisoners without charges or trial. No move was made by the administration to end this system until six months after it had been put into effect. State authorities claimed the system was necessary and justified under martial law in order to prevent those guilty of the crimes from escaping. But that does not appear sufficient reason, especially in view of the fact that after April 29 no violence or disturbance of any kind occurred, though martial law continued in force for many months thereafter.

The thing most to be condemned in the affair was the act of General Merriam in lending the support and prestige of the army to such an obvious anti-union plan as the permit system. It was the claim of the state authorities that the permits were necessary in order to drive the lawless elements out of the district. Under the system it was assumed that every member of the union was a criminal and deserved no employment. Thus some 1500 men who refused to renounce their union membership were, with their families, driven from the district, although they had been neither indicted nor convicted of any offense.[1] It was not until three

---

[1] *House Com. Rep., op. cit.,* p. 132.

weeks after the system had been put into operation that the President made any attempt to forbid the use of the federal troops in support of it.

From a study of the Coeur d'Alenes affair one is brought to the conclusion that it was serious negligence on the part of the President to have sent the troops in without specific directions as to their activities, and to have permitted them to be used for purposes not warranted by the ends of justice. The history of later administrations shows that Mr. Mc-Kinley's successors profited by his mistakes, and attempted to prevent the use of troops for any purposes other than to end violence and to maintain peace. They were more prompt to investigate conditions, more careful that the activities of the troops be limited to legitimate purposes, and more insistent that the army should not be used as the tool of some faction within a state.[1]

[1] For good statements of the cases for and against the President in the Coeur d'Alenes affair, see the majority and minority reports of the House Committee on Military Affairs, House Report 1999, 1st Sess., 56th Cong., already cited here.

CHAPTER III

President Roosevelt, 1901-1909

I. THE ANTHRACITE STRIKE OF 1902

THE first important instance on record in which a President of the United States took an active part in attempting to mediate a labor controversy was that which culminated in the appointment of the Anthracite Coal Strike Commission in October, 1902.

In the latter part of 1899 and in the spring of 1900 the United Mine Workers of America, which, since 1897, had become a factor of great importance among the workers in the bituminous coal fields, sent organizers into the anthracite districts of Pennsylvania.[1] In the early summer of 1900 only about 8000 anthracite workers belonged to the union. At a convention held in July of that year a request was drawn up and sent to the operators asking them to meet the union representatives in order to formulate a wage scale. This request was refused, and on September 17 large numbers of men went on strike. In two weeks, according to the estimate of the union's leader, 90 per cent of the 144,000 workers were idle. For a while the operators refused all overtures for a settlement. The presidential election of 1900 was approaching, however, and Mark Hanna, then Chairman of the National Republican Committee, fearing the possibly injurious influence of a coal famine on the

[1] Sydenstricker, *Collective Bargaining in the Anthracite Coal Industry*, Bureau of Labor Statistics, Bulletin 191, Washington, 1916, p. 18.

candidacy of President McKinley, tried to end the strike.
Probably as a result of his efforts the anthracite operators,
on October 3, posted a notice of a 10 per cent increase in
wages.[1]

This concession of the operators proved unacceptable to
the miners. No promise had been given that the increase in
wages would remain in effect for any definite period.
Various other demands which had figured in the strike had
been left unnoticed. On October 20 another notice was
posted by the operators, offering to increase wages 10 per
cent, to reduce the price of powder, to pay wages semi-
monthly in cash, and to adjust some of the other grievances.
The executive committee of the miners accepted these concessions and advised the miners to return to work. This
they did on October 29. It will be seen that the union received no actual recognition. But the result of the strike
was a considerable increase in membership.[2]

Several times in February, 1901, John Mitchell, the president of the United Mine Workers, sent messages to the
operators requesting a joint conference to consider wages and
conditions in the anthracite fields for the following year.
These requests met with refusal.[3] Finally a conference was
arranged in April, at which President Thomas of the Erie

[1] Mitchell, *Organized Labor,* Philadelphia, 1903, pp. 365-366. Over a
year and a half later George F. Baer, president of the Philadelphia &
Reading Coal & Iron Co., and a leader of the anthracite operators, told
Commissioner of Labor Carroll D. Wright, who was then investigating
the 1902 strike at the request of the President, that Mr. McKinley had
sent someone to him personally to assure him that Ohio and Indiana
were in danger of being lost to the Republicans in the election of 1900
if some adjustment were not made to end the strike. See Wright,
Report to the President on the Anthracite Coal Strike. Bureau of
Labor, Bulletin 43, November, 1902, p. 1204.

[2] Mitchell, *op. cit.,* pp. 365, 366, 367.

[3] *Report of the Anthracite Coal Strike Commission,* Washington, 1903,
p. 31.

Railroad, Senator Hanna, President Mitchell, and the district presidents of the anthracite unions were present. At this time an understanding was reached that the conditions of 1900 should be continued until April, 1902.[1]

With the approach of April, 1902, the officials of the union, on February 14, addressed letters to the presidents of the various anthracite companies asking them to attend a joint conference between miners and operators to be held March 12 for the purpose of reaching a wage agreement for the coming year.[2] All of the operators refused to attend the conference. President Baer, of the Philadelphia & Reading said, " This company does not favor the plan of having its relations with the miners disturbed every year." He claimed that having two masters in business meant having lack of discipline in mining, and he objected to a conference with persons not interested in and ignorant of anthracite mining. Furthermore, he objected to a uniform wage for all mines, conditions at different mines being different. The answers of the other operators were in a similar vein.[3]

In the middle of March the operators posted the following notice:

The rates of wages now in effect will be continued until April 1, 1903, and thereafter, subject to 60 days' notice. Local differences will, as heretofore, be adjusted with our employees at the respective collieries.[4]

At about the same time the anthracite miners, in convention, formulated demands asking for a 20 per cent increase in wages for piece workers, a corresponding increase for men paid by the day in the form of a reduction in hours of work

[1] Mitchell, *op. cit.*, p. 370.

[2] *Ibid.*, p. 370.

[3] Wright, Bulletin 43, *op. cit.*, pp. 1176-1178.

[4] *Ibid.*, p. 1184.

from ten to eight with the same pay as theretofore received for ten hours, that men previously paid per car should receive payment according to the legal ton, and that these terms should be incorporated in an agreement made with the union.   On March 22 the convention sent telegrams to the anthracite presidents again asking them to meet with the union representatives to discuss the miners' grievances. During the month the National Civic Federation also tried to arrange conferences, but the operators refused to attend. Meanwhile the miners' officials had been given power to call a strike.   For the sake of avoiding a suspension the men offered to compromise by proposing a 10 per cent increase in wages and a nine-hour day.   The operators, however, refused to grant any concessions.

On May 8 the union officers sent another telegram to the anthracite presidents offering to submit the miners' demands to an arbitration commission of five persons to be selected by the Industrial Branch of the National Civic Federation, or else to a commission to consist of Archbishop Ireland, Bishop Potter, and one other to be selected by these two. This offer was also unanimously refused.   President Baer, in reply, declared that " anthracite mining is a business, and not a religious, sentimental, or academic proposition. . . . I could not if I would delegate this business management to even so highly respectable a body as the Civic Federation, nor can I call to my aid as experts in the mixed problem of business and philanthropy, the eminent prelates you have named."

Finally the district executive committees of the union, meeting at Scranton on May 9, called for a temporary suspension of mining to start May 12.   On May 15 a convention of delegates instructed to vote on the question decided to make the strike permanent.[1]   Almost the entire body of

---

[1] Mitchell, *op. cit.,* pp. 370-373.

anthracite miners, nearly 150,000 men, remained on strike during the five months or more of its continuance.

On June 7 President Roosevelt directed Commissioner Wright to investigate the causes of the strike and make recommendations concerning it. For the next few weeks the commissioner heard the statements of each side and on June 20 he reported to the President.[1] He made suggestions for a settlement as follows: (1) the organization of an anthracite coal miners' union, independent of the United Mine Workers but perhaps affiliated with it, and to be financially responsible for its contracts; (2) concession of the nine hour day as an experiment, in order to test its influence on production, with a guarantee of permanency if production were not materially reduced; (3) the new union and the operators to form a joint committee on conciliation to consider grievances. Several other recommendations of less importance were also made.[2]

As the summer wore on and the fall approached no sign of a termination of the strike appeared. But as cold weather came nearer the public began to demand that something be done. The Governor of Massachusetts and the Mayor of New York both notified President Roosevelt " that if the coal famine continued, the misery throughout the Northeast, and especially in the great cities, would become appalling, and the consequent public disorder so great that frightful consequences might follow." Describing the situation further in his Autobiography, the President continues, " It is not too much to say that the situation which confronted Pennsylvania, New York, and New England, and to a less de-

---

[1] The legal authority for the investigation was contained in the organic law of the Bureau of Labor, which authorized the commissioner to make special reports on labor conditions to the President or Congress on the request of either.

[2] Wright, Bulletin 43, *op. cit.*, pp. 1166-1167.

gree the states of the Middle West, in October, 1902, was quite as serious as if they had been threatened by the invasion of a hostile army of overwhelming force." [1]

On September 27 President Roosevelt wrote as follows to Mark Hanna, who had tried unsuccessfully for months to bring about a settlement of the strike:

What gives me greatest concern at the moment is the coal famine. Of course we have nothing whatever to do with this coal strike and no earthly responsibility for it. But the public at large will tend to visit on our heads responsibility for the shortage of coal, precisely as Kansas and Nebraska visited upon our heads their failure to raise good crops in the arid belt eight, ten, or a dozen years ago. I do not see what I can do, and I know the coal operators are especially distrustful of anything which they regard as in the nature of political interference. But I do most earnestly feel that from every consideration of public policy and good morals they should make some slight concession. [2]

Despite the hesitation evidenced in this letter the President soon decided on action to end the strike. At his invitation representatives of the operators and of the miners met him on October 3, in response to his request that they come together " upon the common plane of the necessities of the public." When the conference opened, President Mitchell of the miners proposed that all the matters in dispute be submitted to the arbitration of a tribunal selected by the President. [3] In his Autobiography Mr. Roosevelt speaks of the operators as follows: " [They] came down in a most insolent frame of mind, refused to talk of arbitration or other accomodation of any kind, and used language that was

[1] Roosevelt, *Autobiography,* New York, 1921, p. 465.

[2] Croly, *Marcus Alonzo Hanna, His Life and Work,* New York, 1912, p. 397.

[3] Mitchell, *op. cit.,* p. 387.

insulting to the miners and offensive to me." [1]   President
Baer, speaking for the operators, though refusing the proposal for arbitration, promised that if the workers returned
to work and if the employer and employees at any particular
colliery could not reach an agreement on a grievance, it
should go to the judge of the Court of Common Pleas for
that district in Pennsylvania in which the colliery was situated. [2]   He insisted that all that was necessary was for the
state to keep order, using the militia as police, while the
operators ran the mines.   Each side asked the President
to proceed against the other for violation of the interstate
commerce laws. [3]   The conference was a failure as far as
any immediate result was concerned.

Four days later, acting through Commissioner Wright,
Mr. Roosevelt requested that President Mitchell use his efforts to get the men to return to work.   He gave assurance
that after mining was resumed a commission would be appointed to investigate conditions in the anthracite field.   The
President promised, when the report of the commission
and its recommendations were received, to do everything in
his power to induce the operators to accept its findings.
After consideration Mr. Mitchell refused to accept this proposal on the ground that the operators had already declined arbitration and, since the President had no legal
power to enforce the award of such a commission, acceptance
would mean surrender by the miners. [4]

In the meantime the operators had lost considerable of the
support of public opinion for their refusal to arbitrate.   J.
Pierpont Morgan, who much earlier in the strike had made

---

[1] Roosevelt, *op. cit.*, p. 466.

[2] *N. Y. Tribune*, Oct. 4, 1902.

[3] Roosevelt, *op. cit.*, p. 466.

[4] Mitchell, *op. cit.*, p. 467.

ineffectual attempts to have the operators make some concession, was aware of the untenable nature of the operators'
position.   Having considerable influence with the latter
through financial control over the anthracite roads, he appears, about October 7, to have determined to get the operators to make some move to end the strike.   Furthermore, on
the 11th, Secretary of War Root, at the request of the
President, had a long conference with Mr. Morgan in New
York.   He presented the President's point of view so successfully that he persuaded the financier to join him in
drafting an agreement for arbitration.[1]   Mr. Morgan obtained the approval of the operators for this agreement, with
the one modification upon which they insisted, that the members of the commission of arbitration be appointed from certain groups which they named.[2]

On October 13, presumably at the request of the operators,
Mr. Morgan visited President Roosevelt and proposed that
he appoint an arbitration commission to be constituted as
follows: one officer of the engineer corps of the army or
navy, one man with experience in mining, one man of prominence eminent as a sociologist, one Federal Judge of the
Eastern District of Pennsylvania, and one mining engineer.[3]

The President forwarded this proposal to Mr. Mitchell,
who suggested that, since capital was to be represented, labor
should also have a representative.   In addition he also asked
for the appointment of some Catholic ecclesiastic on the
ground that this would strengthen the proposition with the
miners, many of whom were Catholics.   The operators refused to grant either of these points, but were not so em-
phatic about refusing the appointment of a clergyman as

[1] *Review of Reviews*, vol. xxvi, pp. 516, 522, 552-555.

[2] Bishop, *Theodore Roosevelt and his Times*, New York, 1920, p. 212,
Letter of Elihu Root.

[3] Roosevelt, *op. cit.*, p. 467; *N. Y. Tribune*, Oct. 14, 1902.

that of a labor representative. The union officials put the matter into President Roosevelt's hands for settlement.[1]

A final conference between the operators and the President took place on October 15. The former were persistent in contending for a commission appointed according to their own proposition. Suddenly, after two hours of argument, Mr. Roosevelt discovered " that they did not mind [his] appointing any man, labor man or not, so long as he was not appointed as a labor man, or as a representative of labor." [2] He announced at once that he had accepted the terms laid down by the operators. With this understanding he appointed the labor man he had had in mind all the time, Mr. E. E. Clark, head of the Order of Railway Conductors, calling him an " eminent sociologist." On his own authority he put a sixth man on the commission, Bishop Spalding, a Catholic ecclesiastic of Peoria, Illinois.

The operators had expected that Carroll D. Wright would be appointed as a sociologist. Instead the President named him recorder of the commission, and added him as a seventh member when the commission got fairly started. In publishing the list of commissioners the President added, after naming Mr. Clark, " as a sociologist, the President assuming that for the purpose of such a commission, the term sociologist means a man who has thought and studied deeply on social questions and has practically applied his knowledge." [3] The other men appointed were Brigadier General

---

[1] Roosevelt, *op. cit.,* p. 467.

[2] Roosevelt, in his letter to Senator Lodge, of October 17, 1902, said, " It took me about two hours before I at last grasped the fact that the mighty brains of these captains of industry had formulated the theory that they would rather have anarchy than tweedledum, but if I would use the word tweedledee they would hail it as meaning peace." Bishop, *op. cit.,* p. 214.

[3] Roosevelt, *op. cit.,* pp. 468-469.

J. M. Wilson, E. W. Parker, Judge George Gray, and Thomas H. Watkins.

A delegate convention of the anthracite miners was called for October 20. On the next day it voted to end the strike, that work be resumed on October 23, and that all disputed questions be submitted to arbitration by the commission.[1] Thus the strike, one of the most serious in the country's history, was ended after a duration of more than five months.

From October 27, when the first hearing was held, to February 9, 1903, the commission investigated conditions at first hand and heard the testimony of both sides. Its final report, containing the award and recommendations, was presented to the President on March 18. Briefly summarized, the award, which remained the basis for continuing peace and prosperity in the anthracite field for many years, was as follows:

1. Wages were increased 10 per cent, retroactive to November 1, 1902.

2. Coal was to be paid for according to the then existing method.

3. Each of the three anthracite districts was to nominate two men, one representing the operators, the other elected by the miners. The six men thus appointed were to act as a board of conciliation to hear all disputes which could not be settled locally. Its award was to be final and binding. Provision was to be made for arbitration by an umpire in case of disagreement by the board.

4. Check weighmen or check docking bosses, or both, were to be employed wherever a majority of the contract miners requested it.

5. A sliding scale of wages, following increases or decreases in the price of coal in New York, within certain limits, was to be adopted.

[1] *Report of the Anthracite Coal Strike Commission*, p. 12.

6. There was to be no discrimination by either side because of membership or non-membership in the union.

7. The award was to continue in force until March 31, 1906.[1]

In considering the part that President Roosevelt played in settling the strike it should be borne in mind that there existed no precedent for him to follow. He had no authority of a legal nature, and only his own prestige and the country's unquestioned eagerness to be assured of the winter's coal were his supports in prevailing on the operators to agree to arbitration. As he himself put it, " There was no duty whatever laid upon me by the Constitution in the matter, and I had in theory no power to act directly unless the Governor of Pennsylvania, or the legislature, if it were in session, should notify me that Pennsylvania could not keep order, and request me as commander in chief of the army of the United States to intervene and keep order." [2] But the Governor handled the little violence there was with state militia and did not call for federal troops. Furthermore, had he done so, and had his request been promptly met, that in itself would probably not have had any great influence in ending the strike and producing coal for an anxious public. The precedent which President Cleveland had set in obtaining an injunction to end a railroad strike could hardly serve in a case like this.

It may be asked, " Would it not have been wiser for the President to have kept his hands off, since he had no legal authority to intervene?" But to have done nothing under such conditions as threatened with the approach of winter would undoubtedly have occasioned very serious hardship and suffering. Furthermore President Roosevelt had a

[1] *Rep. of the Commission*, p. 80.

[2] Roosevelt, *op. cit.*, p. 466.

theory of executive action which was quite inconsistent with a " hands-off " policy.   He did not believe that a President was limited in his acts by what the Constitution or Congress specifically empowered him to do.   He felt that he was limited only to the extent that he might not do the things which the law of the land specifically forbade.[1]   A President with strict constructionist views of the executive powers might consistently have kept his hands off.   But, in this instance, it would seem to have been fortunate that such a president was not in office, despite the copious criticism to which Mr. Roosevelt's intervention gave rise among his political opponents.

It appears clear that the President's primary motive in this case was to prevent a coal famine.   Was his method of mediation fair to both sides?   Did it aim at bringing about a settlement that was just to both sides?   To attempt an answer to such questions is perhaps superfluous, for each individual would probably answer according to his usual sympathies in industrial struggles.   It is doubtful whether the consideration of fairness and justice was uppermost with the President.   The important principle in his method was that of expediency, moderated to a certain extent by his own standard of fairness, and his probable dislike of the operators for their stubbornness.   But that expediency was the guiding principle seems evident when his proposal to President Mitchell, through Commissioner Wright, is considered.   He asked the miners to give up the strike on the basis of the possibility that the operators would agree to put into operation the award of the proposed commission, though he must have realized as well as the miners that it was improbable that the operators would do this.

One more fact may be given as evidence that he had determined to use whatever method was necessary to end the

---

[1] Roosevelt, *op. cit,* p. 388.

strike.   While the President was trying to get a settlement, he was formulating other plans of a very drastic nature. He had determined that as a last resort he would get the Governor of Pennsylvania to ask him to keep order.   Then he would put the army under the command of a first-rate general with instructions to keep absolute order and to prevent any interference by the strikers or others with those who wanted to work.   He would also instruct the general to dispossess the operators and run the mines as a receiver. Meanwhile he would appoint a commission to investigate the issues and make an award.   He had already asked ex-President Cleveland to serve on such a commission, not, however, mentioning any other detail of his plan to him. Mr. Cleveland had agreed to accept such an appointment. The President expected to appoint a commission which would command such confidence that public opinion would support its award, and he, with the U. S. Army in control, could issue whatever orders were necessary to carry it into effect.

President Roosevelt had actually made most of the necessary arrangements for putting the plan into effect, had arranged matters so that the Governor of Pennsylvana would call for troops when he suggested it, and had gone over the whole plan with Major General Schofield, upon whom he had determined as commander, and who alone, besides the President, knew what the plan was.   But a voluntary settlement made the whole arrangement unnecessary.[2]   It is quite evident, when one considers such a plan, that he was determined to have coal mined, and it is needless to add that his critics would have had much more to say about executive usurpation of authority had he put it into effect.

[1] For the letters between Cleveland and Roosevelt in regard to this matter see Bishop, *op. cit.*, pp. 204, 205, 209, 210, 213.

[2] Roosevelt, *op. cit.*, pp. 473-475.

In addition to his desire to spare the country the effects of a prolonged coal famine there was perhaps another reason for the President's wish to end the strike. This is apparent when one considers his letter to Senator Hanna, previously quoted. Evidently the President was thinking not only of his duty to protect the country from hardship, but he also had in mind the results of such hardship on the political prestige and reputation of his administration; for the campaign of 1904 was approaching and no one doubted his willingness to be a candidate for the presidency.

2. THE MINERS' STRIKE IN ARIZONA, 1903

Early in June, 1903, miners in Morenci, Arizona, went on strike because of the recently passed territorial eight hour law. The passage of the law involved the question of a reduction in pay. The miners asked their previous ten hours' pay for the new eight-hour day. Their request was refused by the mine operators and the strike resulted.[1] On June 10, because of the violence which had developed in the district, the Acting Governor of the Territory sent in territorial troops. At the same time he asked the President to send federal forces to the district.[2]

The President thus describes his action in a letter published in his Autobiography:[3]

The miners struck, violence followed, and the Arizona Territorial authorities notified me they could not grapple with the situation. Within 20 minutes of the receipt of the telegram orders were issued to the nearest available troops, and 24 hours afterwards General Baldwin and his troops were on the ground and 24 hours later every vestige of disorder had disappeared.

[1] *Reports of the War Department,* 1903, vol. 3, p. 31.

[2] *N. Y. Tribune,* July 11, 1903.

[3] P. 494.

On arriving, the troops found that the district was quiet, the territorial forces having the situation well in hand. On the 18th of June the federal soldiers were withdrawn. No further difficulties developed.[1]

It is apparent from Mr. Roosevelt's letter that he was proud of his prompt action in sending the troops. Yet there was evidently no need for them, and a short delay, while some federal officer investigated the need, might have been wiser. President Roosevelt's care to investigate before sending troops in later times is evidence that he realized that promptness in such cases was not an unmixed advantage.[2]

3. THE COLORADO STRIKE OF 1903-1904

In 1903 there commenced a serious and bitter strike of gold miners in the Cripple Creek and Telluride districts of Colorado.[3] Before long considerable violence and rioting developed. State troops were sent in, but disorder continued. On November 16 Governor Peabody of Colorado wired to President Roosevelt, informing him that industrial troubles were becoming more dangerous every day and that a serious emergency existed. " Will you," he asked, " instruct General Baldwin, commanding the Department of Colorado, to furnish me with such aid as I may call for? " [4]

On November 17 Secretary of War Root wrote to the Governor, telling him he hoped matters would not reach

---

[1] *Rep. of the War Dept., op. cit.,* p. 31.

[2] The Western Federation of Miners later denounced the President for sending troops to Morenci in order to kill the strike. *Miners Magazine,* August, 1903. The charge does not appear to have been justified.

[3] For a complete account of the strike see Rastall, *The Labor History of the Cripple Creek District,* Madison, Wis., 1908.

[4] *Report on Labor Disturbances in Colorado,* 3rd Sess. 58th Cong., Senate Document 122, p. 9.

a point beyond the ability of the state authorities to enforce
the laws. If such a situation were to arise the Governor
should make application to the President, since General
Baldwin could not act prior to such application.[1]

The next day Governor Peabody again wired the President. He claimed that armed pickets had taken possession
of property in San Miguel County, that violence was being
committed, that the sheriff was unable to cope with the
situation, and that the state had exhausted every means at
its command to enforce the law, to suppress lawlessness, and
to protect life and property. He again asked that General
Baldwin be instructed to furnish aid.[2] On the 19th Secretary Root, in answer to the Governor, telegraphed that the
President had no lawful authority to comply with the request. The President could send troops at the request of
the Governor only if the disturbance amounted to an insurrection against the state. He could not place troops at the
disposal of the Governor, but must himself direct their
operation,[3] " and he must be furnished with such facts as
shall enable him to judge whether the exigency has arisen
upon which the Government of the United States is bound
to interfere." [4]

The War Department, on November 20, instructed Major
J. C. Bates to make an investigation into conditions of
lawlessness and disturbances reported to exist in Colorado
and to report whether such conditions amounted to insurrection, whether state forces had been used to the extent which
would justify the President in sending in United States
troops, and whether the laws of the United States were being

[1] *Report on Labor Disturbances in Colorado, op. cit.,* p. 9.

[2] *Ibid.,* p. 10.

[3] Compare the way in which troops were used in the Coeur d'Alenes.

[4] *Ibid.,* p. 11.

violated to an extent which would justify the President in sending troops on his own initiative.[1] On November 29 Major Bates reported that a state of insurrection against the state existed justifying the employment of the state militia, but that federal troops were not then needed.[2] Though the strike lasted for many months longer no federal troops were sent to the district.[3]

The course of the President in this instance seems an admirable one when compared to the hasty and ill-advised use of troops in other disturbances. The lesson of the Coeur d'Alenes appears to have been learned by 1903, and the principle that federal troops were not to be used in such cases until all the resources of the state were exhausted was maintained by the President with a firmness not found before that time.

4. THE COAL STRIKES OF 1906

The wage agreements in both the anthracite and bituminous coal fields were scheduled to expire on March 31, 1906. Early in the year the bituminous miners and operators held conferences over the new agreement. In 1905 the miners had undergone a reduction in wages. For the new scale they asked an increase of 5.55 per cent, which would place them on a par with their 1903 wages. They also made other demands. Against these demands the operators were firm. The most they would do was to offer to continue the

[1] *Report on Labor Disturbances in Colorado, op. cit.*, pp. 11-13.

[2] *Ibid.*, p. 14.

[3] President Roosevelt had several investigations made into the general strike situation in Colorado. On May 2, 1904, W. B. Palmer of the Bureau of Labor was sent in and made a thorough investigation, the report of which was made public in January, 1905, and is the source of information here used. On May 16, 1904, John Graham Brooks was also sent to investigate and report to the President. But the administration had no further connection with the strike, other than to ascertain that federal laws were being obeyed.

existing conditions. This offer was almost unanimously rejected by the bituminous miners in convention, and they at
the same time made preparations for a strike.[1]

Meanwhile the anthracite miners, whose wages, under the
award of the Anthracite Strike Commission, had not changed
since 1902, were also planning to fight for an increase in
wages and for certain other changes.[2]

The attitude of the operators and miners indicated that
strikes in all fields were likely to occur. Accordingly, on
February 24, President Roosevelt wrote a letter to President
Mitchell of the miners, of which the following is a part:

A strike such as is threatened on April 1 is a menace to the
peace and general welfare of the country. I urge you to
make a further effort to avoid such a calamity. You and Mr.
Robbins [3] are joint chairmen of the Trade Agreement Committee of the National Civic Federation and it seems to me
that this imposes additional duty upon you both, and gives an
additional reason why each of you should join in making a
further effort.[4]

A similar letter was sent to Mr. Robbins. As a result
both operators and miners at once made further attempts to
come to an agreement. In the bituminous conferences,
however, no settlement had been reached by March 29.
Most of the operators refused to grant an increase. The
miners' convention, under the circumstances, voted to strike,
but with the understanding that work would be continued at
those mines which put the 1903 scale into effect.[5] In a
number of cases the increase was conceded. But not until

---

[1] *Philadelphia Public Ledger,* Feb. 1 and 2, 1906.

[2] *Ibid.,* March 12, 1906.

[3] F. L. Robbins was the leader of the bituminous operators.

[4] *Ibid.,* Feb. 27, 1906.

[5] *Ibid.,* March 30, 1906.

July 13 was an agreement signed which virtually ended the strike in the bituminous fields. The miners succeeded in getting their increase, but lost out on several other demands.[1]

The anthracite miners also went on strike when their agreement ended. Throughout the month of April conferences were held with the operators, at which arbitration was proposed and rejected. Finally, on May 7, with the approval of the anthracite miners' convention, the union leaders signed an agreement with the operators continuing the award of the Anthracite Coal Strike Commission for three years to March 31, 1909.[2]

It is evident that the strikes, occurring as they did in the spring, were not very serious, and though President Roosevelt's letters perhaps hastened the conferences between operators and miners, it is doubtful whether the strike would have continued much longer had he not interfered. A dispatch from Washington stated that the President and his cabinet, on March 30, had decided not to interfere in the coal situation unless public interest suffered from a coal famine, or general disorder occurred in the mining regions, or the operators and miners should agree to be bound by the award of a commission of arbitration.[3]

5. THE MINERS' STRIKE IN GOLDFIELD, NEVADA, 1907

In the late fall of 1907 the gold miners of the Goldfield district of Nevada went on strike against payment of wages in the form of bank scrip. The operators claimed that currency was not available, due to the panic of that year. The miners, on the other hand, maintained that the scrip was not accepted at par by the bank and by the merchants. Back of this direct cause of the strike there existed discontent due

[1] *United Mine Workers Journal,* July 19, 1906.

[2] *Ibid.,* May 10, 1906.

[3] *Philadelphia Public Ledger,* March 31, 1906.

to the hostile attitude of the operators toward the Western Federation of Miners, and to the desire for higher wages.[1]

On December 5, 1907, Governor Sparks of Nevada appealed to President Roosevelt for federal troops. He asserted that violence and unlawful conspiracies obstructed and hindered the execution of the laws and were depriving citizens of rights guaranteed by the Constitution, that the state authorities were unable to apprehend and punish the criminals, and that there had occurred " unlawful dynamiting of property, commission of felonies, threats against lives and property of law abiding citizens, the unlawful possession of arms and ammunition, and the confiscation of dynamite with threats of the unlawful use of the same by preconcerted actions ". He asked that two companies of United States troops be sent to Goldfield immediately.[2]

General Funston, commanding the Department of California, was at once instructed to send such troops to Goldfield as he thought necessary to cope with the situation.[3] After conferring with a mine operator from Goldfield the general sent nine companies into the strike district. On the 6th it was learned that the Governor had appealed for troops after having been requested to do so by the operators, and that the call on the President was made without consulting the local sheriff as to the need for troops.[4]

On December 10 Colonel Reynolds, in charge of the troops at Goldfield, reported that conditions were quiet. As a New York editor put it, the troops found everything " as quiet and peaceful as any slumbering New England town." [5]

The President, on the next day, sent the following instructions to Colonel Reynolds :

[1] *Outlook*, vol. 87, p. 838; vol. 88, p. 57; *Overland*, vol. 51, p. III.
[2] *N. Y. Evening Post*, Dec. 6, 1907.
[3] Wilson, *Federal Aid in Domestic Disturbances*, p. 310.
[4] *N. Y. Evening Post*, Dec. 6, 1907.
[5] *Ibid.*, Dec. 10 and 21, 1907.

The troops are not sent to take the part of either side in a purely industrial dispute, as long as it is kept within the bounds of law and order. They are to be neither for nor against the strikers or the employers. They are to prevent riot, violence, and disorder, under and in accordance with the Constitution and laws of the land. No man is to be interfered with so long as he conducts himself in a peaceful and orderly manner. . . . Do not act until President issues proclamation.[1] Notify adjutant general at once whenever anything occurs making proclamation necessary, and then wait further orders. Better twenty-four hours of riot, damage, and disorder than illegal use of troops.

There was no occasion for the issue of the proclamation, and at no time were the troops used against the strikers.[2]

On December 11 President Roosevelt appointed the following commission to go to Nevada and make a thorough investigation into the strike and the need for troops: Assistant Secretary of Commerce and Labor Murray, Commissioner of Labor Neill, and Commissioner of Corporations Smith.[3]

On the 17th he telegraphed to Governor Sparks, informing him that the troops were not sent to provide a substitute for the exercise by the state of its police functions, that in view of the fact that the Nevada legislature had not been convened to ask that they remain, it was fair to assume that the state officers were adequate to the situation, and that he would direct the troops to leave at once unless further cause for keeping them could be shown. Three days later, having received no answer, the President sent another message

---

[1] Rev. Stat. 5300 provides that the President shall issue a proclamation when troops are used, ordering the insurgents to retire peacefully to their homes.

[2] Wilson, *op. cit.*, p. 310.

[3] *N. Y. Evening Post*, Dec. 11, 1907.

to the Governor.   He said that he had been informed by
the commission which he had sent to Nevada that the Governor would neither convene the legislature nor take steps
to form a military force, and that there was no disturbance
in the state which the latter could not control if it made the
attempt to do so.   " Federal aid," he wrote, " should not be
sought by the State as a method of relieving itself from the
performance of this duty, and the State should not be permitted to substitute the Government of the United States
for the Government of the State in the ordinary duty of
maintaining order within the State."   He informed the
Governor that he had given orders for the withdrawal of
the troops on December 30.[1]

The Governor finally replied to the President on December 26.   He asserted that the miners had been armed for
the past year, that this was enough to overpower the civil
authorities, and that in his judgment, therefore, a state of
violence and insurrection had arisen.   He believed that the
troops should be kept at Goldfield indefinitely until both sides
ceased being armed camps, that it was practically useless to
convene the legislature, because it would require three weeks
to get the members together, and he intimated that even if
the legislature met he did not think it would call for the
retention of the troops.[2]

To this telegram President Roosevelt replied on December
28.   He maintained that even though the legislature might
refuse to call on the federal government, the Constitution
nevertheless put that duty on it.[3]   " The state government,"

[1] *N. Y. Evening Post,* Dec. 21, 1907.

[2] *Miners Magazine,* Jan. 2, 1908.

[3] Article IV, Section 4, of the Federal Constitution says, " The United
States shall guarantee to every State in this Union a republican form
of government, and shall protect each of them against invasion; and
on the application of the legislature, or of the executive (when the
legislature cannot be convened) against domestic violence."

he continued, " certainly does not appear to have made any serious effort to do its duty by the effective enforcement of its police functions." He insisted that troops would be permitted to remain only if the legislature asked for them. " You have," the message concluded, " fixed the period of three weeks as the time necessary to convene and organize a special session. If within five days from the receipt of this telegram you shall have issued the necessary notice to convene the Legislature of Nevada, I shall continue the station of the troops at Goldfield during such period of three weeks. If within the term of five days such notice has not been issued, the troops will be immediately returned to their former stations." [1]

On December 30 Governor Sparks called an extra session of the legislature to convene on January 14. On the 16th the legislature passed a resolution asking the President to keep the troops at Goldfield until it could provide for the formation of a state constabulary. A law enacting such a force was passed on February 1, and on March 7, 1908, the last of the federal troops were withdrawn.[2]

Meanwhile, on January 12, the report of the President's commission was made public. The commission asserted that there was no warrant whatever for calling on the President for troops, that there was no insurrection when the troops were called, that none of the conditions enumerated in the statutes empowering troops to be sent existed, and that the call for the troops was plainly the effort of the state to have the United States perform police duties for it. The commission reported that the operators had instigated the call for troops, that after having heard their side of the case the commission was satisfied that no justification for

[1] Wilson, *op. cit.*, p. 310.
[2] *Ibid.*, p. 310; *Miners Magazine*, Jan. 9, 1908.

bringing in the soldiers existed, and that the mine operators, as soon as they had arrived, had issued a statement announcing a 20 per cent reduction in pay, and their intention not to employ members of the Western Federation. Concerning this, the commission said :

The action of the mine operators warrants the belief that they had determined upon a reduction in wages and the refusal of employment to members of the Western Federation of Miners, but they feared to take this course of action unless they had the protection of federal troops, and that they accordingly laid a plan to secure such troops and then put their program into effect.

The report of the investigators pointed out that the bulk of the testimony showed not the existence of past or present disorder, but the possibility of future disorder if the troops should be withdrawn, because of the operators' intention to reduce wages and not to employ Federation miners. The commission accordingly recommended that troops be kept at Goldfield for a short time longer.[1]

The incident again shows the necessity for investigation by some impartial agent before the President orders troops sent to the scene of a strike.   The alarming tone of Governor Sparks' first telegram to the President probably caused the latter to fear the evil consequences of delay, but, as he himself said to the officer in charge of troops at Goldfield, " Better twenty-four hours of riot, damage, and disorder than illegal use of troops."   Though his action in sending soldiers so hastily is deserving of criticism, his insistence that they be strictly impartial and his pressure on the Governor to have the legislature convened and to make provision for doing its own policing, when he realized that he had been placed in a false position, are worthy of praise.

[1] *N. Y. Tribune,* Jan. 13, 1908.

6. THE THREATENED WAGE REDUCTION ON THE LOUISVILLE
& NASHVILLE RAILROAD, 1908

Before proceeding to a discussion of railway labor disputes it is necessary to describe briefly the machinery set up by law for their adjustment, which might be invoked by the President in case of strike. In 1898 the Erdman Act [1] was passed to supersede the Act of 1888, already referred to in connection with the Pullman Strike. It provided that whenever a dispute occurred between a carrier and its employees in train service or operation either side might ask the Commissioner of Labor or the Chairman of the Interstate Commerce Commission to act as a mediator. If he were not successful attempts were to be made to get the parties to submit to arbitration. In case they agreed to this, each party was to choose one arbitrator, and the two thus appointed were to choose a third. If they could not agree, one of the commissioners mentioned above might appoint the third member. Though submission and arbitration were to be voluntary, the award was compulsory and provision was made for its enforcement through the federal courts. No strike or lockout might take place within thirty days after the granting of the award, according to the terms of the law. In case either party were dissatisfied it might carry an appeal to the courts. Only one effort was made to use this law during the first eight years of its existence, but beginning in 1906 it was invoked, particularly in its conciliation provisions, in many instances.

In the winter of 1907-1908 a number of roads in the Southeast, claiming the falling off in revenues due to the crisis as a reason, served notice on engineers and some other employees of their desire to change wage schedules. All of the unions declined to agree to any wage reductions, de-

[1] 30 Stat. 424.

claring their intention of striking if the roads insisted on
reducing wages.[1]   In a statement announcing a reduction
to go into effect on March 1, issued about the first of February, the Louisville & Nashville Railroad gave as one of
the reasons for the proposed cut, that drastic railroad legislation had " resulted and will undoubtedly continue to result
in loss of revenue and increased expense." [2]

This statement aroused President Roosevelt, a firm sup-
porter of the railroad legislation which had been recently
passed by Congress.   On February 18 he wrote an open
letter to the Interstate Commerce Commission, pointing out
that the Louisville & Nashville had laid the necessity of a
wage reduction to railroad legislation.   He directed the
commission to make an investigation of conditions on that
road, and others as well, to find out whether the need of the
wage cut was due to legislation or to misconduct on the
part of the roads.   He expressed his hope that any wage
controversy between the railroads and their employees might
find peaceful solution through the machinery of the Erdman
Act.   For this purpose the commission should be in a position to have relevant data pertaining to the carrier concerned,
for the use of a board of conciliation or arbitration.   Should
conciliation fail, and arbitration be rejected, accurate information should be available to develop public opinion.[3]

It is difficult to say to what extent the events which followed were the results of the President's letter.   On February 22 a committee representing the railway Brotherhoods
was assured by a number of important eastern roads that
there would be no wage cuts.   Union officials in public

[1] Neill, *Mediation and Arbitration of Railway Labor Disputes in the
U S.*, Bureau of Labor, Bulletin 98, p. 22.

[2] *Washington Post*, Feb. 21, 1908.

[3] Roosevelt, *An Autobiography*, p. 496.

statements expressed their belief that the letter of the President had had a good effect.[1]

Unable to secure an agreement with the unions for a wage reduction, the Southern Railway, late in February, invoked the mediation provisions of the Erdman Act. Shortly afterwards the engineers and other employees on seven of the southern roads, including those of the Louisville & Nashville, did likewise, to avoid what they regarded as the necessity for a strike should wages be reduced. Commissioners Knapp and Neill, the mediators under the law, agreed to dispose of their cases after the negotiations in the Southern Railway case had been concluded. It became generally understood that the agreement reached in the latter case would be followed by the other roads. On April 1 an agreement continuing the existing wage schedule was reached.[2] Meanwhile the Louisville & Nashville, soon after the publication of the President's letter of February 18, had let it be known that for the present at least the existing wage scale would be maintained.[3] The settlement of the Southern Railway case virtually put an end to any further danger of strikes on any of the southern roads.

If the letter of the President was the principal factor in preventing a railroad strike at this time, and no further evidence than the foregoing is available to prove it, it is interesting to observe the motive in the case. Apparently this is an instance in which the affection of a fond father for his legislative children led him to come to their defense with such vigor that it caused the offenders to retreat, and so neither a strike nor a wage reduction took place.[4]

---

[1] *Washington Post*, Feb. 23, 1908.   [2] Neill., *op. cit.*, pp. 22-23.

[3] *Washington Post*, March 9, 1908.

[4] The next four years was a period of comparative prosperity, with few important labor disputes. This must be assigned as the reason for the fact that there is on record no instance in which President Taft used his powers or influence to prevent or settle a strike.

CHAPTER IV

President Wilson, 1913-1917

I. THE THREATENED STRIKE OF CONDUCTORS AND TRAINMEN ON THE EASTERN RAILWAYS, 1913

At a meeting of the General Committees of the Order of Railway Conductors and the Brotherhood of Railway Trainmen, representing the employees on the eastern railways, which was held in Rochester, N. Y., on October 19, 1912, demands were formulated to be presented to the roads. The employees asked that wages be increased 15 per cent, which would place the wages on the eastern roads on a level with the western scales, that in all freight service ten hours or less constitute a day's work on runs of 100 miles or less, that overtime in excess of ten hours be paid for at the rate of time and a half, and that in cases where two engines were used double rates should be paid.[1]

Early in July, 1913, after conferences with the railway managers, the latter rejected the demands of the men, and also refused to consider their offer of arbitration under the Erdman Act on the ground that it placed the whole decision in the hands of one man, the third member of the board. Furthermore, the managers claimed, the act had been framed to settle disputes on a single railroad, and not on all the railroads in a large territory.[2]   Some time before, disputes

[1] *Report of the Board of Arbitration*, Eastern Railways, 1913, pp. 13-16, vol. i.

[2] *N. Y. Times*, July 5, 1913.

between the roads and the engineers and firemen had been settled by arbitration.   In both instances dissatisfaction with the provisions of the Erdman Act had developed, and long before July, 1913, both the roads and the men thought the law should be amended.[1]

On July 8 the conductors and trainmen voted overwhelmingly in favor of a strike and gave their officers power to call one if necessary.[2]   Both the managers and the men seemed to feel that a settlement without a strike was possible if some change could be made in the Erdman Act.   At the request of a committee of railway presidents, the chiefs of the railway Brotherhoods, and some officials of the National Civic Federation, arrangements were made through the Secretary of Labor for a conference with President Wilson to discuss changes in the act.   The President called the representatives of the roads and the Brotherhoods to meet him for that purpose on July 14.[3]

In the meantime identical bills to amend the act, satisfactory to both the Brotherhoods and the railways, had been introduced in the Senate and the House on June 17.   The Senate soon passed the bill before it without amendment.[4] It set up a permanent U. S. Board of Mediation and Conciliation, to consist of a Commissioner of Mediation and Conciliation, and not more than two other members, all of whom were to be appointed by the President, who was also to appoint an Assistant Commissioner of Mediation and Conciliation.   The Commission might, if it thought advisable, attempt to mediate on its own initiative.   In case mediation proved unsuccessful provision was made for

[1] Fisher, *Use of Federal Power in Railway Labor Disputes,* Bureau of Labor Statistics, Bulletin 303, 1922, pp. 45-47.

[2] *N. Y. Times,* July 9, 1913.

[3] *Ibid.,* July 10 and 12, 1913.

[4] *Congressional Record,* vol. 50, p. 2182.

arbitration by a board of three, or if desired by the disputants, of six members, with powers similar to those of the boards under the Erdman Act.[1]

In the House the bill was so amended that it was equally unsatisfactory to the railway companies and to the men.[2] At this stage, the conference, which President Wilson had called, took place.   Besides representatives of the roads and the Brotherhoods, the President had also called in Congressman Clayton, Chairman of the House Committee on the Judiciary, and Congressman Mann, Republican leader in the House.   The conference went to work earnestly to find some way to avert what threatened to be a most disastrous strike, and it succeeded in reaching a settlement on the first day.   Congressman Clayton promised the two parties to the dispute that he would offer to the House the bill which had already passed the Senate, and would urge its passage. On their side, the railways and the unions promised to submit the dispute to arbitration when the bill became a law.[3] On the next day, July 15, the House passed the bill and the President signed it.[4]

Although the country was greatly relieved at what had happened, the way to a settlement was not yet quite clear. On July 17 the railroads published their own set of grievances, which they insisted should be arbitrated along with the demands of the men.   Against their inclusion the Brotherhoods stood quite firm.   They maintained that the proper subjects for arbitration were their own demands and those alone, and that rather than yield the point they would go on strike as originally planned.   Finally, on July 26, the

---

[1] 38 Stat. 63rd Congress, Chap. 6.

[2] *N. Y. Times,* July 10, 1913.

[3] *Congressional Record,* vol. 50, p. 2432.

[4] *Ibid.,* pp. 2442, 2471.

railways gave in and joined the unions in signing a formal agreement to arbitrate under the Newlands Act, as it was called.[1]   In due course an arbitration board of six men was constituted and considered the disputed questions.   On November 10, 1913, it rendered its award, giving the men a compromise increase in wages averaging 7 per cent, but rejecting the other important demands of the Brotherhoods.[2]

This case is significant for several reasons.   In the first place, the calling of a conference by the President, and his efforts in the conference, averted a disastrous strike. Secondly, it was the first of many times that President Wilson called a conference to settle a strike.   And finally, it is one of the few instances in which a settlement was effected and a strike directly avoided by the passage of an act of Congress.   For it must again be emphasized that the railways were thoroughly determined not to arbitrate under the Erdman Act, and equally determined not to arbitrate under an extra-legal board carrying no statutory sanction whatever.[3]

2. THE COLORADO STRIKE OF 1913-1914

The Colorado strike of 1913-1914 was one of the bitterest that the country has ever seen.   It is particularly interesting because there were directly involved in it only about fifteen thousand men, but the issues it aroused and the antagonisms it stirred up were so important that they quite overshadowed its apparent insignificance.

For years the miners in Colorado had made unsuccessful attempts to obtain recognition of their union.   Since 1883 strikes had occurred about every ten years, all of them end-

---

[1] *N. Y. Times*, July 27, 1913.
[2] *Report of the Board of Arbitration, op. cit.*, vol. iii, p. 34.
[3] *Congressional Record*, vol. 50, pp. 2430-2442.

ing unsuccessfully and most of them disastrously. Chief
among the coal companies, and the leader of the industry in
the state, was the Colorado Fuel & Iron Company, controlled
by the Rockefeller family, and at the time of the strike of
1913, under the particular supervision of John D. Rockefeller, Jr. The unrest among the miners was not alone due
to unsatisfactory industrial conditions. Added to these
there existed political and social conditions which did much
to arouse the workers. The men claimed, and most investigators believe, with justice, that the coal companies, particularly the Colorado Fuel & Iron Co., dominated political
and economic affairs to such an extent that they were able to
turn matters to their interest whenever they desired. The
workers further maintained that this domination was
achieved through ruthless suppression of unionism, through
the blacklist, armed guards, spies, venal political officials,
summary discharge, the suppression of free speech, free
press, free assembly, and by various other means.[1]

It was this center of unrest and dissatisfaction that the
United Mine Workers of America determined to unionize.
It sent in organizers who built up small organizations in
many of the non-union districts. On August 26, 1913, the
Policy Committee of the union sent letters to every coal
operator in the state, asking him to meet the union in joint
conference for the purpose of adjusting matters in the industry. The letter was not answered, except by two small
operators. Undaunted, on September 8, the committee sent
letters to the operators again, notifying them of a joint convention of operators and miners to be held at Trinidad,
Colorado, on September 15, and asking them to be present.

This convention met on the date appointed, but no opera-

[1] G. P. West, *Report on the Colorado Strike,* 1915, U. S. Commission
on Industrial Relations, pp. 12-16.

tors appeared. The convention, which the employers claimed was made up of members hand picked by the U. M. W. officials, adopted a number of demands to be presented to the operators, and voted to strike September 23 if these were not granted.[1]   These demands, which were at once submitted as a basis of settlement, were as follows :

   1. Recognition of the union.

   2. A 10 per cent advance in tonnage and day rates of pay.

   3. An eight-hour day for all classes of labor.

   4. Pay for all narrow and dead work, including brushing, timbering, removing falls, handling impurities, etc.

   5. Checkweighmen at all mines, to be elected by the miners without any interference by company officials.

   6. The right to trade in any store they pleased, and the right to choose their own boarding houses and their own doctors.

   7. The enforcement of the Colorado mining laws, and the abolition of the " notorious and criminal guard system, which has prevailed in the mining camps of Colorado for many years ".

The miners claimed that demands 3, 5, 6, and 7 were already embodied in state laws, but that the operators did not comply with them, that the state law forbidding discrimination between union and non-union men was also continually violated, that wages in Colorado were the lowest paid in any Rocky Mountain state, and that workers were paid for work done under demand number 4 in all other states.[2]

The operators, on the other hand, maintained that 90

[1] *Facts Concerning the Struggle in Colorado*, Series 1, Coal Mine Managers, Sept. 21, 1914, p. 7; *Report of the Commission on Industrial Relations*, vol. vii, p. 6515.

[2] *Rep. of the Com. on Ind. Rel.*, vol. viii, p. 7025.

per cent of their workers did not belong to the unions, and
to grant recognition of the union would be to force them in,
that miners' wages in the state were 20 per cent higher than
in the districts with which it competed, that the pay
asked under the fourth demand had been paid for many
years, and that all the other demands were granted under
state laws which were not and had not been violated by the
operators.[1] The strike, as was expected, started on September 23, most of the miners going out.

Even before the strike had begun the federal government,
realizing that it might bring about serious consequences, had
made an attempt to avert it. In the act which created the
Department of Labor and the office of Secretary of Labor,
passed early in 1913,[2] one section provided that " the Secretary of Labor shall have power to act as mediator and to
appoint commissioners of conciliation in labor disputes
whenever in his judgment the interests of industrial peace
shall require it to be done." No restriction was made as to
the industries in which mediators might be named, and under
this provision the department built up a valuable and active
bureau of mediation which settled many disputes. It was
under this law that the administration attempted to avert,
and later to end, the Colorado strike.

About a week before the Trinidad convention of September 15, Ethelbert M. Stewart of the Department of
Labor called at the New York office of John D. Rockefeller,
Jr., to see the latter concerning the threatened strike in
Colorado. At that time he was told that Mr. Rockefeller
was on vacation, but that he would be back on September 15.
Mr. Stewart called again on that day, but Mr. Rockefeller
had not yet appeared and had instructed a member of his
staff to talk with Mr. Stewart in his place. The latter called

[1] *Facts etc., op. cit.,* pp. 7, 8, 9.

[2] 37 *Stat.-at-Large* 736.

attention to the letter of the miners to the operators and the operators' failure to reply. The miners had then appealed to the Secretary of Labor to appoint a mediator. Mr. Stewart asked if it would be worth while going to Colorado, as he did not care to make a fruitless trip. He was told that the matter would have to be handled by the executive officers in Colorado. He answered that he thought that the policy could be determined in New York, but he was told that New York would not interfere with the Colorado officers unless the latter saw fit to submit the matter.[1] This interview is reported at some length because it indicates the policy that was followed by John D. Rockefeller, Jr., throughout the strike.

Failing in his efforts in New York, Mr. Stewart went to Colorado. The strike had already started, and he made unsuccessful attempts to bring the operators and miners together in conference to end it. He had various meetings with L. M. Bowers, manager of the Col. F. & I. Co., with other operators, and with the miners. In a letter to John D. Rockefeller, Jr., written September 29, Mr. Bowers said that he had told Mr. Stewart that the company would continue to work whatever mines it could, and that it would stand out against the union " until our bones [are] bleached as white as chalk in these Rocky Mountains." [2]

On October 6 Mr. Rockefeller, in answer to Mr. Bowers, wrote as follows:

We feel that what you have done is right and fair and that the position you have taken in regard to the unionizing of the mines is in the interests of the employees of the company. Whatever the outcome may be, we will stand by you to the end.[3]

[1] *Rep. of the Com., op. cit.,* vol. ix, p. 8413.

[2] *Ibid.,* vol. ix, p. 8420.

[3] *Ibid.*

On October 9 Mr. Stewart met representatives of the three most important coal companies, called at the request of Governor Ammons, in the latter's office. He made them the following proposals:

1. That the operators and strike leaders hold a conference.

2. That the operators meet with Governor Ammons, officials of the U. M. W., and himself, for an informal discussion of the situation.

3. That the operators suggest some method of ending the strike.

Each of these proposals was rejected in turn. On this Mr. Stewart stated that he would report to the Secretary of Labor and make recommendations for a Congressional investigation. This first attempt at mediation thus came to an end.[1]

During the rest of October Governor Ammons and various others continued their efforts to bring about a settlement, but to no avail. Meanwhile mine guards had been brought into the strike area in large numbers and efforts to work some of the mines continued. This situation soon developed much ill feeling in the strike districts, and finally the violence became so pronounced that the Governor, on October 27 and 28, sent in state troops to keep order.[2]

In November the Governor learned that Secretary of Labor Wilson was coming West, and he wrote to President Wilson asking that the Secretary be sent to Denver to attempt to bring about a settlement.[3] On November 20 Secretary Wilson sent the following telegram to John D. Rockefeller, Jr.:

[1] *Rep. of the Com., op. cit.,* vol. vii, p. 6595; *United Mine Workers Journal,* Oct. 9, 1913.

[2] *Rep. Com., op. cit., vol. vii,* p. 6512.

[3] *Ibid.,* vol. vii, p. 6413.

The governor of Colorado has asked me to lend my efforts toward settlement of coal strike there. He says the situation is critical and growing worse hourly. Can you help by using your influence to have representatives of the coal companies in Colorado meet representatives of miners with view to finding a mutual basis for settlement? . . .[1]

To this Mr. Rockefeller answered as follows:

. . . . So far as Colorado Fuel and Iron Co. is concerned the matter is entirely in hands of its executive officers in Colorado. They have always been quite as solicitous for the well being of the employees as for the interests of the stockholders. The men who have brought about this strike are not representatives of our miners, as only a small percentage of our men are members of unions, and all but an inconsiderable fraction of those have protested against the strike. The action of our officers in refusing to meet the strike leaders is quite as much in the interest of our employees as of any other element in the company. Their position meets with our cordial approval, and we shall support them to the end. The failure of our men to remain at work is due simply to their fear of assault and assassination. The governor of Colorado has only to protect the lives of bonafide miners to bring the strike to a speedy termination.[2]

After much effort Secretary Wilson arranged a meeting between three operators, three union men who were employees of the coal companies, and Governor Ammons, on November 26. At this conference it was agreed to submit identical propositions for a settlement to the operators and miners on the following day. On the 27th Secretary Wilson and Governor Ammons drew up a letter submitting the following as a solution, and sent it to both sides: there was to be strict enforcement of all the statutes, including that

[1] *Rep. Com., op. cit.,* vol. ix, p. 8422.
[2] *Ibid.*

forbidding discrimination against union or non-union men;
all employees on strike were to be reemployed except where
their places were filled, or where they were guilty of unlawful acts; and where the strikers' places were filled, other
places were to be furnished as soon as possible.[1]

On the same day Secretary Wilson and the Governor
submitted another proposal to the effect that with the acceptance of the other terms the following questions were to
be submitted to a board of arbitration: (a) the question of
an increase in wages; (b) the question of devising a method
whereby future grievances and disputes might be adjusted
without recourse to strikes.[2]

The operators accepted the first proposal, but objected to
the second on the ground that the other should first be accepted by the miners. The arbitration proposal was then
withdrawn.[3] Concerning it Manager Bowers wrote to Mr.
Rockefeller on November 28:

I can see no particular objection to the formation of an arbitration board as suggested by Secretary Wilson, providing the
three miners are non-union men who have remained in the
employ of the coal operators during this strike, but to this I
am sure neither Secretary Wilson nor the labor leaders would
consent.[4]

Meanwhile the miners' leaders had sent out the first proposal to be voted on by local unions throughout the state.
It was overwhelmingly rejected by the men on the ground
that to go back to work under the conditions proposed would
leave them in precisely the same position they were in be-

[1] Rep. Com., op. cit., vol. viii, p. 7037.

[2] Testimony before the Subcommittee of the House Committee on
Mines and Mining, Investigating the Colorado Strike. Washington,
1914, p. 411.

[3] Rep. Com., op. cit., vol. vii, pp. 6413-6414.

[4] Ibid., vol. ix, p. 8424.

fore the strike, since they would have to rely on the operators' promises to obey laws which the latter had claimed
had always been obeyed.[1] Finding the administration's
second attempt at mediation no more successful than the
first, Secretary Wilson returned to Washington.[2]

Before and during the period when Secretary Wilson
was endeavoring to bring the strike to an end, the President
was making similar efforts, through letters to Manager
Bowers. The following extracts from correspondence between J. Starr Murphy, of Mr. Rockefeller's personal staff in
New York, Mr. Rockefeller himself, and Mr. Bowers, in-
dicate the content of the President's proposals and the nature
of their reception.

Letter from Murphy to Bowers, December 1, 1913, in
which the former submits to the latter, at the request of Mr.
Rockefeller, a suggestion with regard to President Wilson's
proposal for arbitration by an impartial board:

. . . . whether it might not be a tactical advantage to say that
while we refuse to consent to arbitraion, we are not only willing, but we strongly urge an investigation of all the facts as
to the relation between the company and its employees and the
circumstances leading up to the strike. . . . The investigators
should not be politicians, but we might suggest that the President appoint any three Federal judges.

Letter from Bowers to Murphy, December 6, 1913:

On the surface the President's suggestion looks plausible but
we are too well advised to believe that it would be possible to
secure an impartial committee named by him. . . .

[1] *Rep. Com., op. cit.*, vol. viii, p. 7038-7039.

[2] President Welborn of the Col. F. & I. Co., in a letter to J. H.
McClement of New York, on Dec. 4, 1913, wrote, " Wilson says he
expects to go back to Washington tonight and we hope he will." *Ibid.*,
vol. viii, pp. 7117-7119.

We know that the President will not ignore the head of the Department of Labor, but will let his Secretary of Labor name the committee, if such an agreement was entered into. . . . . No whipping around the bush is necessary on the part of the President, if he really wants to end the strike; but he is too fearful of the labor voters who are in the unions to come out into the open and demand an end of the strike by those who are responsible for it. . . .

The writer has satisfied himself that the labor leaders in charge would laugh at any report of any committee that would leave recognition of the union open for the operators to decide for themselves. So we prefer to let the President ask Congress to make an investigation and take our chances.

Letter from Bowers to Rockefeller:

His Excellency [President Wilson] had an excellent opportunity to end this correspondence upon receipt of my second letter, but unwisely, we all think, he allowed himself to write another one, which, if from a less dignified statesman, would be regarded as a bluff, as he was well aware that the efforts of Congressman Keating, of Colorado, and some other representatives catering to labor unions have utterly failed to induce Congress to make an investigation. We are confidentially advised that President Wilson's recommendation for a congressional investigation will be no more effective. Anyhow, he can meditate over his decidedly weak reply to my second letter and take such action as he sees fit.[1]

Evidently the President ceased his efforts with Mr. Bowers, for there is no mention of any further letters. But on January 27 the House of Representatives provided for an investigation into the Colorado strike to ascertain if the Constitution or any federal laws were being violated. A subcommittee of the House Committee on Mines and Mining held hearings on the strike from February to April,

[1] *Rep. Com., op. cit.,* vol. ix, pp. 8425-8427.

1914, made a report to Congress rather favorable to the strikers for the most part, and published the testimony taken by it. The latter furnished the public much needed information concerning the strike.[1]

Throughout the winter much enmity had developed between the miners and the militia stationed in the strike districts. As spring came on conditions seemed to become more peaceful and plans were considered for removing most of the soldiers. The Governor had also had difficulty in raising money to support them, and this was an additional reason for the withdrawal plans. About April 1 a considerable number of troops were sent to their homes, and arrangements were made for the departure of the few remaining about April 22.[2] In reality, however, though violence may have diminished, the antagonism between the miners and the soldiers, who had used their efforts in aiding the operators in their attempts to run the mines with strikebreakers and had done various other things calculated to arouse the men (for example, the imprisonment of Mother Jones), was by no means diminished.

The miners and their families, having been evicted from the company houses they had previously occupied, had settled in several tent colonies in the mountains near the mines. At one of these colonies, Ludlow, a rumour spread shortly before April 20 to the effect that the militia were planning to descend on the colony and wipe it out. The colonists prepared for the expected attack by getting ready their arms and making arrangements to protect their families. On April 20, seeing a party of militia approaching the colony and believing that its intention was to attack them,

[1] *Report on the Colorado Strike Investigation*, 3rd Sess., 63rd Cong., House Document 1630.

[2] *Ibid.*, vol. vii, pp. 6415-6416.

the colonists are believed to have opened fire. That was the beginning of what soon became known the country over as " the Ludlow Massacre ". The soldiers, whatever their intent may have really been in the beginning, did just what the miners feared they were going to do. A large number of men were killed that day and the next, both among the militia and among the miners, and after the battle had cleared a group of women and children, who had escaped into a dugout beneath a tent to escape the gun fire, were found smothered to death by the fires which the soldiers had started to destroy the colony.

Some time afterward a military board of investigation made up of officers of the state militia reported: " Beyond a doubt, it was seen to intentionally that fire should destroy the whole of the colony. This, too, was accompanied by the usual loot. . . . So deliberate was this burning and looting that we find that cans of oil found in the tents were poured upon them and the tents lit with matches." [1]

On hearing of what had happened, Governor Ammons, who had gone to Washington to see the federal authorities in order to get them to make another attempt to end the strike, at once started back to Denver without an opportunity to accomplish his purpose. On the way he asked the administration to send troops into the state, but did not receive a favorable answer at first. He at once ordered the militia which had been relieved into the strike zone again. [2]

Before sending any federal troops to the scene of the disturbance President Wilson determined first to do what he could to bring the strike to an end and thus do away with

---

[1] *Ibid.*, vol. ix, p. 8765. There have been many contradictory descriptions of this unfortunate event, but that here given seems, after an examination of the testimony before the Commission on Industrial Relations and of other reports, to be nearest the truth.

[2] *Ibid.*, vol. vii, pp. 6415-6416.

the need for troops.   On April 26 he had a conference with
Representative Foster of Illinois, who had been chairman
of the House investigating committee, and with a number
of Colorado congressmen.   They all joined Governor
Ammons in urging him to send troops.   He also conferred
with Secretary Wilson and Secretary of War Garrison.[1]
On the same day he sent a message to John D. Rockefeller,
Sr., asking him to intervene to bring about peace in Colorado.   The elder Mr. Rockefeller answered that he had
turned the control of the Colorado Fuel & Iron Company
over to his son, but that he would ask the latter to take up
the matter.   Accordingly the President at once sent Mr.
Foster to New York to see John D. Rockefeller, Jr.   On
the 27th a meeting between the two took place.   Mr. Foster
asked Mr. Rockefeller to agree to have a commission appointed to settle the strike, so that federal troops would not
have to be sent.   This request met with a flat refusal.   Mr.
Rockefeller was also asked to shut down the mines pending
arbitration, but this request met a similar answer.[2]   The
next day Mr. Rockefeller published a statement regarding
the conference.   He said that Mr. Foster could suggest
nothing as a solution which did not mean either recognition
of the union or arbitration, and he defended his company's
stand against the demands of the strikers.

On the same day, April 28, realizing that a settlement was
unlikely, the President ordered federal troops to Colorado.
In a telegram notifying the Governor of his action he said
that he expected the latter to call the attention of the legislature, which was due to meet on May 4, to the necessity for
considering the whole situation and coming to prompt
action, " in order that the use of the Federal power may

[1] *N. Y. Times,* April 27, 1914.
[2] *Ibid.,* April 28, 1914.

be limited within its contemplated confines, and in order that the state may take up its duty as soon as it is possible for it to do so." He also asked that the state militia be withdrawn as soon as federal troops had arrived and taken control.[1]

Meanwhile Representative Foster continued his efforts. On April 29 he sent a telegram once more asking Mr. Rockefeller to end the strike, especially in view of an announcement which had recently been made by William Green, Secretary-Treasurer of the United Mine Workers, to the effect that the miners would waive their demand for recognition of the union in order to settle the strike. Mr. Rockefeller replied that he was forwarding the telegram to the Colorado officers of the company, who were the only ones competent to deal with it.[2] On the 30th the Colorado operators wired Mr. Foster, recounting the violence committed by the strikers and refusing to enter negotiations, but stating that they conceived it to be the duty of the United Mine Workers to call off the strike. On the same day Mr. Rockefeller wired to President Welborn in Colorado asking that the operators call Mr. Foster's attention to their acceptance of the Ammons-Wilson proposal of November 27. This the operators did in a telegram sent on May 1. That day and the next Mr. Foster sent further messages, asking that the operators arbitrate regardless of whose fault the trouble was. On May 4 the operators again sent a telegram to Mr. Foster refusing negotiations with the union, and reiterating their position that the men could always bring their grievances to the company officers.[3]

In the meantime the limelight into which the whole strike,

[1] *N. Y. Times*, April 29, 1914.
[2] *Rep. of the Com., op. cit.*, vol. vii, p. 6713.
[3] *Ibid.*, vol. vii, pp. 6713-6718.

and especially the affair at Ludlow, had thrown John D. Rockefeller, Jr., became distasteful, and his support of Messrs. Bowers and Welborn in their stand against any concessions whatever had aroused considerable public opinion rather unfavorable to the company. In this situation the Colorado operators, not including the Col. F. & I. Co., sent a long telegram to President Wilson. They pointed out that their companies operated 60 to 70 per cent of the mines, that they deplored the injustice done to John D. Rockefeller, Jr., and they took upon themselves independently of him and the Colorado company the responsibility for the conduct of the strike and the refusal to arbitrate or to recognize the union.[1]

The federal troops which the President had ordered out arrived in the strike district about May 1. On May 2 Secretary of War Garrison, by authority of the President, issued a proclamation calling upon and directing all persons in the district not in the military service of the United States, who had arms or ammunition in their possession or under their control, to deliver them to the army officers.[2] For some time afterwards the troops endeavored to enforce the proclamation, disarming both mine guards and miners, and though it was claimed they were not entirely successful, no violence occurred after they were settled in the district. On May 10 President Wilson, acting through the War Department, instructed the officer in charge of the troops to permit no importation of strike breakers.[3] Immediately afterwards the officer in charge ordered that all mines which were closed before the strike began, or at the beginning of the strike, should not open, but that all mines not closed before April 20 might reopen.[4]

[1] *Rep. Com., op. cit.* vol. vii, pp. 6718-6720; vol. ix, p. 8416.

[2] *United Mine Workers Journal*, May 17, 1914.

[3] *N. Y. Times*, May 11, 1914.

[4] *Ibid.*, May 12, 1914.

The policy of the federal troops in this strike is worthy of further attention.   In a letter sent to Mr. McClement, of New York, on May 27, 1914, President Welborn writes:

The policy of the Federal troops is not entirely satisfactory to us. . . . They will not permit us to bring in any men from outside the state and require that all of those seeking employment shall go direct to the mines where they want to work and make their application, rather than making it through our office here.[Denver] or in Trinidad.

In a later letter written on August 18 he says, " No change has taken place in the policy of the Federal troops with respect to the employment of men, although I do not think their rules are as rigidly enforced as at the beginning." [1]

The unions also felt that the enforcement of the rules was becoming less strict, for on September 1 the Secretary of War had occasion to send the following telegram to a union official in Aguilar, Colorado, who had complained that troops were permitting the importation of strikebreakers in his district:

I was not aware that the orders of the department were being interpreted differently in the different districts.   To prevent any such difference of interpretation I have communicated with all the commanders, advising them that hereafter orders shall be carried out as follows, with respect to those mines which are running: First—Operators are not to be permitted to gather men and ship them into such mines.   Second— Miners who apply at the mines may be there employed provided they are residents of the state of Colorado, and have complied with the laws of Colorado relative to miners.[2]

As a whole it may be said that the miners were well satis-

[1] *Rep. Com., op. cit.,* vol. viii, pp. 7120-7123.
[2] *United Mine Workers Journal,* Sept. 3, 1914.

fied with the federal troops; so much so that on October 29
Mother Jones, one of their organizers, and James Lord, of
the Mining Department of the American Federation of
Labor, called on President Wilson and asked him not to
withdraw them.[1] It is evident from what has been said
concerning the troops that the operators were eager to have
them afford such protection and aid that they might operate
the mines and thus defeat the strike; and it is equally
evident that President Wilson was determined that the
strike, if it were defeated, should not be defeated because
of the activities of the federal troops, a position which appears widely divergent from that taken by President Cleveland in the Pullman Strike, as well as from that taken by the
officer in command of troops in the Coeur d'Alenes.

It will be recalled that the President, in sending the
troops, had notified the Governor that he expected the
Colorado legislature to take such action as would make it
possible for the state to assume its whole duty in the matter. On May 16, hearing that the legislature was preparing to adjourn without acting on all the emergency measures before it, the President sent the following telegram to
Governor Ammons:

Am disturbed to hear of the probability of the adjournment
of your legislature, and feel bound to remind you that my
constitutional obligations with regard to the maintenance of
order in Colorado are not to be indefinitely continued by the
action of the state legislature. The federal forces are there
only until the state of Colorado has time and opportunity to
resume sovereignty and control in the matter. I cannot con-
ceive that the state is willing to forego her sovereignty or to
throw herself entirely upon the government of the United
States, and I am quite clear that she has no constitutional right

[1] *United Mine Workers Journal*, Nov. 5, 1914.

to do so when it is within the power of her legislature to take effective action.[1]

Governor Ammons replied on the same day, saying that the legislature had authorized a million-dollar bond issue, that as soon as these bonds could be issued funds would be available and the state could control the situation, that a commission of mediation had been appointed to settle the strike, and that other measures had been passed.[2] However, on May 19 the operators announced that they would not consider mediation by the commission, since they had "nothing to mediate."[3] And the Governor found that it was easier to have the legislature authorize a sale of bonds than it was to sell them.[4] The activities of the state of Colorado did not obviate the necessity for federal troops until after the strike was over.

On April 29 President Wilson had directed the Secretary of Labor to make another attempt to mediate the strike. For that purpose the latter asked Hywel Davies, president of the Kentucky Mine Operators Association, and W. R. Fairley of Alabama, an officer of the United Mine Workers, to go to the strike district and attempt a settlement.[5] These two spent several months in Colorado, the one mostly with the operators getting their side of the case, the other with the miners. Finally, late in the summer of 1914, they drew up a "tentative basis of adjustment", to be approved by both operators and miners in order to bring the strike to an end.

This plan was submitted to President Wilson, and on

[1] *United Mine Workers Journal*, May 21, 1914.

[2] *N. Y. Times*, May 17, 1914.

[3] *Ibid.*, May 20, 1914.

[4] *Rep. Com., op. cit.*, vol. vii, p. 6416.

[5] *N. Y. Times*, April 30, 1914.

September 5 he proposed it to both sides.   The basis of adjustment was to be as follows:

There should be enforced a three-year truce, subject to the following conditions:

1. The mining laws of the state were to be enforced.

2. All strikers not guilty of violation of law were to be given employment.   Where the miner's place was filled he was to be given employment as a miner at the same or at another mine of the company.

3. There was to be no intimidation of union or non-union men.

4. The current scale of wages, rules, and regulations for each mine was to be printed and posted.

5. Each mine was to have a grievance committee elected by employees.   The members of the committee were to be employees of at least six months standing, and married men were to be in the majority.   Grievances not settled individually were to be taken up by the committee.   If it could not settle a matter it was to go to a commission of three men, one of them representing the miners, one the operators, and the third to be appointed by the President.

6. During the life of the truce, as a condition of the establishment of the above machinery,

a. The claim for contractual relations was to be waived.

b. No mine guards, with the exception of the necessary watchmen, were to be employed.

c. The presence of troops was to be made unnecessary.

d. There was to be no picketing, parading, colonizing, or mass campaigning by representatives of labor organizations, which would interfere with mine work during the truce.

e. The decisions of the commission were to be binding and final during the truce.

f. There was to be no suspension of work during investigation and adjustment.

g. There was to be no suspension of the mines over six consecutive days pending the dispute.

h. Wilful violations of these conditions were to be subject to the penalties of the commission, the expenses of which were to be shared equally by employers and employees.

In a letter accompanying the proposal, the President wrote:

I feel justified in addressing you with regard to the present strike situation in Colorado because it has lasted so long, has gone through so many serious stages, and is fraught with so many possibilities that it has become of national importance. . . .

I am now obliged to determine if I am justified in using the Army of the United States indefinitely for police purposes. . . . I recommend [the tentative basis] for your most serious consideration. I hope that you will consider it as if you were acting for the whole country, and I beg that you will regard it as urged upon your acceptance by myself with very deep earnestness.[1]

The President's proposal was considered by a special miners' convention called for the purpose at Trinidad, Colorado, and on September 16 it was approved by a vote of 83 to 8.[2] Meanwhile the Colorado Fuel and Iron Co., with the help of Mr. Rockefeller's staff,[3] was preparing its answer to the President. On September 22 President Welborn replied to the proposal, accepting it as regards the enforcement of the statutes, but rejecting practically all the

---

[1] *Report of the Secretary of Labor*, 1914, pp. 40-41.

[2] *Ibid.*, p. 42.

[3] See Letter Welborn to Murphy, Sept. 18, *Rep. Com., op. cit.*, vol. vii, p. 6691.

rest.[1] On the same day the other operators sent their reply to the President, taking the same position.[2] For some time after hopes were entertained at the White House that the postion of the operators might change, but by the middle of October the President admitted that chances of acceptance of the plan had passed.[3]

The strike continued, and numerous plans were suggested to the President for handling the situation. Chief among them was a proposal made by the miners that the government take over the mines and operate them. It was also suggested that the government close the mines and not permit them to operate until the companies were willing to settle. The administration especially considered the first plan, but upon consultation with officials as to its legality, decided that it had no legal warrant.[4]

On November 30 the President made his final move in the direction of a settlement. He appointed Seth Low, Charles W. Mills, and Patrick Gilday as a commission to go to Colorado. In a statement explaining the purpose of the commission the President said:

I think the country regretted [the operators' decision concerning the proposal of September] and was disappointed that they should take so uncompromising a position. I have waited and hoped for a change in their attitude, but now fear that there will be none. And yet I do not feel that I am at liberty to do nothing in the presence of circumstances so serious and distressing. Merely to withdraw the federal troops and leave the situation to clear and settle itself would seem to me to be doing something less than my duty after all that has occurred.

[1] *N. Y. Times*, Sept. 23, 1914.
[2] *Ibid.*, Sept. 24, 1914.
[3] *United Mine Workers Journal*, Oct. 22, 1914.
[4] *N. Y. Times*, Nov. 25, Dec. 9, 1914.

I have, therefore, determined to appoint the commission contemplated in the plan of temporary settlement, notwithstanding the rejection of that plan by the mine operators, and thus at least to create the instrumentality by which like troubles and disputes may be amicably and honorably settled in the near future, in the hope . . . . that both parties may . . . . make use of this instrumentality of peace and render strife of [this kind] . . . . impossible of repetition.[1]

By this time the strikers were in distressing circumstances, the strike had evidently been proven a disastrous failure, and the union officials realized the fruitlessness of continuing it. On December 8 the Executive Board of the United Mine Workers recommended to a miners' convention at Denver that the strike be called off, calling attention to the President's appointment of a commission, and deeming it "the part of wisdom to accept his suggestion and terminate the strike". Two days later the convention formally voted the strike at an end, directed the miners to apply at once for their former positions, and recommended that efforts to organize the miners in Colorado be continued.[2]

On hearing of the miners' action President Wilson wired Governor Ammons, asking if it would be safe to withdraw federal troops. The Governor replied, requesting that troops be kept in the strike zone for the time being, since he feared that the strikers might attempt reprisals on the mines, the companies having thus far refused all their applications for work.[3] The troops were permitted to remain for the rest of the month, but on January 1, 1915, conditions having become more satisfactory, their withdrawal commenced. By January 10 all of them had departed.[4]

[1] *United Mine Workers Journal*, Dec. 3, 1914.
[2] *Ibid.*, Dec. 17, 1914; *N. Y. Times*, Dec. 9, 1914.
[3] *N. Y. Times*, Dec. 11, 1914.
[4] *Annual Reports of the War Department*, vol. i, 1915, p. 152.

The strike over, the commission appointed by the President found itself in a rather awkward position. It proceeded to Colorado, however, made an investigation, and reported on February 23, 1915.[1] Its report appears strangely insignificant, after an examination of all the other available material on the strike. It describes conditions in Colorado as more or less harmonious, and it approves the newly introduced Colorado Plan, the company union arrangement to which Mr. Rockefeller was converted by Mackenzie King, but which was quite actively opposed by the Colorado Fuel and Iron Company officials during the strike as a concession to the union which the latter would publish to the world as a victory.[2]

This strike is perhaps the best instance available of the unsuccessful use of the Presidential influence to end a dispute.[3] It is rarely that one can find an instance in which continually repeated requests for settlement addressed by the executive to a contestant elicit no concessions. There are on record in this case five entirely distinct and separate attempts on the part of the President and his officials to bring the strike to an end by mediation, with at least four of which attempts he had a direct connection. It is not often that a group of employers or of employees dares to face such a long and concentrated attack of public opinion as must come from a persistent refusal to be affected by the requests of the President of the United States. That the President in this case did all that he could do in the way of mediation is apparent.

[1] House Document 859, 64th Cong., 1st Sess.

[2] See letter of Bowers to Rockefeller, Aug. 16, 1914, *Rep. Com., op. cit.*, vol. ix, p. 8441.

[3] The fact that the miners gave the appointment of the commission as a reason for ending the strike seems more like a polite gesture than a statement of fact.

Enough attention has also been given to the use of federal troops in the strike to show that the policy followed for the most part was an enlightened and satisfactory one. Especially does this appear true when comparison is made with the use of troops in some of the earlier instances. In Colorado the President himself saw to it that troops were used for the only valid reasons which excuse their use in domestic troubles, that is, to preserve the peace and the law, and to prevent disturbances when the state government is unable to do these things itself. Neither side in the strike could with justice complain of the partiality of the troops, and the public interest was at the same time entirely protected by their use.

The question that remains unanswered is whether Mr. Wilson should have made attempts of a different sort in order to end the strike. There were no precedents which he could have followed, had he decided to take over the mines and put them under federal operation or to close them. It is doubtful, under the circumstances, whether such a step would have been a wise one. Such procedure was, as already indicated, of questionable legal validity. The further consideration that after all the strike was comparatively unimportant as far as it affected the welfare of the country as a whole is to be called to mind. The coal produced in Colorado, though important locally, was only a small proportion of the total tonnage, and the strike itself concerned only a few thousand men.[1]

[1] There was one other instance in 1914 of the President's sending troops to the scene of a strike. In April of that year the Bache-Denman Company, operating coal mines in Hartford Valley, Arkansas, tried to introduce the open shop. Considerable picketing and some violence took place when the men struck. The company obtained an injunction from the federal court to prevent interference with its operations. Later the court appointed Franklin Bache, one of the owners of the company, as a receiver under the court's orders. From

3. THE THREATENED STRIKE OF ENGINEERS AND FIREMEN ON THE WESTERN RAILWAYS, 1914

In October, 1913, the officers of the Brotherhood of Locomotive Engineers and the Brotherhood of Locomotive Firemen and Enginemen presented demands for important wage increases and changes in working rules, largely connected with wages, to the managers representing 98 western railroads. The managers and the union officials held conferences in Chicago during the next seven or eight months, but found it impossible to come to any agreement. Meanwhile a strike vote had been taken and the employees were ready to quit work if no satisfactory agreement could be obtained.[1]

Finally, on July 14, negotiations were broken off and a serious strike threatened the country.[2] A week later the United States Board of Mediation and Conciliation, established under the Newlands Act, took a hand in trying to effect a settlement. The mediation proceedings extended for some time, but were unsuccessful because the railway representatives declined to accept any of the proposals of the

then on more violence occurred, until finally, early in November, the court asked for federal troops to aid in enforcing its orders. President Wilson sent 250 men to the scene, the troops arriving November 4, and he issued at the same time a proclamation ordering the dispersal of unlawful assemblages in the district. The miners were not averse to the sending of federal trooops, which they preferred to the presence of state militia. The strike was finally settled when the control of the property passed by purchase into the hands of the United Mine Workers on January 19, 1915. The federal troops left the district in the middle of February. See the *N. Y. Times,* Nov. 4 and 5, 1914, Jan. 21, 1915; Wilson, *Federal Aid in Domestic Disturbances,* pp. 317, 321.

[1] Lauck, *Railway Labor Arbitration,* Report of the U. S. Board of Mediation and Conciliation. Washington, 1916, p. 457. For the demands of the men see *ibid.,* pp. 459-463.

[2] *N. Y Times,* July 15, 1914.

mediators unless certain counter demands of the railroads were also considered. Against this stand the employees' representatives strongly protested. The mediators then tried to induce the parties to arbitrate the men's demands under the Newlands Act. The men finally agreed to this, but the railway managers insisted that their own counter demands be arbitrated with those of the employees.[1]

With the situation at a standstill the Board of Mediation asked President Wilson to use his influence. On July 31 the Brotherhood presidents made a public statement announcing that the strike order would go into effect August 7 if the railway managers did not accept the plan of settlement which had been proposed by the Board of Mediation. They asserted that since the managers were the first to appeal to the board for its aid in avoiding a strike they ought to accept the plan which it supported.[2] The next day President Wilson had separate conferences with the managers and with the Brotherhood chiefs at the White House,[3] and urged them to arbitrate the controversy. The managers promised him that they would give the proposal their further consideration.[4]

Meanwhile the war in Europe had just begun. The panic and uneasiness which the reports announcing the entry into it of one great nation after another caused in this country will be readily recalled. Taking this feeling of disquiet as his leading motive, the President wrote on August 2 to A. W. Trenholm, Chairman of the Conference Committee of Railway Managers. After referring to the previous day's conference at the White House he continued:

[1] *Report of the U. S. Board of Mediation and Conciliation,* 1913-1917. Washington, 1918, p. 21.

[2] *N. Y. Times,* Aug. 1, 1914.

[3] *Rep. of Board., op. cit.,* p. 22.

[4] *N. Y. Times,* Aug. 2, 1914.

I am sure that you appreciate the extreme gravity of the situation into which the country and your roads would be plunged if the strike now threatened should unhappily occur. In view of world wide conditions, unparallelled in recent history, which have arisen in the last few days, it is obvious that the suspension of business on roads serving more than half the territory of the United States would be a calamity of incalculable magnitude. The situation has reached a crisis which hardly permits a full consideration of the merits of the controversy, and I feel that in the circumstances I can appeal with confidence to your patriotism and to your regard for the public welfare to make whatever sacrifice is necessary to avert a national disaster. The mediators under the Newlands law were impelled to propose a certain plan of arbitration because they were fully convinced, as I am also convinced, that under existing conditions no other peaceful solution of the dispute is possible. For these reasons, I very earnestly urge the acceptance of that plan, even though you may regard it as in some respects unfair to the interests you represent; and I am certain that in so doing you will perform an invaluable public service which will be everywhere deeply applauded and deeply appreciated.

The next day, after a meeting, the managers notified the President through Mr. Trenholm that they would yield to his request. The concluding part of their message follows:

In view . . . . of the situation as you have presented it, and of your appeal to our patriotism and to our regard for public welfare, we beg to express to you herewith our acceptance of the plan of arbitration proposed.[1]

On the same day, August 3, the managers and employees signed an agreement to arbitrate under the Newlands Act. By August 11 the four members of the board of arbitration representing the parties to the dispute had been chosen.

[1] *Rep. of Board., op. cit.,* p. 22.

These four found it impossible, however, to agree on the two impartial members, and under the terms of the law the latter were named by the U. S. Board of Mediation and Conciliation on November 21. The men thus chosen were Judge J. C. Pritchard, of the U. S. Circuit Court, and Charles Nagel, an attorney of St. Louis. On November 30 the hearings before the board commenced, and on April 30 the award was handed down.[1] It conceded only a small increase to the employees, and made only a few of the changes in working rules which had been demanded. It was an award distinctly unfavorable to the Brotherhoods.[2]

Meanwhile considerable complaint and difficulty were occasioned because of the membership of Charles Nagel on the board. On April 26, 1915, Brotherhood Presidents Stone and Carter had sent sharp protests to President Wilson, to Judges Chambers and Knapp of the U. S. Board of Mediation and Conciliation, and to Judge Pritchard, of the board of arbitration. They asserted that Mr. Nagel was a co-executor in the Busch estate, which owned stocks and bonds in 21 railways, and protested against the decisions which a board with him on it as a neutral member would hand down. After a conference on the 27th President Wilson and Messrs. Chambers and Knapp asked the Brotherhood chiefs that the protests be withheld from the board of arbitration. It was too late to do this, however, since they had already been filed.[3]

On April 30, after a conference with Judge Knapp, President Wilson decided that there was no good reason for the withdrawal of Mr. Nagel, since the employees knew that he was a trustee of the Busch estate and had not protested

[1] *Rep. of Board, op. cit.* pp. 23, 24, 25.

[2] *Ibid.,* pp. 23-25; Lauck, *op. cit.,* p. 493; editorial, *N. Y. Times,* May 2, 1915.

[3] *N. Y. Times,* May 1, 1915.

his selection when he was appointed. On the same day, however, Messrs. Stone and Carter denied that they had known of Mr. Nagel's connections, and issued a statement saying that "candor compels us to state that we have been grossly deceived in being compelled to submit our cases to a jury upon which sat not only two railroad officials, but also one alleged neutral arbitrator, who has shown by his conduct and demeanor throughout the whole hearing that he was a violent partisan of the railroads.[1]

The next day the delegates of the Brotherhoods met at Chicago. They declared that the award was a joke and the arbitration a farce; that they had "played in a game with the cards stacked against them"; that the wage increase didn't "amount to carfare"; that Mr. Nagel had been moved throughout by his "class consciousness"; but they ended by deciding to accept the award and to file no protest against it.[2]

The incident of the protest against Mr. Nagel was greatly to be regretted. The fault seems to have rested on the U. S. Board for appointing him under the circumstances, and on him for having accepted appointment. It is probable that no one at the time gave any thought to his connection with an estate owning railroad securities. President Wilson's decision, under the circumstances, seems to have been justifiable. It was rather late for the Brotherhoods to protest. The affair is worth consideration because it increased the dislike of the railway employees for arbitration by "so-called neutral" outsiders, a dislike which later occasioned the necessity for further exercise of the President's influence to avert strikes.

The whole incident is significant not alone because it

[1] *N. Y. Times,* May 1, 1915.
[2] *Ibid.,* May 2, 1915.

shows the influence of the President in averting a strike involving over 50,000 men and threatening serious harm to a large part of the United States, but also because it was among the first of many similar pleas for industrial peace made by President Wilson, based on grounds of patriotism and war necessity.

4. THE EASTERN OHIO COAL STRIKE, 1914-1915

The President, in 1915, made an unsuccessful attempt to settle a strike of coal miners in eastern Ohio. The strike, which was due to a dispute over the terms of an agreement embodying the provisions of a recently passed Ohio law which required that miners be paid on the run-of-the-mine basis rather than the screened-coal basis, began April 1, 1914, and was not finally settled until more than a year later. In January, 1915, mediators from the Department of Labor attempted a settlement, but the miners refused to accept less than 47 cents per ton for machine-mined coal and declined to arbitrate, while the operators insisted on not paying more than 44.61 cents. The mediators, therefore, failed to accomplish their purpose.

Further attempts were made by the Secretary of Labor early in March, but as these also failed, President Wilson met the operators on March 12. After this meeting the President consulted with the mediators and asked them to submit a basis of settlement to him. This they did on March 17. It was expected for some time after that Mr. Wilson would submit this basis to the miners and ask them to arbitrate the issue, but there is no record of such a request from him. The miners having refused previous offers to arbitrate, and being unwilling to accept less than 47 cents, the President seems to have preferred to keep his hands off. The strike was finally settled through the efforts

of the Governor of Ohio, who brought the parties together and on May 8 succeeded in getting an agreement.[1]

5. THE THREATENED RAILWAY STRIKE OF 1916.
THE ADAMSON ACT

On March 29, 1916, the four railway Brotherhoods,
consisting of engineers, conductors, firemen, and trainmen
on practically all roads in the United States, adopted demands to be presented to the railway managers. These demands were concerned principally with the introduction of
the eight-hour-day-100-mile-run standard as a day's work in
the freight service, and the payment for all time over eight
hours per day at the rate of time and a half. At the same
time the chiefs of the Brotherhoods, which were acting con-
certedly, notified the railway managers of the desired changes
and requested that all the railroads join together for the purpose of handling the proposals at one and the same time
through a joint committee of all the roads.

About a month later the roads replied in a more or less
uniform manner, neither accepting, rejecting, nor modifying
the demands made on them, but proposing that the whole
question of compensation in the classes of service affected
be opened up for consideration and disposal. On May 18,
according to the union's request, the railroads organized the
National Conference Committee of Railway Managers.[2]

From June 1 to June 15 the representatives of the railways and of the Brotherhoods held wage conferences in
New York City. On the 14th the men made a definite de-

---

[1] For the incidents of the strike and the issues involved see *United
Mine Workers Journal* from March 1914 to June 1915, especially the
issues of April 2 and April 30, 1914, and Jan. 21, Feb. 4 and 18, April
1, and May 13, 1915. See also the *Cincinnati Enquirer*, March 11, 13,
19, and 25, 1915; *The Survey*, May 29, 1915, vol. 34, p. 190, and the
Report of the Secretary of Labor for 1915, p. 24.

[2] *Report of the U. S. Eight Hour Commission*, Washington, 1918, p. 8.

mand for information as to whether the managers would
accept and apply the propositions for the eight-hour day and
time and a half for overtime.   On the next day the managers declined to accept the proposals and suggested that
the whole matter, including their own as well as the Brotherhood demands, be submitted to arbitration by the Interstate
Commerce Commission, or by a board constituted under
the provisions of the Newlands Act.   This proposal was declined by the men, whose experience with arbitration had
not left them favorably disposed toward it.   The Brotherhood chiefs, on the break-up of the conference, ordered that
a strike vote on the demands be taken.[1]

At a joint meeting of the managers and the men, taking
place on August 8, the former were notified that the men
had voted overwhelmingly in favor of a strike if no satisfactory agreements were made.[2]   The managers again offered to arbitrate and again the men refused.   On the next
day the railway representatives proposed that the unions
join them in invoking the aid of the U. S. Board of Mediation and Conciliation to effect a settlement.   This the men
declined to do, but they consented to give the board a chance
to mediate the controversy.[3]

Some time previously Judge Chambers of the U. S. Board
had consulted with President Wilson concerning the threatened strike, and when the meeting of August 8 took place
he was in New York, ready, with the President's approval,
to offer the services of the board if a break came.[4]   Accordingly, the board responded promptly to the manager's call
and commenced work on August 9.   After working for

[1] *Report of the U. S. Eight Hour Com., op. cit.,* p. 9; *The Railway
Conductor,* July 1916, p. 528.

[2] *Rep. Com., op. cit.,* p. 8; *N. Y. Times,* Aug. 9, 1916.

[3] *The Railway Conductor,* Sept., 1916, p. 671.

[4] *N. Y. Times,* Aug. 4 and 9, 1916.

several days with both sides, the mediators, who could obtain no concession from the men and none except the arbitration proposal from the managers, announced on August 12 that their efforts at obtaining a settlement had failed.[1]   At the same time they notified the parties concerned that the President desired conferences with them before a final break was made.

On the 13th Mr. Wilson sent requests for conferences to the two sides, of which the following letter to Elisha Lee, Chairman of the National Conference Committee of Railway Managers, is an example:

I have learned with surprise and with keen disappointment that an agreement concerning the settlement of the matters in controversy between the railroads and their employees has proved impossible. A general strike on the railroads would at any time have a most far-reaching and injurious effect upon the country. At this time the effect would be disastrous. I feel that I have the right, therefore, to request, and I do hereby request, as the head of the Government, that before any final decision is arrived at I may have a personal conference with you here. I shall hold myself ready to meet you at any time you may be able to reach Washington.[2]

On the 14th and 15th the President had separate conferences with the managers and the four Brotherhood chiefs. The latter told the President that they had no power to agree to arbitrate, and that only the 600 district chairmen, who were in New York at the time, had that power. Mr. Wilson then requested that they come to Washington, and on the 16th they arrived in the city.[3]

A day or two later the President made the following proposals for a settlement of the controversy:

[1] *N. Y. Times,* Aug. 13, 1916.

[2] *Ibid.,* Aug. 14, 1916.

[3] *Ibid.,* Aug. 15, 16, 17, 1916.

Concession of the eight-hour day.

Postponement of the other demand, as to payment for overtime, and the counter suggestions of the railway managers, until experience actually discloses the consequences of the eight-hour day.

In the meantime the constitution, by authority of Congress, of a commission or body of men, appointed by the President, to observe, investigate, and report upon those consequences, without recommendation.

Then such action upon the facts as the parties to the present controversy may think best.[1]

The proposals were a compromise of the demands of the men. Under the then existing conditions, with a standard ten-hour-day-100-mile-run basis, the men were paid for a day's work after completing ten hours, or after accomplishing a run of 100 miles even though this might be done in less than ten hours. Were the President's plan accepted the men would receive a day's pay after eight hours of work, regardless of the run accomplished, or after a run of 100 miles, whether accomplished in eight hours or less. Thus an actual increase in wages would accrue to them even without the time and a half rate, for on runs that took over eight hours or were more than 100 miles in length they would receive extra pay pro rata, whereas under the then existing conditions, such pay would not be received until ten hours had elapsed. The proposal was by no means all that the men asked for, but it was a generous concession, granting more than half of their demands.[2]

The plan, which had been previously discussed rather fully by the managers, was rejected by them on the 17th. The President immediately sent the following telegram to the presidents of the railways:

[1] *Hearings on the Threatened Strike*, Senate Committee on Interstate Commerce, 1st Sess., 64th Congress. Senate Document 549, p. 41.

[2] *Ibid.*, p. 68.

Discussion of the matters involved in the threatened railway strike has reached a point which makes it highly desirable that I should personally confer with you at the earliest possible moment, and with the presidents of any other railroads affected who may be immediately accessible. Hope you can make it convenient to come to Washington at once.[1]

On the next day, after a meeting of the 600 Brotherhood officials, the unions formally accepted the President's proposals. On the same day thirty-one railway presidents likewise met Mr. Wilson and discussed his plan of settlement. They failed to accept it, however, but agreed to consider the matter further before giving the President their last word.[2] The next day the President issued a statement giving his plan to the public, and saying, " This seems to me a thoroughly practical and entirely fair program, and I think the public has the right to expect its acceptance."

The railway executives again met the President on August 19, rejected his proposals, and demanded arbitration as a matter of principle. Replying to them Mr. Wilson said that " this is a condition and not a principle which we face. . . . . We must face the naked truth in this crisis. We must not discuss impractical things. We must get down to a basis on which this situation can be solved." He pointed out that he favored arbitration, but that under the law it was impossible if one side refused it. " If it should prove through experience that the eight-hour day imposed a new and heavy added burden to the cost of operation I will lend my influence personally and officially to influence the rate making body of the government to grant an increase in freight rates, if the findings of the federal commission show

[1] *N. Y. Times.* Aug. 18, 1916.
[2] *Ibid.,* Aug. 19, 1916.

that such a course would be just." At the conclusion of
his appeal to the railway heads the President said, " If a
strike comes, the public will know where the responsibility
rests. It will not be upon me." After the meeting he sent
telegrams to sixty-three other railway presidents not in
Washington, evidently desiring that the responsibility should
be borne by all of them.[1]

For the next few days Mr. Wilson had further conferences with the railway presidents and managers, who, though
still unwilling to accept the proposal, displayed a fear that
if it were accepted they had no guarantee of being able to
raise their rates to meet the increased wages. Meanwhile
the 600 union representatives were growing unruly and
tired of waiting in Washington. Being notified that they
were ready to leave the city, the President, on August 25,
informed the railway heads that he must have their answer.

The latter framed two separate sets of counter proposals
for the President to submit to the union officials, who rejected them and stood out for the President's own plan.
The first proposal recommended an investigation by some
government authority or commission into all the facts of
the case. Meanwhile there was to be no strike, and a law
was to be passed similar to the Canadian law requiring investigation before the calling of any strike. After a report had been made and the facts ascertained the railroads
would be in a position to make a prompt answer to the
President's proposals. The second proposal of the railways suggested that beginning September 1 they would
keep separate accounts of the rates of pay on the eight-hour
and on the ten-hour basis, and would pay over the difference to the men if the question should be adjudged in their
favor. Meanwhile the President was to appoint a com-

[1] *N. Y. Times,* Aug. 20, 1916.

mission to inquire into the matter and make an award, by which the roads would abide.[1]

There still being a possibility of the acceptance of the President's own plan if they were assured of an increase in rates to make up for an increase in costs involved in its acceptance, Mr. Wilson, on August 26, consulted with administration leaders in Congress, and asked them to have the Interstate Commerce Commission increased by two members so that it could handle rate cases promptly. He also asked that the Commission be empowered to take wage schedules into account in fixing rates, that Congress provide for a permanent arbitration board to hear railway labor disputes, and that it pass a resolution declaring itself of the opinion that rates should be increased if the eight-hour day put an extra burden on the railways.[2]

On August 27 the 600 district chairmen left Washington with conditional strike orders in their pockets. The next day it developed that in these secret orders, which were not to be opened until a few days later, directions had been given that the strike commence on all the roads at 7 A.M., September 4. On hearing of this, the President summoned the Brotherhood chiefs, who acknowledged the truth of the report, and on the President's request that they have the orders rescinded, answered that they were beyond recall and that they could not be rescinded, according to the vote of the 600 chairmen, unless the President's proposal were accepted by the railroads. On the same day the railway executives again rejected the plan and insisted on their final counter-proposal.[3]

Mr. Wilson having exhausted his resources in attempting

[1] *Hearings, op. cit.,* p. 41; *N. Y. Times,* Aug. 22-Aug. 26.

[2] *N. Y. Times,* Aug. 27, 1916.

[3] *Ibid.,* Aug. 28 and 29, 1916; *Hearings, op. cit.,* p. 66; *Congressional Record,* vol. liii, Part 15, Appendix, p. 1956.

to effect a voluntary settlement, and the most serious strike in its history facing the nation as a practical certainty unless the eight-hour day were granted, he appeared before Congress on August 29, and requested that the following be enacted into legislation:

1. Immediate provision for the enlargement and administrative reorganization of the Interstate Commerce Commission, so that it might deal with the many duties before it with more promptness and thoroughness.

2. " [The] establishment of an 8 hour day as the legal basis alike of work and wages, in the employment of all railway employees who are actually engaged in the work of operating trains in interstate transportation."

3. " [The] authorization of the appointment by the President of a small body of men to observe the actual results in experience of the adoption of the 8 hour day in railway transportation, alike for the men and the railroads; its effects in the matter of operating costs, in the application of the existing practices and agreements to the new conditions, and in all other practicable aspects, with the provision that the investigators shall report their conclusions to Congress at the earliest possible date, but without recommendation as to legislative action; in order that the public may learn from an unprejudiced source just what actual developments have ensued."

4. Explicit approval by Congress of consideration by the Interstate Commerce Commission of whatever increase in freight rates would be necessitated by the adoption of the 8 hour day.

5. Amendment of the Newlands Act to provide compulsory investigation into railway disputes before a strike or a lockout might be lawfully attempted.

6. Lodgment in the President's hands, of power, in case

of military necessity, to take such control of the railroads as is necessary for military use, " with authority to draft into the military service of the United States such train crews and administrative officials as the circumstances require for their safe and efficient use."

This action of the President has been subject to so much adverse criticism that it seems best to give several excerpts from his address to Congress in support of his proposals. After describing the great hardships which would result from a strike of such magnitude the President continues:

It has seemed to me, in considering the subject matter of the controversy, that the whole spirit of the time and the preponderant evidence of recent economic experience spoke for the 8 hour day. It has been adjudged by the thought and experience of recent years a thing upon which society is justified in insisting as in the interest of health, efficiency, contentment, and a general increase of economic vigor. The whole presumption of modern experience would, it seemed to me, be in its favor, whether there was arbitration or not, and the debatable points to settle were those which affected its establishment. . . .

I unhesitatingly offered the friendly services of the administration to the railway managers to see to it that justice was done the railroads in the outcome. I felt warranted in assuring them that no obstacle of law would be suffered to stand in the way of their increasing their revenues to meet the expenses resulting from the change so far as the development of their business and of their administrative efficiency did not prove adequate to meet them. The railway managers based their decision to reject my counsel in this matter upon their conviction that they must at any cost to themselves or to the country, stand firm for the principle of arbitration which the men rejected. I based my counsel upon the indisputable fact that there was no means of obtaining arbitration. The laws supplied none; earnest efforts at mediation had failed to influence the men in the least. To stand firm for the principle of arbitration and yet not get arbitration seemed to me futile, and something more than futile, because it involved incalculable distress to the country, and consequences in some respects worse than those of war, and that in the midst of peace. . . .

I yield to no man in firm adherence, alike of conviction and purpose, to the principle of arbitration in industrial disputes; but matters have come to a sudden crisis in this particular dispute and the country has been caught unprovided with any practicable means of enforcing that conviction in practice (by whose fault we will not now stop to inquire). . . .

Having failed to bring the parties to this critical controversy to an accommodation, therefore, I turn to you, deeming it clearly our duty as public servants to leave nothing undone that we can do to safeguard the life and interests of the nation.[1]

Immediately after the President's address numerous measures to meet the strike situation were introduced in Congress. They provided that the roads be placed under federal control and management under certain conditions, that the Brotherhoods be requested to postpone the strike for a week to give the Senate a chance to investigate, that receivers be appointed for the railroads in certain cases, that arbitration be made compulsory, etc., etc. On August 31 Representative Adamson introduced House Resolution 17700, entitled " A bill to establish an 8 hour day for employees of carriers engaged in interstate and foreign commerce, and for other purposes." The measure was referred to the House Committee on Interstate and Foreign Commerce.[2] On the next day the committee reported the bill favorably, with only slight modifications, and no changes in principle. As thus reported the bill passed the House

[1] *Congressional Record*, vol. liii, pp. 13335-13337.

[2] *Ibid.*, vol. liii, p. 13540.

on the same day by a vote of 239 to 56.[1]   The measure was
then taken up by the Senate and discussed on September 1
and 2.   On the latter day, the Senate having become acquainted with the situation through hearings before the
Committee on Interstate Commerce on August 31, the bill
was passed by a vote of 43 to 28.[2]   On September 3 President Wilson approved the bill, but it being Sunday, and
the next day being Labor Day, he signed it a second time
on September 5.[3]

The bill, which came to be known as the Adamson Act,
provided that " beginning January first, 1917, eight hours
shall, in contracts for labor and service, be deemed a day's
work and the measure or standard of a day's work for the
purpose of reckoning the compensation for services of all
employees " on railroads engaged in train operation in interstate commerce, excepting those not over 100 miles in
length and excepting electric street and interurban roads;
that the President appoint a commission of three to observe
the operation and effects of the eight-hour standard work-
day and report its findings to the President and Congress;
" that pending the report of the commission herein provided
for and for a period of 30 days thereafter the compensation of railway employees subject to this Act for a standard
eight hour work day shall not be reduced below the present
standard day's wage, and for all necessary time in excess
of eight hours such employees shall be paid at a rate not less
than the pro rata rate for such standard eight-hour work-
day "; and finally, that violation of the Act be a misde-
meanor punishable by fine or imprisonment, or both.[4]

It will be observed that the measure practically enacted

[1] *Congressional Record,* vol. liii, pp. 13608-13609.
[2] *Ibid.,* pp. 13566, 13610, 13655.
[3] *Ibid.,* p. 14158.
[4] *39 Stat. at Large,* p. 721.

into law the provisions of the President's original proposals to the railroads and the men, and further, that it enacted only two of his six recommendations to Congress. Those two, however, were the ones which were particularly designed to avert the threatened strike.

Immediately on the passage of the act by the Senate the Brotherhood officials, on September 2, without waiting for the President to sign the bill, rescinded the strike order.[1]

The President and Congress, by their prompt action, had averted a great strike, but they had not settled the dispute. In November and December, 1916, the railroads brought many suits to enjoin the enforcement of the Adamson Act. By agreement between railroad counsel and the Attorney General it was arranged to continue all these cases except one, which was made a test case, to be expedited as much as possible. The roads agreed to keep their books and accounts so that if the constitutionality of the act were upheld the men could be paid from January 1, 1917, in accordance with the terms of the law. The case was argued before the Supreme Court on January 8, but the Court's decision was delayed for some time.[2]

Meanwhile, however, considerable dissatisfaction prevailed among the railroad employees. The law which gave them the eight-hour day did not provide for a wage agreement with the roads for putting it into effect. When January 1 came they were in the same position as before, and the situation promised that they would remain in that position for some time to come. By March unrest had reached such a point, due to the continuation of the old conditions, and the fear that the Supreme Court would decide against the Adamson Act, that the Brotherhood chairmen notified

[1] *N. Y. Times*, Sept. 3, 1916.
[2] *Report of the Eight Hour Commission*, p. 10.

the railway managers that a strike applying to men in the freight service would go into effect at 6 P.M., March 17, unless some satisfactory settlement were reached.[1]

On the 15th the union heads met with the railway managers. In answer to the men's demands that the eight-hour day be put into effect at once, retroactive to January 1, the employers refused to do anything until the Supreme Court rendered its decision, and offered, in case the law was declared unconstitutional, to arbitrate the matter through the Eight-Hour Commission. This proposal the Brotherhoods rejected, and notified the employers that the strike would go into effect on the 17th as planned.[2]

With danger of a strike once more at hand President Wilson, on March 16, wrote to the managers and the Brotherhood heads and appealed to them to reopen the question at issue: " It is now the duty of every patriotic man to bring matters of this sort to immediate accommodation. The safety of the country against manifest perils affecting its own peace and the peace of the whole world makes accommodation absolutely imperative and seems to me to render any other choice or action inconceivable." The President further notified them that he had appointed a committee of mediation, representing the Council of National Defense, to confer with them in order to bring about a settlement. The members of this body were Secretary of the Interior Franklin K. Lane, Secretary of Labor William B. Wilson, President Daniel Willard of the Baltimore and Ohio, and Samuel Gompers.[3]

On the 17th, at the request of the mediators, the Brotherhood chiefs sent out an order delaying the strike for 48

[1] *N. Y. Times,* March 12, 1917.
[2] *Ibid.,* March 16, 1917.
[3] *Ibid.,* March 17, 1917.

hours. Conferences continued throughout that day and the next. Shortly after midnight of the 18th, when the conference seemed hopelessly deadlocked, the mediators received word from the President, that in view of the increasing gravity of the international situation caused by the sinking of three American vessels by German submarines on the same day, he had decided that under no conditions should there be a strike. On receipt of this message the two sides immediately came to an agreement. By daybreak of the 19th the agreement had been signed.[1] It put into effect the terms of the eight-hour law, but defined somewhat more specifically the application of the eight-hour basis to existing schedules, and provided for a Commission of Eight, representing the roads and the men, to decide disputed questions arising under it. On the same day, March 19, the Supreme Court upheld the constitutionality of the Adamson Act.[2] It is probable that the railroad managers, expecting the result, were in the position of conceding more gracefully to the President's demand for a settlement on the night before. The basic eight-hour day had become an accomplished fact, and all danger of a strike on that issue was past.[3]

It is apparent that though the passage of the Adamson Act averted a strike, it did not obtain the eight-hour day for railroad employees. That was not obtained until the railroads signed the agreement of March 19, 1917, though undoubtedly the enactment of the law made it easier to win the assent of the employers to this agreement.

[1] N. Y. Times, March 19, 20, 1917.

[2] Wilson v. New et al., 243 U. S. 332.

[3] Rep. Eight Hour Com., p. 10. Of course, neither the agreement between the roads and the men nor the Adamson Act itself limited hours of labor on the railways. Since they provided only proportionate pay for over-time, they served rather to increase wages than to decrease hours.

There can be little question that it was the influence of the President which prevented the threatened strikes of September, 1916, and March, 1917.   As regards the latter, little discussion seems necessary.   War between the United States and Germany threatened at any time.   Two weeks later it was actually declared.   To permit a great strike at such a time would have been without justification.   The President, in using pressure to avert it, seems to have been entirely justified.

Concerning his connection with the Adamson Act, however, there has been much unfavorable criticism.   He was accused of surrendering the country to the Brotherhoods, of using a pliable Congress to create political support for himself in the campaign of 1916 at the expense of the rest of the country, etc., etc.   It seems that such charges, whether there be truth in them or not, are aside from the point.   The facts were that the President had proposed a settlement which appeared fair and just.   The Brotherhoods accepted this proposal and the railroads rejected it.   The Brotherhoods were probably at fault in refusing to consider arbitration.   They were perhaps also in the wrong in refusing to delay the strike, though their belief that the railroads were profiting by every day of delay through the perfection of their arrangements to defeat the strike was doubtless justified by the facts.[1]   But by August 29, 1916, it was not a question of which side was in the right.   It was a question of whether or not the most disastrous strike in our history was to be averted.   The employees had positively refused to arbitrate or to delay the strike.   The railroads had just as positively refused to do anything but arbitrate.   There was no existing law which could have forced the men to arbitrate, or the employers to concede their demands, and

[1] *Hearings, op. cit.,* pp. 61, 67.

the President had already done his utmost to bring about a voluntary settlement.

There appear to have been several courses open to the President. One was to get an injunction against the strike on the ground that it would be a conspiracy in restraint of trade. But the Clayton Act, passed but two years earlier, had exempted labor unions from the provisions of the anti-trust laws. President Wilson had given his strong support to that act. To have sought an injunction under such conditions would have been inconsistent and apparently unwarranted. Furthermore, even had an injunction been obtained, experience has shown that that would not in itself have prevented the strike. There is a great difference between obtaining an injunction and enforcing it.

A second course would have been to ask Congress for power to enable the administration to take over the railroads and operate them while a commission of arbitration was deciding the eight-hour question, the assumption being that the railroad employees would not strike against the government. It is extremely doubtful if Congress would have given the administration such power on a moment's demand in 1916, with the United States not in the war, and the government quite unprepared to administer such power. It is to be doubted also whether the railway workers would have given up the strike simply because the government rather than the roads became their employer.

Mr. Wilson might have chosen a third course by asking Congress to pass a law requiring arbitration of railway labor disputes. In his address to that body in August he did ask for an amendment to the Newlands Act providing for compulsory investigation of railway disputes before a strike or a lockout might be lawfully attempted. But he cannot be said to have emphasized such a measure, and his readiness to sign the Adamson Act without any provision

having been made for compulsory investigation indicates that
he did not consider it a means of preventing the threatened
strike.   Yet it is reasonable to ask why, if the President
favored arbitration in principle, he was not ready to ask
Congress for a law which would make the calling of the
threatened strike unlawful unless the disputants first submitted to arbitration.   In his address to Congress the President pointed out that the laws supplied no means of compelling arbitration.   Neither did the laws provide for a
basic eight-hour day on the railroads.   It would have been
as easy, as far as his power was concerned, to have asked
for the enactment of one as for the other.   For the President to have asked Congress for the enactment of a compulsory arbitration law would, of course, have evoked a
tremendous opposition from labor.   The President, having
already placed all his influence behind a certain plan of
settlement, which was accepted by the employees, would have
been severely criticized had he given up this plan and insisted on the arbitration which the employers, refusing his
proposal, had themselves demanded.   It would probably
have been better for the President to have postponed the
making of a definite proposal until he knew that there was
a likelihood of its being accepted.   As it was, he shot his
bolt early, and could consistently do nothing but insist on
the acceptance of his plan.   His sympathy with the demand
for an eight-hour day, his pique at the employers because of
their persistent refusal to accede to his request, and the certain opposition of great numbers of voters were he to change
his stand, were also probably important factors in determining his policy.   Moreover Mr. Wilson, though favoring
arbitration in principle, was probably opposed to compulsory arbitration in times of peace.   Had he asked Congress
for a law making the arbitration of the dispute compulsory,
his request, though arousing tremendous opposition the

country over, might have been granted, but there is a question whether the enactment of such a law would have been effective in preventing the strike. The feelings of the railway employees were at fever heat, they were determined not to arbitrate, and after their hopes had been raised by the proposals of the President the shock of a disappointment might easily have resulted in a decision to defy the government.

A fourth course would have been for the President to step aside and let the employees strike if they so wished, there being the probability that public opinion would have been so outraged that the strike could only last a short time before a settlement was forced. Such a course would have involved more criticism and complaint than the course actually taken. A strike involving but one class of employees, or one small section of the country, might be permitted to take place without a great deal of harm to the country as a whole. But this strike would have involved 400,000 employees, practically all of those engaged in train operation throughout the country. Such a strike, at the end of a few days, would have caused untold hardships.

There remained the course actually taken by the President. It subjected him to the charge that he had permitted labor to hold up the government, but it seems to have been the course most certain to prevent the strike, and it must be judged from that point of view, unless one assumes that a strike would have been preferable to what critics called "a surrender to the domination of a class."

However necessary one may consider Mr. Wilson's action, one cannot ignore the possible consequences. In the last analysis the affair resolved itself into an attempt at enforcement by law of the President's proposals for settlement. It is evident that labor itself realized the danger of such a precedent, for its leaders promptly declared that they had not asked for Congressional legislation in its behalf. They saw clearly that the legislation might as easily have provided for the enforcement of proposals unfavorable to them.   In war-time such compulsion as the government finds necessary for the successful accomplishment of its work or for the purpose of safeguarding public interest is doubtless permissible, but it may be seriously questioned whether such a method can be justified in times of peace.   Its use in the case of the threatened railway strike of 1916 cannot easily be defended, despite the fact that the occasion was as serious a one as any President is likely to face.

CHAPTER V

PRESIDENT WILSON : WAR-TIME ACTIVITIES

FROM the moment that the United States declared war against Germany in April, 1917, there were two outstanding methods of participation on which the government concentrated its energies. One was to make preparations for giving our allies aid in the shape of fighting men. The other was to produce as much as possible of the food and supplies needed by the allies and ourselves. To that end it was necessary to correct as far as possible peace-time inefficiency and all other causes leading to decreased production. It was felt that all industrial disturbances involving suspension of production must be avoided. In order to accomplish this, the governmental agencies engaged in war production began, in the summer of 1917, to establish various boards for the settlement of labor disputes. Such boards were all the more necessary because the continually rising cost of living caused strikes for higher wages to become more frequent. All of these war-time agencies cannot be discussed here.[1] Discussion will be limited to those boards in the creation of which the President took an active part, and to those instances in which he used his personal influence to end or avert a strike.

[1] For a thorough discussion of them see Bing, *War Time Strikes and their Adjustment*, New York, 1921; and Watkins, *Labor Problems and Labor Administration in the United States during the World War*, Urbana, 1919.

I. THE PRESIDENT'S MEDIATION COMMISSION

In the summer of 1917 considerable unrest and numerous strikes developed in the Far West, especially in the copper and lumbering industries, in which continued production was essential for war purposes. The strikes in the copper districts of Arizona involved not alone a serious decrease in production. In Bisbee they were accompanied by forcible deportation of strikers, by objectionable treatment of union officials, and by other outrages. These conditions the Arizona Federation of Labor reported to President Gompers of the American Federation, requesting that he use his influence to have them investigated. Mr. Gompers thereupon presented the employees' position to President Wilson, who brought the matter to the attention of Secretary of War Baker, the Chairman of the Council of National Defense, and asked that the Council take it under advisement and determine what ought to be done.

Late in August the Council reported to the President and suggested that he appoint a commission to investigate labor conditions in the western states, from which reports of unrest and strikes continued to come.[1] On September 19 the following letter to the Secretary of Labor, made public the next day, was written by the President:

I am very much interested in the labor situation in the mountain region and on the Pacific Coast. I have listened with attention and concern to numerous charges of misconduct and injustice that representatives both of employers and employees have made against each other. I am not so much concerned, however, with the manner in which they have treated each other in the past as I am desirous of seeing some kind of working arrangement arrived at for the future, particularly during the period of the war, on a basis that will be fair to all parties concerned. To assist in the accomplishment of that

[1] *American Federationist*, October, 1917, p. 846.

purpose, I have decided to appoint a commission to visit the
localities where disagreements have been most frequent as my
personal representatives.   The commission will consist of Wm.
B. Wilson, Secretary of Labor; Col. J. L. Spangler, of Pennsylvania; Verner Z. Reed, of Colorado; John H. Walker, of
Illinois; and E. P. Marsh, of Washington.   Felix Frankfurter,
of New York, will act as secretary of the commission.
It will be the duty of the commission [to lend] sympathetic
counsel and aid to the state government[s] in the development
of a better understanding between laborers and employers, ...
to deal with employers and employees in a conciliatory spirit,
seek to compose differences and allay misunderstanding and
in any way that may be open to them to show the active interest of the National Government in furthering arrangements
just to both sides . . . , [to call whenever] it is deemed advisable conferences of employers and employees . . . . with
the purpose of working out a mutual understanding between
them which will insure the continued operation of the industry
on conditions acceptable to both sides . . . , to learn the real
causes for any discontent which may exist on either side . . . .
I would be pleased to have the commission report to me from
time to time such information as may require immediate attention.[1]

The commission thus appointed, which became known as
the President's Mediation Commission, soon began its task.
It carried on investigations into conditions, used its good
offices in settling various strikes, and accomplished much
valuable work.   More specifically, on November 6, 1917, it
made a special report to the President on the Bisbee deportations, recommending action by the Attorney General
and by other authorities to punish offenders against the law.[2]
It settled the strikes in the copper-mining districts of
Arizona, and set up agencies to handle future disputes and

[1] *Official Bulletin,* Committee on Public Information, Sept. 21, 1917.
[2] *Report on the Bisbee Deportations,* Washington, 1918.

to improve relations between employers and employees. It settled an important dispute in the California oil fields and appointed administrators to take care of future relations. It ended a serious strike of telephone employees which had tied up to a considerable extent telephone communication in California, Oregon, Washington, Idaho, and Nevada, and, as in the other cases, set up machinery for future adjustment. It investigated unrest in the lumber industry of the Pacific Northwest, and although the strike of the summer was practically over and had been defeated, it recommended the granting of the eight-hour day, for which the strike was fought, and the establishment of some means of collective bargaining. The commission was also instrumental in effecting the settlement of a strike in the packing industry, involving nearly 100,000 men, and of serious consequences to the meat supply of the nation. In addition to ending the strike it secured the acceptance of Judge Samuel Alschuler as an arbitrator to determine wages, hours, and working conditions.[1] The award [2] of the arbitrator, made on March 30, 1918, secured peace in the industry for the duration of the war and for some time afterwards.

In its report of January 9, 1918, the commission made valuable recommendations concerning war-time labor policies. During the same month it investigated the Mooney case, reported to the President its belief that the conditions under which Mooney was sentenced were unjust, and recommended that he use his good offices to secure a new trial.[3] Later in the year the President succeeded in securing a commutation of Mooney's sentence to life imprisonment.[4]

[1] *Report of the President's Mediation Commission,* Jan. 9, 1918, Washington, 1918.

[2] *Monthly Labor Review,* May, 1918, p. 115.

[3] *Official Bulletin,* Jan. 28, 1918.

[4] *N. Y. Times,* Nov. 29, 1918.

In February, 1918, the commission, at the request of the Council of National Defense, tried to bring about the amicable settlement of a street-car strike in St. Paul and Minneapolis, but was unsuccessful.[1] After that its activities seem to have come to an end. It attempted in all its settlements to introduce the principle of collective bargaining and to set up machinery which would substitute quick settlement of disputes and amicable relations for industrial unrest and warfare. It is apparent that its appointment by the President filled an important war need. By the time its activities had ceased other agencies had been created to handle the problems which it had for the most part treated so successfully.

2. MINERS' WAGES AND STRIKE PENALTIES

The Lever Act of August 10, 1917, put control over food and fuel in the hands of the President, in order that he might safeguard production in any way he thought desirable. On August 23 he appointed H. A. Garfield as U. S. Fuel Administrator. Soon after the Fuel Administration started to function, Mr. Garfield took over the matter of supervising wage agreements between miners and operators. A bituminous agreement was reached on October 6, 1917, providing for an increase in wages, and for an automatic penalty clause to be introduced into wage contracts to prevent strikes and lockouts. The agreement was to be extended for the continuation of the war and not to exceed two years from April 1, 1918. It was to be put into effect provided the government, which had assumed control of fuel prices, permitted an advance in the price of coal sufficient to meet the burden of increased wages.

A committee of the Fuel Administration soon after reported as to the amount of price increase necessary for the

[1] *Monthly Labor Review,* April, 1918, pp. 302-304.

purpose. This report the Fuel Administrator submitted to the President, who on October 27 ordered an increase in the price of coal, subject to certain conditions, one of which was that the increase should apply only to those districts in which the operators and miners agreed on a penalty clause providing for the automatic collection of fines from employers and employees for lockouts and strikes. The penalties, which in most cases were fixed at $1 per day per worker to be paid by whichever side was responsible for the suspension, played a considerable part in preventing strikes and lockouts in the bituminous industry during the war.[1]

In November, 1917, the President, at the request of the Fuel Administrator, granted an increase in the price of anthracite coal to permit an increase in wages, but in this case, Mr. Garfield pointed out that the Anthracite Board of Conciliation sufficed to prevent strikes, and no automatic penalty clause was required.[2]

3. RAILWAY LABOR DISPUTES

In the fall of 1917 the rapidly increasing cost of living led to considerable agitation for wage increases among railroad employees. Attempts made by the Brotherhood officials to secure increases from the railroads proved unsuccessful. By November talk of a strike became quite common, and several of the unions had decided to take strike votes.[3] Preliminary efforts made by Judge Chambers of the U. S. Board of Mediation and Conciliation to secure an agreement to arbitrate or mediate the controversy did not prove successful.[4]

On November 14 President Wilson wrote to Judge

[1] *Final Report, U. S. Fuel Administrator*, 1917-1919, p. 209.
[2] *Official Bulletin*, Dec. 3, 1917.
[3] *N. Y. Times*, Nov. 14, 1917.
[4] *Ibid.*, Nov. 15, 1917.

Chambers, expressing his interest in the latter's efforts to prevent a strike, and continuing:

I take it for granted that your efforts will succeed, because it is inconceivable to me that patriotic men should now for a moment contemplate the interruption of the transportation which is so absolutely necessary to the safety of the nation and to its success in arms, as well as to its whole industrial life. . . .
The last thing I should wish to contemplate would be the possibility of being obliged to take any unusual measures to operate the railways, and I have so much confidence that the men you are dealing with will appreciate the patriotic motives underlying your efforts that I shall look forward with assurance to your success.

A few days later the Brotherhood chiefs agreed to permit mediation of the controversy, and on the 19th the railway managers, in a letter to Judge Chambers, agreed not only to arbitrate the issue, but went on to say that, as " no interruption of continual railroad operation can be tolerated under war conditions, we are ready, should any crisis now arise, unreservedly to place our interests in the hands of the President for protection, and for disposition as he may determine is necessary in the public interest." [2]
Two days later President Wilson met the four Brotherhood heads and received a promise from them that they would not call a strike. They agreed to abide by any form of settlement the President might urge in case no agreement with the carriers could be reached.[3] Further negotiations between the roads and their employees again having met with failure, and dissatisfaction and unrest still threatening

[1] *Official Bulletin,* Nov. 15, 1917.
[2] *N. Y. Times,* Nov. 17, 20, 1917.
[3] *Ibid.,* Nov. 23, 1917.

a strike, the President, who in a proclamation of December 26 had announced government control of the railways to take effect on December 28, called the leaders of the Brotherhoods for another conference. The latter agreed, at the President's request, to withhold their wage demands until government control got started, and for a period of thirty days after December 31.[1]

On January 18, 1918, Secretary of the Treasury William G. McAdoo, who had been appointed Director General of the Railways, issued an order creating a Railroad Wage Commission. After an exhaustive study of general wage conditions the commission recommended a wage increase on April 30, 1918. Some weeks later Mr. McAdoo ordered an increase in wages to meet the conditions which had threatened to produce a railway strike in the previous winter. Adjustment boards to handle labor problems were set up and strikes on the roads were avoided during the war by means of them.[2]

4. THE SHIPBUILDING LABOR ADJUSTMENT BOARD

On August 20, 1917, the Emergency Fleet Corporation, which was in charge of the government's war-time shipbuilding program, entered into an agreement with the Metal Trades Department of the American Federation of Labor, creating the U. S. Shipbuilding Labor Adjustment Board. The board was to have jurisdiction over disputes concerning wages and working conditions in shipbuilding plants operated by the U. S. Shipping Board, or under contract with it; and, under certain conditions, over similar disputes in plants operated by the Navy Department. The decisions of the board were to be binding on all parties to the agreement.[3]

[1] *Ibid.*, Dec. 28, 30, 1917; *Official Bulletin*, Dec. 27, 1917.

[2] *Annual Report of the Director General of the Railroads*. Washington,, 1919, pp. 3, 4.

[3] *History of the Shipbuilding Labor Adjustment Board*, 1917-1919. Bureau of Labor Statistics, Bulletin 283. Washington, 1921, pp. 8, 9.

On September 7 Chairman Hurley of the Shipping Board set up the claim that the awards of the Adjustment Board should be subject to the approval of the Emergency Fleet Corporation. The board, which had already been appointed, refused to agree to this procedure. After many conferences the question was laid before the President, and an understanding was reached that the decisions of the board should be final and not subject to review by any of the parties concerned.[1]

Meanwhile conditions on the Pacific Coast had become so unsatisfactory to the workers that on September 17 the shipbuilding trades in San Francisco struck for higher wages. Some time earlier the shipyard workers in Seattle and Portland had also voted to strike. Chairman Hurley asked the workers not to quit pending a settlement by the Adjustment Board, and invited the representatives of the unions to come to Washington to talk the matter over. They arrived in the capital in time to find the controversy concerning the board's status going on, and returned home.[2] By the last week of September the Seattle and Portland unionists had followed the example of those in San Francisco and gone on strike.[3]

On September 21 President Wilson and Chairman Hurley requested Gavin McNab, of San Francisco, to attempt a temporary settlement of the strike in that city, pending the arrival of the Adjustment Board. Two days later Mr. McNab obtained a temporary agreement ending the strike and submitting the dispute to the board for settlement. The President, on the same day and before the agreement was actually made, wired his approval of this method of ending

[1] *History of the Shipbuilding Labor Adjustment Board, 1917-1919, op. cit.,* p. 12.

[2] *Ibid.,* p. 11.

[3] *Ibid.,* p. 15.

the strike, and recommended similar temporary settlements to the unions in Seattle and Portland.[1]

The Adjustment Board started for the coast on October 3, and succeeded in getting temporary settlements at Seattle and Portland about the middle of October. It then proceeded to San Francisco, and after hearings and deliberations handed down an award on November 4, 1917, fixing basic wage rates for the whole Pacific Coast.[2] The board then returned East and devoted its attention to controversies in the shipyards of the Delaware River district.

During the winter of 1917-1918 the carpenters working in shipyards near New York harbor became dissatisfied with the wages paid for government work, claiming that the rates on the Pacific Coast were much higher, and that the Emergency Fleet Corporation had delayed increases unnecessarily. The carpenters' union had been the only organization in the Metal Trades Department of the A. F. of L. which had declined to abide by the terms of the agreement creating the Shipbuilding Labor Adjustment Board, the signature of its representative signing the agreement having been withdrawn several weeks after the board was set up.[3] W. L. Hutcheson, president of the international union, conferred with Chairman Hurley early in February, 1918, but refused to agree to submit the demands of the carpenters to the Adjustment Board or to abide by its award.

On February 11 considerable numbers of the men quit work. Three days later, the strike having spread to the Baltimore shipyards, Mr. Hurley wired President Hutcheson, asking him to get the men back to work and let the board handle the dispute. "You will be well advised," the

---

[1] *History of the Board, op. cit.,* p. 20; San Francisco Chronicle, Sept. 22, 24, Oct. 2, 1917.

[2] *History of the Board, op. cit.,* pp. 18, 20, 21.

[3] *Ibid.,* p. 10.

telegram said, " to follow the methods of well-managed and patriotic labor organizations, at least until you have tested whether or not your Government, for which as shipbuilders you are now working, can be fair." [1]

The next day Mr. Hutcheson replied to this telegram, saying that the strikers were willing to resume negotiations and go back to work if their demand for the Pacific Coast rate of pay were granted, and if certain conditions, which really amounted to the closed shop, were put into effect. In answer to this Mr. Hurley again asked that work be resumed, and refused to grant the demands for what he believed were special privileges for which not even all the carpenters asked. Referring to the Adjustment Board agreement he said, " You are the only international President of all crafts working in the shipyards who refused to become a party to this agreement. Are the other international Presidents less patriotic or less careful of the interests of their crafts than yourself? " [2]

After this there followed an exchange of telegrams between President Wilson and Mr. Hutcheson which show so clearly the President's attitude toward questions of a similar nature during the war that they are given in full:

NEW YORK, FEBRUARY 16, 1918.

The President.

My Dear Mr. President: The situation now existing in the shipyards is of a nature that requires immediate attention. I, as President of the United Brotherhood of Carpenters and Joiners of America, endeavored to reach an understanding with the officials of the U. S. Shipping Board but was unable to do so. I feel that if given the opportunity to lay the matter fully before you that a solution should be quickly arrived at. I desire to inform you, my dear Mr. President, that I as

[1] *N. Y. Times*, Feb. 16, 1918.

[2] *Ibid.*, Feb. 16, 1918.

a patriotic citizen am desirous of rendering every assistance to you and our country to carry on the work necessary to bring about a successful conclusion of the world war in which we are engaged.

Yours, most respectfully and sincerely,

WILLIAM L. HUTCHESON.

FEBRUARY 17, 1918.

William L. Hutcheson. . . .

I have received your telegram of yesterday and am very glad to note the expression of your desire as a patriotic citizen to assist in carrying on the work by which we are trying to save America and men everywhere who work and are free. Taking advantage of that assurance, I feel it to be my duty to call your attention to the fact that the strike of the carpenters in the shipyards is in marked and painful contrast to the action of labor in other trades and places. Ships are absolutely necessary for the winning of this war. No one can strike a deadlier blow at the safety of the Nation and of its forces on the other side than by interfering with or obstructing the shipbuilding program. All the other unions engaged in this indispensable work have agreed to abide by the decisions of the Shipbuilding Wage Adjustment Board. That board has dealt fairly and liberally with all who have resorted to it.

I must say to you very frankly that it is your duty to leave to it the solution of your present difficulties with your employers and to advise the men whom you represent to return at once to work pending the decision. No body of men have the moral right in the present circumstances of the Nation to strike until every method of adjustment has been tried to the limit. If you do not act upon this principle you are undoubtedly giving aid and comfort to the enemy, whatever may be your own conscious purpose. I do not see that anything will be gained by my seeing you personally, until you have accepted and acted upon that principle. It is the duty of the Government to see that the best possible conditions of labor are maintained, as it is also its duty to see to it that there is no lawless and conscienceless profiteering and that duty the Government has accepted and will perform. Will you co-operate or will you obstruct?

WOODROW WILSON.[1]

On receipt of this message from the President the officers of the carpenters' union gave orders to all the local officials to get the men back to work immediately. At the same time Mr. Hutcheson again wired the President, informing him that he had no power to sign an agreement to abide by the award of the Adjustment Board " which would deprive our members of their constitutional rights," and asked for a conference, as he felt that was the only way to solve the question. The President, however, refused to grant a conference unless the carpenters submitted the dispute to the board.[2]

In a few days the strike, which had for a brief time paralyzed shipbuilding work in New York, was completely at an end. Soon afterwards the Adjustment Board took up the demands of the carpenters along with those of the other employees in the North Atlantic district, and on April 6, 1918, handed down an award granting increases in wages. The award, though not entirely satisfactory to the men, was accepted and lived up to in good faith by them.[3]

5. THE NATIONAL WAR LABOR BOARD

One of the principal difficulties encountered by the government in handling its war labor problems in 1917 was the great difference in the methods and policies of the various war-production agencies. In September of that year the National Industrial Conference Board, an employers' organization, submitted to the Council of National Defense a

[1] *Official Bulletin,* Feb. 18, 1918.
[2] *N. Y. Times,* Feb. 18, 19, 1918.
[3] *History of the Board, op. cit.,* pp. 37-39.

proposal for the creation of a federal board to adjust labor disputes, and suggested that a set of war labor principles be drawn up by a conference appointed for that purpose. In December the Council called a conference of representatives of the various governmental production departments. This conference, on December 20, recommended the setting up of national adjustment machinery "in accordance with the principles to be agreed upon between labor and capital and without stoppage of work." The matter was then taken up with the Secretary of Labor, who submitted it to President Wilson. On January 4, 1918, the President appointed the Secretary as labor administrator along the lines of the interdepartmental conference report.[1]

In order to assist him in carrying out this program Secretary Wilson appointed an advisory council of seven members. The council met on January 16, and three days later presented a report to the Secretary recommending the appointment of a board of twelve persons for the purpose of negotiating agreements for the war period and of establishing war labor principles and policies. It suggested that the board consist of five representatives of the employers and five of the employees, each of these groups to choose a joint chairman of the board, who would also represent the public.[2]

These recommendations were approved by the Secretary of Labor, who on January 28 created the War Labor Conference Board and called upon the National Industrial Conference Board and the American Federation of Labor to appoint representatives of capital and labor respectively to the board. The personnel of the board thus chosen was as follows:

Joint chairmen: William Howard Taft, chosen by the employers; Frank P. Walsh, chosen by the employees.

---

[1] *National War Labor Board*. Bureau of Labor Statistics, Bulletin 287. Washington, 1921, p. 9.

[2] *Ibid.*, p. 10.

Employers' representatives: L. A. Osborne, C. E. Michael, W. H. Van Dervoort, B. L. Worden, and L. F. Loree.

Employees' representatives: F. J. Hayes, W. L. Hutcheson, W. H. Johnston, Victor Olander, and Thomas H. Rickert.[1]

The board began its sessions February 25, 1918, and on March 29 handed down a unanimous report suggesting the appointment of a National War Labor Board for the purpose of adjusting labor disputes, to be appointed in the same way as the War Labor Conference Board. It also outlined the powers and functions of such a board, and set forth the principles and policies to govern industrial relations in war industries during the war. In the opinion of the Secretary of Labor the persons best fitted to carry out the policies and suggestions were those who had unanimously agreed on them. He accordingly appointed the members of the board as the members of the new National War Labor Board.[2]

On April 8, 1918, President Wilson issued a proclamation in regard to the new organization. After approving the appointments of the Secretary of Labor the proclamation continued:

The powers, functions, and duties of the National War Labor Board shall be: To settle by mediation and conciliation controversies arising between employers and workers in fields of production necessary for the effective conduct of the war, or in other fields of national activity, delays and obstructions which might, in the opinion of the national board, affect detrimentally such production; to provide, by direct appointment or otherwise, for committees or boards to sit in various parts of the country where controversies arise and secure settlement by local media-

[1] *National War Labor Board, op. cit.* p. 10.
[2] *Ibid.*, p. 11.

tion and conciliation; and to summon the parties to controversies for hearing and action by the national board in event of failure to secure settlement by mediation and conciliation. The principles to be observed and the methods to be followed by the national board in exercising such powers and functions and performing such duties shall be those specified in the said report of the War Labor Conference Board dated March 29, 1918, a complete copy of which is hereunto appended.

The national board shall refuse to take cognizance of a controversy between employer and workers in any field of industrial or other activity where there is by agreement or Federal law a means of settlement which has not been invoked. And I do hereby urge upon all employers and employees within the United States the necessity of utilizing the means and methods thus provided for the adjustment of all industrial disputes, and request that during the pendency of mediation or arbitration through the said means or methods there shall be no discontinuance of industrial operation which would result in curtailment of the production of war necessities.[1]

The principles of the board, approved by the President and appended to his proclamation, may be summarized as follows:

There are to be no strikes or lockouts during the war.

The right of workers to organize into trade unions and to bargain collectively is affirmed and shall not be interfered with by employers in any manner whatsoever.

The right of employers to organize into associations and to bargain collectively is affirmed and shall not be interfered with by workers in any manner whatsoever.

Workers shall not be discharged for trade-union membership or for legitimate union activities.

Workers shall not use coercive methods to induce persons to join unions or employers to bargain with them.

[1] *National War Labor Board, op. cit.,* p. 34.

Where the union shop and union standards exist they shall be continued.

Where the open shop exists its continuance is not to be considered a grievance.

Established safeguards for the protection of health and safety of workers shall not be relaxed.

Where it is necessary to employ women on men's work they must be allowed equal pay for equal work.

The basic eight-hour day is recognized.

Maximum production of all war industries should be maintained, and all methods of employees or employers hindering it should be discouraged.

In fixing wages and conditions regard should be had to standards prevailing in the localities affected.

The right of all workers to a living wage is hereby declared.

In fixing wages minimum rates of pay shall be established which will insure the subsistence of the worker and his family in health and reasonable comfort.[1]

The proclamation of the President and his approval of the board's method of procedure and policies gave it great prestige and insured its success. The board functioned about sixteen months, in almost all cases as arbitrator, rather than as conciliator. A total of 1251 cases came before it, and its awards and findings directly concerned more than 1100 establishments, employing about 711,500 persons, about 90,500 of whom were street railway employees. Of the 1251 cases before it, it made awards and findings in 490 and dismissed or referred most of the remainder to other boards because the cases did not come under its jurisdiction. To expedite its work the board decided many cases in section; that is, the case was investigated and the award drawn up by one employer representative and one worker repre-

---

[1] *National War Labor Board, op. cit.*, pp. 32-33.

sentative, the award being then approved by the remainder of the board. Its first decision was rendered June 12, 1918. Thereafter the number of cases increased each month until in November, 1918, 275 were submitted.[1]

After November 11, 1918, when the armistice was signed, objections were made to accepting the board's decisions on the ground that it was created only for the war period. At the request of the President, however, the board decided to continue its work. On December 5, in view of increasing complaints, it decided to hear only those cases which were jointly submitted by both parties to the dispute after mediation by the Department of Labor had failed.[2] After this cases continued to be submitted, but the activity and the effectiveness of the board gradually declined. On August 12, 1919, it held its final meeting and formally dissolved.[3]

The President's relation to the board extended beyond the fact that he approved its appointment and upheld its principles and policies. In several important instances in which a party to a dispute refused to accept the award of the board, the President used his war-time powers to force an acceptance. These cases, because they are such important evidence of his power and his attitude with regard to labor controversies during the war, are worth discussing at some length.

a. *The Western Union Case.*

In April, 1918, over 20,000 telegraph operators employed by the Western Union and the Postal Telegraph Companies, members of the Commercial Telegraphers' Union of

---

[1] *National War Labor Board, op. cit.,* pp. 16-22.

[2] *Ibid.,* p. 35. Previously the board had heard and decided many cases in which only one side submitted the grievance. Until after the armistice, however, there were very few cases, even of this sort, in which the award was not accepted by both sides.

[3] *Ibid.,* p. 13.

America, voted to strike because some of their number had been discharged for belonging to the union. On April 28, the strike, which was scheduled to commence the next day, was postponed, the War Labor Board having invited the men to present their grievances to it.[1] The board in a few days appointed Joint Chairmen Taft and Walsh to attempt to settle the controversy.

Mr. Taft, at the suggestion of Mr. Walsh, submitted to the heads of the Western Union a proposal to the following effect: That the company receive back the men whom it had discharged upon condition; (1) that the company receive committees of its own men to present requests for better conditions, and if an agreement could not be reached the matter would be submitted to the board; (2) that the company should not be required in any way to deal with or to recognize the union; (3) that the Commercial Telegraphers' Union should agree not to permit any strike and to submit its grievances to the board and abide by its award; (4) that if any member of the union employed by the company should fail to conform to the agreement the company might discharge him and the board would sustain such discharge.

Newcomb Carlton, head of the Western Union, declined to accept this proposal on the ground that the company could not give uninterrupted and competent telegraph service if its operators belonged to the union. He offered to permit the employees to vote as to whether they desired to join the union. In case a majority voted to join he promised to withdraw his objections to union membership, but would not deal with the union. If the employees opposed the union the company would continue the existing practise. To this proposition Mr. Taft replied on May 27: " I do not think our principles include the closed non-union shop in

[1] N. Y. Times, April 29, 1918.

the status quo to be maintained," and rejected the company's offer. He again urged the acceptance of the compromise plan previously suggested, but Mr. Carlton persisted in his refusal.

On June 1 Messrs. Taft and Walsh reported to the board, recommending the publication of their report. The board thereupon approved the report, all the workers and the Joint Chairmen voting for it while all the employers opposed it.[1]

On June 11 President Wilson addressed the heads of the Postal Telegraph and the Western Union Companies. After referring to the decision of the War Labor Board and the companies' refusal to accept it, he continued:

May I not say that in my judgment it is imperatively necessary in the national interest that decisions of the National War Labor Board should be accepted by both parties to labor disputes? To fail to accept them is to jeopard the interests of the Nation very seriously. . . . I do not hesitate to say that it is a patriotic duty to cooperate in this all-important matter with the Government . . . . I, therefore, write to ask that I may have your earnest cooperation in this matter. . . .

The next day Mr. Mackay of the Postal Telegraph Company replied to the President, agreeing not to discharge union men during the war.[2] Mr. Carlton, of the Western Union, however, denied the right of the board to enforce its recommendation and refused to accede to the President's request.[3] The persistent opposition of the company to the union affiliation of its employees continued and the telegraphers' union again decided to strike, the time being set for July 8.[4]

[1] *Official Bulletin,* June 4, 1918.
[2] *Ibid.,* June 15, 1918.
[3] *Annual Report of the Secretary of Labor,* 1918, p. 108.
[4] *N. Y. Times,* July 8, 1918.

Toward the end of June a resolution was introduced in the House of Representatives providing that the President be given power to take over possession and control of the telephone and telegraph systems. On its introduction Postmaster General Burleson sent a letter to Chairman Sims of the House Committee on Interstate Commerce, urging the passage of the resolution. " At this moment," he wrote, " paralysis of a large part of the system of electrical communication is threatened, with possible consequences prejudicial to our military preparation and other public activities that might prove serious or disastrous."

This letter was referred by Mr. Sims to the President, who on June 29 replied, " I indorse heartily the enclosed letter from the Postmaster General, . . . and think that the reasons are stated by him truly and comprehensively." [1] Meanwhile the telegraphers' strike was called off at the request of Secretary Wilson, who pointed out the likelihood of government control.[2] The resolution providing for government control was passed by the House on July 5 and by the Senate eight days later.[3] On July 16 the President approved the act and at midnight of July 31 control of the telegraph and telephone lines passed over to the government.[4]

For a few weeks after government control went into effect the Western Union continued to discharge union members, but the Postmaster General soon issued orders forbidding discrimination and the company ended the practice.[5]

[1] *Official Bulletin,* July 2, 1918; *Congressional Record,* vol. lvi, p. 8716.

[2] *N. Y. Times,* July 8, 1918.

[3] *Cong. Rec.,* vol. lvi, pp. 8735, 9094.

[4] *Official Bulletin,* July 24, 1918.

[5] *Report of the Secretary of Labor,* 1918, p. 108; *N. Y. Times,* Aug. 2-8, Aug. 22, 1918.

b. *The Bridgeport Case.*

In August, 1917, machinists employed in the manufacture of munitions in Bridgeport, Connecticut, began to demand wage increases and the adjustment of other grievances, which included discrimination against union men, and the alleged intimidation of workmen through threats of applying the military draft to them. Various efforts at local conciliation proved unsuccessful, and in March and May, 1918, numerous strikes occurred at the larger plants. Finally the wage adjustment board of the Ordnance Department took up the demands. It handed down on June 7 an award which was accepted by the employees only after much complaint. Some of the employers, however, who had not bound themselves to abide by the award, refused to put it into effect.

After consideration of the problem the Secretary of War, on June 24, formally referred the entire controversy to the War Labor Board. In a short time the board took up the matter, and succeeded in obtaining, on July 3, the formal agreement of all the employers and of the union to abide by its decision.[1] In August, however, the board announced its failure to agree unanimously upon the award, such an agreement being necessary under its rules in case of joint submission, and chose O. M. Eidlitz, of New York City, Director of the Bureau of Housing of the Department of Labor, as umpire to determine the undecided points in the controversy.[2]

The umpire's decision, which was announced on September 4, was duly made the award of the board and forwarded to the parties at Bridgeport. The decision, though

---

[1] *Report of the Activities of the War Department in the Field of Industrial Relations during the War.* Washington, 1919, pp. 32-33.

[2] *Official Bulletin,* Aug. 16, 1918. The board's rules provided that such cases were to be referred to an umpire having final authority.

it upheld some of the workers' contentions, granted increases in wages very unsatisfactory to the men, who, having waited nearly a year for a settlement of the question, were bitterly disappointed.[1] Early in September, contrary to the advice of their leaders, many of the men went on strike against the award.

At this point President Wilson, acting on the joint recommendation of the Secretary of Labor, the Acting Secretary of War, and the Chairmen of the War Labor Board, addressed the striking employees on September 13, and threatened to have them drafted into the military service unless they returned to work.[2] The letter, after pointing out that the employees had agreed to accept the award of the board, continued as follows:

[Whatever] the merits of the issue it is closed by the award. Your strike against it is a breach of faith calculated to reflect on the sincerity of national organized labor in proclaiming its acceptance of the principles and machinery of the National War Labor Board. . . . I desire that you return to work and abide by the award. If you refuse, each of you will be barred from employment in any war industry in the community in which the strike occurs for a period of one year. During that time the U. S. Employment Service will decline to obtain employment for you in any war industry elsewhere in the United States, as well as under [any] Government agencies, and the draft boards will be instructed to reject any claim of exemption based on your alleged usefulness on war production.[3]

The letter had an immediate effect, the strikers voting to return to work on September 17. On the same day the President was informed by the representatives of the strikers

[1] *Official Bulletin*, September 4, 1918; *War Dept. Rep., op. cit.*, p. 33.
[2] *War Dept. Rep., op. cit.*, p. 33.
[3] *National War Labor Board, op. cit.*, p. 36.

that the manufacturers were refusing to reinstate the men. He at once wrote to the employers, concluding his letter thus: " In view of the fact that the workmen have so promptly complied with my directions, I must insist upon the reinstatement of all these men." [1]   The strikers were then taken back and the provisions of the award were put into effect.

c. *The Smith and Wesson Case.*

At about the same time that President Wilson brought pressure to bear upon the Bridgeport strikers to abide by the award of the War Labor Board it became necessary for him to use his power in a similar way in an attempt to get a recalcitrant employer to abide by another award of the board.   In the early summer of 1918 the employees of the Smith and Wesson Company, of Springfield, Massachusetts, manufacturing munitions under contract with the War Department, appointed a committee from among their own number to confer with the management for the purpose of negotiating an increase in wages.   The company refused to see this committee and discharged its members. Thereupon the employees asked the machinists' union to organize the plant.   From time to time the company continued to discharge men for union activity.

Finally, on July 12, about half the employees went on strike.   The company being engaged in the manufacture of supplies that were greatly needed, the War Department intervened on the 17th, under a clause in the contract with the company giving the Secretary of War the right to mediate labor difficulties.   On the advice of his assistants the Secretary formally referred the dispute to the National War Labor Board, which investigated the case and handed down an award on August 21.   The award granted a

[1] *National War Labor Board, op. cit.,* p. 36.

number of the demands of the employees, directed the company to reemploy all men discharged for union affiliation, and ordered the establishment of a system of collective bargaining.[1]

The company, on August 30, wrote to the War Department refusing to recognize the jurisdiction of the War Labor Board or to put its award into effect, and offered to turn the plant over to the government in preference to doing so. It saw " no reason why it should abandon its lawful and legitimate method of doing business known and proved by it to be conducive to industrial peace and high efficiency for the fantastic method outlined by the War Labor Board in its recommendations for dealing with its employees." This position was considered to be so serious in its implications that the War Department urged the company to reconsider its action, but this the management declined to do.[2]

On September 14 the War Department announced that it had taken over the plant and business of the company with the consent of the President. " The language employed by the company," said the statement, " [in its refusal to abide by the award] was held to be calculated to induce other employers to avoid the jurisdiction of the War Labor Board and to defeat the object of the President in its creation, and the company's general attitude toward the reasonable findings of the board was deemed such as might be expected to disturb industry and interfere with production. . . . It is the policy of the War Department to give effect to the decisions of the War Labor Board in all cases coming under the jurisdiction of the Department." [3]

[1] *War Dept. Rep., op. cit.,* p. 34; *Nat. War Labor Board, op. cit.,* p. 260.

[2] *Official Bulletin,* Sept. 14, 1918; *War Dept Rep., op. cit.,* p. 34.

[3] *Official Bulletin,* Sept. 14, 1918. The plant was commandeered for the duration of the war under Section 120 of the National Defense Act, and an officer of the Ordnance Department was placed in charge.

d. *The New York Harbor Strike, January, 1919.*

Brief mention should be made of one other instance in which the President used his influence in connection with an adjustment made by the War Labor Board. In December, 1918, various private employers engaged in harbor work in New York refused to agree to accept the decisions of the New York Harbor Wage Adjustment Board, which had been functioning during the war in connection with disputes in longshore and harbor work. The Railroad Administration, which employed men in the same work, also refused to abide by the board's decisions, claiming with the other employers that the board had no jurisdiction after the signing of the armistice.

The Adjustment Board then recommended that the employees' demands be referred to the National War Labor Board, which held hearings on the matter on January 7, 1919. The private owners and the Railroad Administration, however, refused to accept the board's jurisdiction and would not agree to be bound by its award. Under the conditions, the board announced that it could not undertake to settle the controversy.

On January 9 all of the 16,000 harbor workers in New York went out on strike, and in addition about 50,000 longshoremen were thus forced out of work. The strike paralyzed harbor traffic, including ferry boats and those boats operated by the federal government.

Two days later President Wilson, who was then in Europe for the purpose of attending the Peace Conference, having been informed by Secretary of Labor Wilson as to the seriousness of the strike, addressed a cablegram to the Joint Chairmen of the National War Labor Board. He asked the board to take up the case again and expressed himself as certain that all the government agencies interested would use all their power to make the findings effective. In conclusion he stated that it was his earnest hope " that in the present period of industrial transition arising from the war the board should use all means within its power to stabilize conditions and prevent industrial dislocation and warfare."

After this the Railroad Administration could hardly continue its opposition to the board. The men voted to return to work January 11, and on the 13th hearings before the War Labor Board began once more. The private boat owners still persisted in their refusal to submit, but the board proceeded to hear the case on the joint submission of the public owners and the employees.[1]

6. CONCLUSION

The war period showed Woodrow Wilson at his best. It gave him the opportunity to take the part of a strong leader such as he believed the President should be. Until after the armistice, when the treaty of peace and the League of Nations Covenant absorbed his attention, he acted the part of a fair-minded and intelligent statesman in dealing with the industrial situation. Realizing that the essential thing was to raise production to the highest point and keep it there, he threw his energies into preventing the suspension of work in essential war industries. To this end he approved the creation of the various adjustment agencies and lent them his full support whenever it was necessary. But he did not rely on such agencies alone. Early in the war he obtained the promise of Samuel Gompers, president of the American Federation of Labor, to do everything possible to work with the government in avoiding strikes,[2] and by putting Mr.

[1] B. M. Squires, " The New York Harbor Strike." *Monthly Labor Review,* February, 1919, p. 330. For a good account of war and after-war adjustments in New York Harbor see other articles by the same author in the same publication, September, 1918, and August, 1919.

[2] *N. Y. Times,* April 9, 1917.

Gompers in the position of aid and advisor to the administration he gained from the first the good will and cooperation of the A. F. of L. and its affiliated unions in carrying out his war labor policies.

It is true that more strikes occurred during the war than at any previous period in our history. In 1917 the U. S. Bureau of Labor Statistics reported a total of 4450 strikes and lockouts. For the next year, when our war efforts had attained their highest point, 3337 such cases were reported.[1] But these figures do not minimize the importance of the efforts of the administration to prevent strikes. The establishment of the numerous government boards of arbitration, the support given by the President to the principles and methods of the National War Labor Board, and the readiness of the President, while under the already great strain of other war-time responsibilities, to step in and use his power to aid the various boards, all undoubtedly tended to lessen the severity and frequency of strikes, especially in the war industries. It should be remembered also that most of the important agencies of adjustment, including the War Labor Board, were created and supported without any specific authorization or appropriation for the purpose from Congress. Their activities and accomplishments were possible largely because of the initiative of administration officials and the determination of the President and his assistants to lend them support.

The vigor with which Mr. Wilson upheld the National War Labor Board in its awards might, in time of peace, have subjected him to the accusation of being arbitrary and high-handed, but few would criticize the staunch support which helped the board maintain the dignity and prestige so necessary in time of war.

[1] *Monthly Labor Review*, June, 1920, p. 506.

The record of the President in industrial disputes during the war was one of which he might be justly proud. By including in his proclamation creating the War Labor Board the statement of the principles which should govern it in its dealings with labor, Mr. Wilson established a definite governmental labor policy for the first time in our history. Thereafter, during the war period, the administration gave its support to the right of workers and employers to organize as they wished and to bargain collectively, to the basic eight-hour day, to the principle of the living wage, and to the maintenance of established safeguards of health and safety. By the same act the government put itself in opposition to strikes or lockouts during the war, to discrimination against workers for legitimate trade-union activities, and to the use of coercion on the part of trade unions. By giving his approval to these principles the President made possible the establishment of a constructive government labor policy which was as a whole characterized by intelligence and a desire to act fairly. Undoubtedly it was the war-time spirit of cooperation which was largely responsible for the success of this policy. But the carrying out of a definite set of principles so efficiently indicates that even in ordinary times the adoption of a constructive labor policy by the administration would not only be possible, but would be attended by some degree of success.

CHAPTER VI

President Wilson, 1919-1921

ALTHOUGH the joint resolution of Congress declaring war between the United States and Germany at an end was not approved until July 2, 1921, and peace was not formally proclaimed by the President until November 14, 1921, it seems best to consider that, in the treatment of industrial problems, the post-war period began with the signing of the armistice in November, 1918. The war-time purpose of the President, that is, his desire to prevent interruption in the production of goods for war purposes, cannot be said to have been a guiding motive in his attitude toward industrial controversies after the war. The strikes and threatened strikes of 1919 and thereafter were handled by the President from a viewpoint quite different from that of the war period. The motives to action on his part were more like those which prevailed before war was declared.

I. THE RAILROAD SHOPMEN'S STRIKE OF 1919

It has already been observed that the rapidly rising cost of living during the war was probably the most important factor in producing strikes and industrial unrest. Contrary to the expectation of many, the year 1919, instead of witnessing a decline in prices due to the absence of the war demand, was accompanied by continued increases in prices. Thus, taking 1913 as a base of 100, the index number of retail food prices in the United States was 160 in January, 1918, 167 in July, 1918, and 185 in January, 1919. By

154   [402

August, 1919, it had reached 192, and by the following
January was up to 201.[1] It was to be expected that under
such conditions considerable unrest and agitation for higher
wages would develop. The fact is borne out by the statistics of strikes and lockouts. Whereas for 1918 the Bureau
of Labor Statistics reported a total of 3337, the number in
1919 had mounted to 3374.[2]

Among those workers whose wages had lagged behind
the continually increasing cost of living the railroad employees were perhaps the most numerous. The railroad
shopmen in particular had become greatly dissatisfied.
They had received a general increase to a 68 cent per hour
minimum on July 2, 1918,[3] but this had still left them
in the position of receiving less pay than did the machinists
in similar work in the shipyards, who received 80 cents per
hour.[4]

In January, 1919, the men asked for an increase of from
68 cents to 85 cents per hour, with proportionate increases
for helpers and apprentices.[5] The consideration of these demands by the Board of Railway Wages and Working Conditions, to which they had been referred in February, was
considerably delayed because of other matters which had
been presented to it previously. Finally, on July 16, the
board announced its inability to agree on the increase to be
made. The matter was thus left to Director General Hines
to decide. On July 28 and 29 he had conferences with the
representatives of the shopmen, who informed him of the
great dissatisfaction among the men, due to the long delay

[1] *Monthly Labor Review*, vol. x, p. 1368.

[2] *Ibid.*, vol. x, p. 1506.

[3] *U. S. Railroad Administration. Wages of Railroad Employees.*
Supplement No. 4, General Order 27. Washington, 1919, p. 32.

[4] Bing, *War Time Strikes and Their Adjustment*, p. 92.

[5] *N. Y. Times*, Aug. 3, 1919.

in the determination of their demands, and to the fact that men engaged in similar work elsewhere were and had been getting much higher wages. Under existing circumstances, however, the Director General did not feel himself to be in a position to grant increases on his own responsibility.

In a letter to President Wilson, written on July 30, Mr. Hines pointed out that many classes of railway workers all over the country were demanding wage increases, that the government was already incurring a deficit because railway rates had not been increased, that were a 12 cent increase to be granted to all railway men the added annual cost to the railroads would be $800,000,000, and that any increase in wages would necessarily entail an increase in rates. Though the President had power under the law to increase the rates, the Director General did not think that this power should be exercised at such a time without specific authority from Congress. Accordingly, he recommended that "Congress be asked promptly to adopt legislation providing a properly constituted body on which the public and labor will be adequately represented, and which will be empowered to pass upon these and all railroad wage problems. . . . Such legislation should also provide that if wage increases shall be decided upon it shall be mandatory upon the ratemaking body to provide, where necessary, increased rates to take care of the resulting increases in the cost of operating the railroads." [1]

The refusal of the Director General to grant them their long delayed wage increase, and his suggestion that the question be referred to a new board and thus delayed still further, so aroused the shopmen that large numbers of them, on August 1, obeyed the call of some of the less conservative leaders and went on strike in defiance of instructions from

[1] *Congressional Record*, vol. lviii, p. 3545.

their international officers.   The strike started with the quitting of many men in and about Chicago.[1]   It soon spread to various sections all over the country, until, at the end of a week, thousands of shopmen had followed the Chicago strikers, despite the orders from the heads of the unions.

Meanwhile, on August 1, President Wilson had written to the chairmen of the Congressional committees on interstate commerce forwarding the suggestions of Mr. Hines, and recommending that they be enacted into legislation.   At the same time, the House having previously decided to take a recess of five weeks, the President asked the Republican leaders to postpone it until he had had an opportunity to make recommendations to Congress for the purpose of dealing with the cost-of-living problem.[2]   On the afternoon of August 1 the House rescinded its recess resolution.[3]

Conditions, in the meantime, were growing more and more unsatisfactory.   Not only was the unauthorized strike of the shopmen spreading, but the railway Brotherhoods and the other railway unions issued a statement on August 2 asserting the impossibility of continuing to work under the rising cost of living unless they received wage increases. They maintained that the railway problem could not be solved if the roads were returned to their former control, and recommended the enactment of the Plumb Plan of railway management as a solution.   At the same time B. M. Jewell, president of the Railway Department of the American Federation of Labor and leader of the shopmen, announced that his unions had decided to send out a call for a strike vote on the question of accepting the proposal of

[1] *N. Y. Times*, Aug. 2, 1919.
[2] *Congressional Record*, vol. lviii, pp. 3626, 3543.
[3] *N. Y. Times*, Aug. 2, 1919.

Mr. Hines to the President as a solution of their demands.[1]
On August 4 the shopmen's representatives called on the
President and rejected the proposal, pending the final decision of the members of the unions as indicated by the strike
vote.[2]

The House Interstate Commerce Committee, after considering the President's proposal, reported back to the House
on August 4 that Congressional action in the situation was
unnecessary, since, during the continuation of federal control, the President had the power to fix railway rates and
could handle the wage question on his own responsibility.[3]
On being informed of this, the President, on August 7,
wrote to the Director General, authorizing him to tell the
shopmen that " the question of wages they had raised will
be taken up and considered on its merits by the Director
General in conference with their duly accredited representatives." His letter continued:

The chief obstacle to a decision has been created by the men
themselves. They have gone out on strike and repudiated the
authority of their officers at the very moment when they were
urging action. . . . In the presence of these strikes and the
repudiation of the authority of the representatives of the
organization concerned, there can be no consideration of the
matter in controversy. Until the employes return to work
and again recognize the authority of their own organization,
the whole matter must be at a standstill. . . .
Concerned and very careful consideration is being given by the
entire government to the question of reducing the high cost
of living. I need hardly point out how intimately and directly
this matter affects every individual in the nation; and if
transportation is interrupted it will be impossible to solve it.
This is a time when every employe of the railways should help

[1] *N. Y. Times*, Aug. 3, 1919.
[2] *Ibid.*, Aug. 5, 1919.
[3] *Ibid.*, Aug. 5, 1919.

to make the processes of transportation more easy and economical rather than less, and employes who are on strike are deliberately delaying a settlement of their wage problems and of the standard of living. They should promptly return to work, and I hope that you will urge upon their representatives the immediate necessity for their doing so.[1]

This letter Mr. Hines forwarded to Mr. Jewell, who, at midnight of the same day on which it was written, sent messages to all the shopcraft unions asking them to have their men return to work at once in accordance with the President's request.[2] On the day following it was reported that many strikers were returning to work.

It was apparent that President Wilson had determined to attempt a solution of the problem by making efforts to reduce the cost of living. Accordingly he appeared before a joint meeting of Congress on August 8 and recommended the enactment of the following measures in order to lower prices: (1) Extension of the food control act to peace-time and the widening of its scope to cover all necessaries; (2) Licensing of all corporations engaged in interstate commerce to insure competitive selling and prevent " unconscionable profits "; (3) Passage of a law to regulate cold storage, limiting the time of storage, and requiring goods to bear the date of receipt and the price at the time they went into storage; (4) Provision of a penalty for violation of the profiteering clauses of the food control act; (5) Passage of a law requiring all goods destined for interstate commerce to be marked when possible with their price when leaving the producer; (6) Enactment of the proposed law for the control of security issues; (7) Additional appropriations for government agencies which would inform the public of the prices at which retailers buy.

[1] *N. Y. Times*, Aug. 8, 1919.
[2] *Ibid.*, Aug. 8, 1919.

The President also informed Congress that the administration would take the following steps on its own account to cope with the situation: (1) Limit wheat shipments and credit to lower the price of flour; (2) Sell the surplus stocks of food and clothing now in the hands of the government without profit; (3) Draw surplus stocks out of storage and put them upon the market, by legal action wherever necessary; (4) Prosecute combinations of producers and trades formed for the control of supplies and prices; (5) Employ publicity, through the Departments of Commerce, Agriculture, and Labor, and the Federal Trade Commission, to acquaint the public with supplies not available because of hoarding, and methods of price fixing.

" I believe, too," he said, " that the more extreme leaders of organized labor will presently yield to a sober second thought, and, like the great mass of their associates, think and act like true Americans. They will see that strikes undertaken at this critical time are certain to make matters worse, not better—worse for them and for everybody else." [1]

By August 13 the backbone of the strike was broken, and a week later the Director General renewed conferences with the shopmen's representatives. These meetings, however, did not result in any settlement of the issue. On the 25th the shopmen's leaders announced that the men had voted 98 per cent in favor of a strike, to start on September 2 if the wage increases were not granted.[2] This result they communicated to the President in conference. Mr. Wilson thereupon requested the leaders to present the question to the men once more, since in his opinion the vote had been taken on the matter of accepting the submission of their claims to a new tribunal, a question which no longer was

[1] *Congressional Record,* vol. lviii, p. 3718.
[2] *N. Y. Times,* Aug. 14, 21, 26, 1919.

pertinent, since such a tribunal was not then contemplated. After referring to the government's measures to reduce the cost of living, the President continued:

A general increase in the levels of wages would check and might defeat all this at its very beginning. Such increases would inevitably raise, not lower, the cost of living. Manufacturers and producers of every sort would have innumerable pretexts for increasing profits and all efforts to discover and defeat profiteering would be hopelessly confused. I believe that the present efforts to reduce the cost of living will be successful if no new elements of difficulty are thrown in the way and I confidently count upon the men engaged in the service of the railways to assist, not obstruct. . . . All that I am now urging is that we should not be guilty of the inexcusable inconsistency of making general increases in wages on the assumption that the present cost of living will be permanent at the very time that we are trying with great confidence to reduce the cost of living and are able to say that it is actually beginning to fall.

The President, at the suggestion of the Director General, at the same time offered the shopmen an increase of 4 cents an hour, instead of the 17 cent increase they demanded, pointing out that the increase offered would bring their wages into alignment with the same basis on which wages of other classes of railway workers were fixed, and that such an increase would bring the shopmen's wages up to the rate of pay for machinists in private employments, as shown by the Department of Labor figures.[1]

In a statement to the public, also made on August 25, the President gave the government's case in the same manner as above, and asserted that the wages of the shopmen, working regularly, many of them in districts in which prices were relatively low, were not comparable with wages paid

---

[1] *Congressional Record*, vol. lviii, p. 4344.

for fluctuating employment in war industries situated in industrial centers where the cost of living was highest.[1]

On August 26 the leaders of the shopmen notified Mr. Hines of their rejection of the 4-cent offer, and sent out a call for a vote by the men as to whether they would accept it or strike.[2]   On the next day, however, after conferences with the heads of the American Federation of Labor, the leaders sent messages to the locals advising the shopmen to accept the offer of the President, pointing out that it would be a fatal mistake to strike at that time.   They referred to a letter of August 26 from the Director General to the Chairman of the Board of Railway Wages and Working Conditions, in which the former directed that the board should not consider general increases in wages pending efforts of the government to reduce the cost of living.   The leaders then pointed out that since all the other unions had also asked for wage increases, which, as Mr. Hines' instructions indicated, would not be granted, and since these unions had not decided to strike, the shopcrafts would be compelled to carry the whole burden of a strike, a very undesirable situation for them.[3]   The offer of the President was then reluctantly accepted.

The shopmen did not finally receive what they asked for in January, 1919, until July 20, 1920, when the new Railroad Labor Board, believing that the cost of living was not likely to decrease very much, granted them a 13 cent increase, which, together with the increase granted by the President, made up the 17 cent advance which they had long before demanded.[4]

[1] *Cong. Rec.*, vol. lviii, p. 4343.

[2] *N. Y. Times*, Aug. 27, 1919.

[3] *Ibid.*, Aug. 29, 1919.

[4] *Decisions of the U. S. Railroad Labor Board*, vol. i, 1920, pp. 15, 16, 23.

Critics of the administration have attacked the action of the President in the shopmen's strike principally along two lines. Many of those who sympathized with the difficult position of labor at this time felt that in strict justice the shopmen were entitled to a larger increase than 4 cents, since their wages had remained stationary over a long period of rising prices. Yet it was probably true that the granting of an increase to them would have involved similar advances to other railway employees, which, taken altogether, would have been an added factor in the increased cost of living. To have increased wages would have necessitated an increase in railway rates, and consequently a vigorous and continued protest on the part of shippers and the general public. Undoubtedly the President was in a difficult position. Congress had refused to take the action he had requested for the establishment of a new wage board and had definitely placed all responsibility in the matter of wages upon him. Under these circumstances Mr. Wilson cannot be judged harshly for asking the shopmen to suffer what was perhaps an undue share of hardship.

There remains one other matter, however, which cannot be so easily defended. The President, after having determined on action to reduce the cost of living, decided on measures, which, even had Congress granted all he asked for, could not have had any important effect on prices. Mr. Wilson does not seem to have realized that his plan for reducing the cost of living could have but little result as long as credit remained uncontrolled. Though profiteering probably had something to do with high prices, it does not appear to have been an important factor. Profiteering itself was a result of the same cause which brought about high prices, that is, the continual expansion of credit on the part of the banks, based on an enormous gold reserve. If the President's efforts to reduce the cost of living were really to be successful it would have been necessary for him to use whatever influence he had, either through Congress or directly, with the Federal Reserve Board, to restrict the rediscounting of commercial paper. Doubtless such a move on his part, did it become generally known, would have given rise to much criticism from those to whom high prices meant prosperity, i. e., to a large proportion of the bankers and business men of the country. But it would probably have been much more effective than the inconsequential measures actually taken by the administration, and upon which the railway employees and all other workers were asked to place their reliance, as an alternative to higher wages.

2. THE SYMPATHETIC RAILWAY STRIKE IN THE SOUTHWEST, 1919

About the 21st of August, 1919, large numbers of railway employees, including shopmen, yardmen, and many engaged in train operation about Los Angeles, went on strike in sympathy with the striking trainmen of the Pacific Electric Railway Company, the employees of which had quit work in order to obtain higher wages. The employees on the other roads, on going out, gave as a cause for their strike their refusal to handle freight from the Pacific electric lines. The suspension spread quickly, and by the 26th had paralyzed rail service throughout Southern California.[1]

In the meantime officials of the railway Brotherhoods ordered the strikers employed on roads under government control to return to work at once. On the 27th the heads of the engineers' and the trainmen's Brotherhoods threatened them with expulsion if they did not return within 24 hours. The strike, however, continued to spread, and soon

[1] *N. Y. Times*, Aug. 26, 27, 31, 1919.

affected not only parts of California, but of Arizona and Nevada as well.[1]

On August 28, President Wilson, learning of large quantities of perishable foodstuffs halted by the strike, authorized the Railroad Administration to exercise the entire power of the government, if necessary, to operate the railroads in the strike region. At the same time the Attorney General, with the sanction of the President, sent messages to the federal district attorneys in all the districts involved, ordering them to aid in the arrest and prosecution of any persons interfering with the operation of the railways under federal control, or whose action might delay the mails. The Director General on the same day issued a statement pointing out that the strike was in violation of agreements with the Railroad Administration, and was illegal under the Brotherhood rules; that he had published advertisements in the California newspapers pointing out the absence of justifiability for the strike and urging the strikers to return to work; but that many still remained on strike. He accordingly announced that the places of all the strikers not at work by 7 A.M., August 30, would be filled. His statement also informed the public of the administration's action in directing U. S. officials to enforce that section of the federal railroad control act which provided for fine or imprisonment of anyone interfering with the operation of the railroads under government control, and announced that the governors of the states and the mayors of the cities in the strike districts had been asked to cooperate with the government by enforcing any local or state laws which might aid operation of the railroads.[2]

The strikers quickly heeded the Director General's warn-

[1] *N. Y. Times,* Aug. 28, 29, 1919.

[2] *Ibid.,* Aug. 29, 1919.

ing, and most of them returned to work by August 30.   In
a short time the sympathetic strike was at an end.[1]

3. THE STEEL STRIKE OF 1919

The great strike of the steel workers in the autumn of
1919 has already received so much attention from other
writers, and the sources of information concerning the
issues involved and the progress of the strike are so readily
available, that the general subject may be treated briefly
here.

At the annual convention of the American Federation of
Labor held in St. Paul in June, 1918, resolutions were
unanimously adopted to the effect that a campaign be inaugurated to organize the steel workers.[2]   On August 1 and
2 fifteen international unions affiliated with the A. F. of L.
organized the National Committee for Organizing the Iron
and Steel Workers, with Samuel Gompers as chairman and
W. Z. Foster as secretary-treasurer.[3]   This committee proceeded with the work of organization, and was so successful that by the time the strike commenced over a year later
they had enrolled over 150,000 steel workers, this number
including only those who had paid the $1 initiation fee re-
quired.[4]

On May 15, 1919, the Amalgamated Association of Iron,
Steel, and Tin Workers, one of the most important of the

---

[1] *N. Y. Times,* Aug. 31, 1919.   A number of suits were brought against
strikers in accordance with the Attorney General's orders.   In the
spring of 1920 30 of them were indicted for violating the Lever Act,
and on June 19, 1920, a jury trying three of the cases together returned
a verdict of guilty as to five defendants, fining them $1000 each, dis-
agreed as to twelve defendants, and declared the remaining thirteen
not guilty. *Report of the Attorney General,* 1920, p. 42.

[2] Foster, *The Great Steel Strike and Its Lessons,* 1920, p. 18.

[3] *Ibid.,* p. 23.

[4] *Ibid.,* p. 65.

organizations making up the National Committee, wrote to
E. H. Gary, head of the United States Steel Corporation and
the controlling factor in the steel industry, asking that he
meet a committee of representatives of the steel workers.
Five days later Mr. Gary replied, refusing a conference because his company did " not confer, negotiate with, or com-
bat labor unions as such. We stand for the open shop. . . .
We think this attitude secures the best results to the employees generally, and to the employers." [1]

On May 27 the National Committee, now representing
twenty-four international unions, met in Washington and
resolved that all the affiliated unions make a joint effort to
enter into negotiations with the steel companies for the
purpose of securing the establishment of better wages,
shorter hours, improved working conditons, and collective
bargaining in the steel industry. A committee headed by
Samuel Gompers was appointed to have charge of the preliminary negotiations with the companies.[2] On June 20
Mr. Gompers sent a letter to Mr. Gary asking for a conference with the committee.[3] After waiting for several
weeks for an answer and receiving none, the National Committee recommended to its affiliated unions that they take
a strike vote of the locals in the steel industry.[4]

On July 20 the National Committee met again, and formulated a set of twelve demands of which those for collective bargaining, the eight-hour day and the six-day week,
and an increase in wages were probably the most important.[5]

---

[1] Foster, *op. cit.*, pp. 70, 71.

[2] *Ibid.*, p. 73.

[3] *Report of the Senate Committee on Education and Labor Investigating the Steel Strike*, 1st Sess., 66th Cong., Senate Report 289, p. 2.

[4] *Foster, op. cit.*, p. 76.

[5] *Ibid.*, p. 77.

The tabulation of the strike vote was completed by August 20, and the organizers claimed that about 98 per cent of the union men had voted for a strike in case no settlement could be reached. The conference committee, with John Fitzpatrick, president of the Chicago Federation of Labor at its head, attempted to see Mr. Gary at his New York office on August 26, but was refused a conference, and was requested to submit its proposition in writing. This was done on the same day, and the committee once more asked for a conference.[1]

To this request Mr. Gary replied the next day, refusing the proposal and pointing out that his company stood for the open shop and did not discuss business with labor unions. The conference committee thereupon tried once more to have Mr. Gary meet them, asserting that " reason and fairness should obtain rather than that the alternative [should] be compulsory upon [them]." [2]

Receiving no reply to this communication, the Executive Council of the A. F. of L. delegated Mr. Gompers to accompany the conference committee and present the matter to President Wilson. About August 28 the committee met the President and asked him to arrange a conference between Mr. Gary and a committee of the employees of his corporation. Mr. Wilson agreed to try to bring about such a meeting. In order to give him an opportunity to do so the unions withheld the setting of the strike date.[3]

On September 4, while the President was on his western trip advocating the League of Nations, the National Committee sent a telegram to him pointing out that the repres-

[1] Foster, *op. cit.*, p. 79.

[2] *Senate Rep.*, *op. cit.*, p. 4.

[3] *Hearings before the Senate Committee on Education and Labor Investigating the Steel Strike*, Washington, 1919, p. 106, Testimony of Mr. Gompers.

sive acts of the officials in the steel towns and the discharge
of union men by the companies were so exciting the workers
that it would be difficult to keep them from striking much
longer. The committee asked the President to reply by
September 9 as to whether a conference with Mr. Gary
could be arranged.[1]

On the 9th the presidents of the unions in the steel industry met to determine on a course of action. There was
laid before the meeting a telegram from the President's
secretary, Mr. Tumulty, informing them that Mr. Wilson
had not yet been successful in arranging a conference, but
that he was continuing his efforts. The meeting then sent
another telegram to the President asking for a definite statement as to the possibility of his being able to arrange a conference with Mr. Gary. The next day Mr. Tumulty answered this telegram in practically the same way as he had
answered the previous one. His message held out no definite hope for a conference, nor did it suggest any other
way out. On receipt of this reply the meeting voted that
the steel strike begin on September 22.[2]

This decision, which was at once published, probably
reached the ears of the President immediately, for on the
same day, September 10, Secretary Tumulty sent the following telegram, which was published in the press the next day,
to Mr. Gompers:

In view of the difficulty of arranging any present satisfactory
mediation with regard to the steel situation, the President de-
sires to urge upon the steel men, through you, the wisdom and
desirability of postponing action of any kind until after the
forthcoming Industrial Conference at Washington.[3]

[1] Foster, *op. cit.*, p. 85.
[2] *Ibid.*, pp. 86-88.
[3] *Senate Report, op. cit.*, p. 4. President Wilson, on September 3,

Mr. Gompers forwarded this message to Chairman Fitzpatrick of the National Committee, expressing the hope " that something can be done without injury to the workers and their cause to endeavor to conform to the wish expressed by the President." [1] On the 12th Mr. Fitzpatrick replied to Mr. Gompers, saying:

It would be a thousand times better for the entire labor movement that we lose the strike and suffer complete defeat, than to attempt postponement now, except under a definite arrangement which would absolutely and positively guarantee the steel workers substantial concessions and protection. If these things cannot be guaranteed, then, in our opinion, our only hope is the strike. [2]

After considering the President's request, and after receiving many protests against postponement of the strike date and threats from the men to go on strike even if it were postponed by the leaders, [3] the National Committee voted

1919, and thereafter, had asked various bodies representing organized labor, employers and farmers to appoint representatives to an Industrial Conference, to meet in Washington on October 6, for " the purpose of reaching, if possible, some common ground of agreement and action with regard to the future conduct of industry." The President himself appointed 22 " representatives of the public," among whom were John D. Rockefeller, Jr., E. H. Gary, B. M. Baruch, Dr. Charles W. Eliot, Henry S. Dennison, Charles Edward Russell, John Spargo, and B. M. Jewell. *Proceedings of the First Industrial Conference,* Oct. 6-23, 1919, Washington, 1920, pp. 4-6.

[1] *Senate Report, op. cit.,* p. 4.

[2] *Senate Hearings, op. cit.,* p. 4. W. Z. Foster, who managed the strike for the unions, said of this request of the President, " It was like asking one belligerent to ground arms in the face of its onrushing antagonist. The employers gave not the slightest sign of a truce. Long before anything could be hoped for from the Industrial Conference, they would have cut the unions to pieces, had the workers been foolish enough to give them the opportunity." Foster, *op. cit.,* p. 90.

[3] Foster, *op. cit.,* pp. 91-92.

to reaffirm September 22 as the strike date.   The committee
then sent a long letter to the President, giving in detail their
reasons for not acceding to his request, and pointing out
especially that the continued discharge of union men by the
Steel Corporation, and preparations on a large scale by the
companies to defeat the strike, would make postponement
fatal.   The letter continued, " If delay were no more than
delay, even at the cost of membership in our organizations,
we would urge the same to the fullest of our ability, notwithstanding the men are set for an immediate strike.   But
delay here means the surrender of all hope ".[1]

On September 22 the strike commenced, about 280,000
men quitting work in the steel mills.   At the end of a week
the total number of strikers exceeded 300,000.[2]   Thereafter the strike continued, accompanied by the persecution
of strikers and their families, suppression by the Pennsylvania State Troopers and local officials of the right of free
speech and free assembly, villification of the strike leaders,
dissemination of propaganda fostered by the companies and
handed out in great quantities to the effect that the strike
was the result of Bolshevik conspiracies, that the workers
received very high pay, etc., etc.[3]

Federal troops were sent to Gary, Indiana, where the
Steel Corporation had a large plant, on October 6, and
were not finally withdrawn until January 1, 1920.[4]   The
best account available concerning the occasion for the use
of troops at Gary and their activities seems to be that given

[1] *Senate Hearings, op. cit.,* p. 5.

[2] *Public Opinion and the Steel Strike,* Commission on Inquiry of the
Interchurch World Movement, N. Y., 1921, p. 132.

[3] For a good account of the strike and its issues, never effectively
answered by the Steel Corporation, see the *Report on the Steel Strike,*
1920, and *Public Opinion and the Street Strike,* 1921, published by the
Commission on Inquiry of the Interchurch World Movement.

[4] *Report of the Secretary of War,* 1920, p. 71.

in the Interchurch Report on the Steel Strike, which is here
quoted at some length:

The walkout on September 22 at Gary was almost complete.
Agreements, subject to various disputes over interpretation,
were reached with city authorities concerning picket line rules.
Huge mass-meetings were held in the open air.   The strikers
made frequent complaints of violent raids carried out by bands
of citizens calling themselves ' Loyal American Leaguers ', who
were charged with clubbing groups of strikers on street corners
at night.   A crowd of strikers leaving a mass-meeting tried
to pull a negro strikebreaker off a street car: the negro was
slightly injured and a number of strikers were clubbed. [Oct-
ober 4.]   On this case of ' mob violence ', the only one alleged,
Indiana state guards were sent in.   Parades were forbidden.
Ex-service men among the strikers, independently of the strike
leadership, put on their old army uniforms and started a march
to exhibit the uniforms to the guardsmen.   There were about
200 of these ex-soldiers and about 10,000 strikers in the streets
fell in behind the procession which wound through the town
in disregard of the guardsmen and quietly disbanded in the
park where meetings were held.   On this second case of ' mob
violence ', known as the ' outlaw parade ', the United States
regulars occupied Gary, with General Wood in personal
charge. . . . [October 6.]   The regulars were equipped with
bayonets and steel helmets and the force included many trucks
mounting machine guns and bringing field artillery.

General Wood declared that ' the army would be neutral '.
He established rules in regard to picketing.   These rules were
so interpreted and carried out as to result in breaking up the
picket line.   One picket, for example, would be permitted at a
certain spot; if the striker who came up to relieve the picket
stopped to converse with him and to receive reports and
instructions, both strikers would be arrested.   Delays and difficulties would attend the release of these men from jail or
' bull pen '.   The picket line thus dwindled and its disappear-
ance signalled to the Gary workers that the strike was break-

ing. Army officers sent soldiers to arrest union officers in other trades, for example for threatening to call a strike on a local building operation. Workers throughout the city believed that the Federal Government opposed them and that the regulars would stay as long as the steel workers remained on strike.[1]

From time to time during the strike unsuccessful attempts were made to have the strike issues arbitrated. The most important of these efforts, and the most significant, in view of the President's suggestion of September 10 that the strike be postponed until after the Industrial Conference had met, was that made by the labor group in the Conference, which began its sessions as scheduled on October 6, 1919. On October 9 Mr. Gompers, on behalf of the labor members, presented the following resolution:

Resolved, That each group comprising this conference select two persons . . . , and these six so selected . . . . constitute a committee to which shall be referred existing differences between the workers and the employers in the steel industry for adjudication and settlement.

Pending the findings of this committee this conference requests the workers involved in this strike to return to work and the employers to reinstate them in their former positions.[2]

On October 21 this resolution was rejected by the conference, a majority of the public group and the employers' group voting against it.[3]

[1] *Report on the Steel Strike*, Interchurch etc., *op. cit.*, pp. 240-242, see also *N. Y. Times, N. Y. World*, Oct. 7, 1919.

[2] *Proceedings of the First Ind. Conf., op. cit.*, p. 58.

[3] *Ibid.*, p. 240. The conference broke up on October 22, when the labor group withdrew, the employer's group having refused to agree to a resolution recognizing the "right of wage earners to organize without discrimination, to bargain collectively, to be represented by representatives of their own choosing in negotiations and adjustments with employers. . . ." *Ibid.*, p. 269.

On December 5, having received the agreement of the National Committee to abide by any plan of settlement which the Interchurch Commission on Inquiry might propose, the Commission conferred with Mr. Gary. He refused to confer with them as mediators in behalf of the strikers, and declared that there was " absolutely no issue " to discuss.[1]

The strike finally ended on January 8, 1920, after the National Committee had ascertained that the steel companies had recruited working forces to about three fourths of normal, and that steel production was 60 per cent to 70 per cent of normal.[2] The tremendous size of the U. S. Steel Corporation and the energy and methods with which it fought the strike, the suppression of strike activities in the steel districts, the hostile attitude of the press, and the lack of wholehearted support from the labor movement in general were probably the most important factors in the defeat of the strikers.[3]

One matter in connection with the President's attitude toward the strike deserves special consideration. Reference has been made to his attempt to get Mr. Gary to confer with representatives of the unions, and to the President's lack of success. It will be recalled that on September 10, hearing that the international presidents had set the strike date for September 22, the President instructed his secretary to request that the strike be postponed until after the Industrial Conference had met. This request quickly reached the press and was given wide publicity. The publication of the telegram at once placed the responsibility for the strike, as far as the public was concerned, upon the shoulders of the

[1] *Public Opinion and the Steel Strike, op. cit.,* p. 339.

[2] Foster, *op. cit.,* p. 192.

[3] *Interchurch Report on the Steel Strike, op. cit.,* p. 15.

unions, who were placed before the nation in the position
of refusing the President's request and thus of bringing on
the strike.   But to one who reads of the events preceding
the setting of the strike date, it is apparent that the responsibility for the strike rests also upon the shoulders of Mr.
Gary, because of his persistent refusal, even at the President's request, to meet the representatives of the unions.

Since the President's telegram requesting a postponement
was published in the newspapers, his failure to make a
public statement telling of Mr. Gary's refusal to confer
seems to have been unfair and unjust to the cause of the
strikers.   Such a public statement would have placed the responsibility where it to a considerable degree belonged, and
might have done more than any other method the President
could have used to bring concessions from Mr. Gary and
thus prevent the strike.

In criticizing President Wilson it is only fair, however,
to remember his position at this time.   He had returned
from Europe worn out by his prolonged labors at the Peace
Conference, and now, with rapidly lessening vigor, he was
face to face with the danger of being repudiated by his own
country.   To him the most important task was to win over
Congress and the nation to an acceptance of the Treaty of
Versailles and the League of Nations Covenant.   Upon this
the President concentrated his powers.   Even though he appeared to take an active part in the settlement of the shopmen's dispute in August, 1919, it is probable that most of
the work in that case was done by Director General Hines.
During the western trip, undertaken in September, Mr.
Wilson's mind was almost wholly occupied by the question
of foreign affairs, and the collapse which ended the trip
necessitated his complete withdrawal from public affairs for
a long period.   Under these circumstances the attempts of
the administration to bring about a conference with Mr.

Gary must have been largely in the hands of Mr. Tumulty, and the latter was probably chiefly responsible for the request to the strike committee to postpone the strike and the failure to make public Mr. Gary's refusal to confer with the union leaders.

There is reason for asserting that the President used poor judgment when he agreed to use his influence with Mr. Gary to bring about a meeting. The well known anti-union policy of the Steel Corporation, and its persistent refusal for many years to deal with unions in any way, made even the possibility of success on the President's part very doubtful. Furthermore, except during war-time, a President has almost never attempted to interfere in disputes other than those concerned with the coal or the transportation industries, in which a suspension of production might involve serious public hardship. The steel industry has no such direct influence on public welfare. Under these conditions it would have been the part of wisdom to avoid interference until public opinion was further roused to support the move. However, had Mr. Wilson possessed his oldtime thoroughness and vigor he might have been successful even under such heavy odds. As it was, nothing but failure for the administration could be expected.[1]

[1] One other matter regarding the administration's part in the strike should be mentioned briefly. It is concerned with the confusion of the Department of Justice with regard to the real purpose of the strike. The Department, aided in Gary by federal soldiers, raided strikers' headquarters and arrested strikers and other workers for radical activities, evidently on the assumption that the strike was part of a Bolshevik plot. The arrests were very often made on alleged information furnished to the Department by detective agencies working for the steel companies. In Gary the attorney for the strikers was seized by the troops as a dangerous radical. For these activities see the *N. Y. Times*, the *N. Y. World*, the *Chicago Tribune*, October 8, 9, 10, and subsequent dates; also the Interchurch *Report on the Steel Strike*, p. 225.

4. THE BITUMINOUS COAL STRIKE OF 1919

On September 22, 1919, a convention of the United Mine Workers approved a set of demands to be presented to the bituminous operators, and to be embodied in a new contract to be effective from and after November 1, 1919, for a period of two years. Most important among the demands were those asking for a 60 per cent increase in wages and the introduction of the six hour day—five day week schedule.[1] The next day the program of the miners was presented to a joint conference of miners and operators of the central competitive field. Thereafter various conferences were held, but on October 11 the meetings came to an end without an agreement having been reached.[2].

The miners' convention of September 22 had instructed Acting President John L. Lewis to issue a strike order effective November 1 in case no agreement with the operators could be secured. On October 14, having heard that the strike order was about to be issued, Secretary of Labor Wilson wrote to Mr. Lewis, asking that the order be withheld until he had conferred with him. A request was also sent to T. T. Brewster, representing the operators, asking for a conference. On the next day Mr. Lewis wired the Secretary that the order had already been issued in accordance with the instructions of the convention.[3] On the 16th the Secretary met Messrs. Brewster and Lewis. The former refused to enter into negotiations for a new wage

[1] *Report of the Secretary of Labor*, 1920, p. 104. The demand for the six hour day was made because of the miners' desire for steady and continuous work throughout the year, in place of the prevailing conditions of long hours part of the year and little or no work the remainder. The demand, instead of being one for less work, as the newspapers interpreted it, was one for steady work.

[2] *Ibid.*, p. 104.

[3] *Ibid.*, p. 104.

scale until the strike order was recalled. President Lewis, on the other hand, was equally firm in his contention that he had no authority to call off the proposed strike.[1]

Thereupon Secretary Wilson called the joint scale committees of the operators and the miners to meet him. The conference met at the Department of Labor headquarters on October 21, and continued in session for four days. While it was in progress President Wilson wrote to the Secretary of Labor:

Whatever their differences may be, no matter how widely divergent their viewpoints may be from each other, it is a duty that they owe to society to make an earnest effort to negotiate those differences and to keep the mines of our country in operation. After all, the public interest in this matter is the paramount consideration of the Government.... If for any reason the miners and operators fail to come to a mutual understanding, the interests of the public are of such vital importance in connection with the production of coal that it is incumbent upon them to refer the matters in dispute to a board of arbitration for determination, and to continue the operation of the mines pending the decision of the board.[2]

This letter, however, was without effect on the contending parties, for on the 24th the conferees adjourned without reaching an agreement, the difficulty still being the refusal of the miners to withdraw the strike order before wage negotiations took place.[3]

In the meantime, on October 21, Attorney General Palmer had petitioned the United States District Court in Indianapolis for an injunction restraining the officers and members of the United Mine Workers from carrying on the proposed strike. The petition was based on the Lever Act of

[1] *Monthly Labor Review*, December, 1919, p. 1730.
[2] *Congressional Record*, vol. lviii, p. 7845.
[3] *Rep. Sec. Labor, op. cit.*, p. 104.

August 10, 1917, providing for federal war-time control
of food and fuel, particularly on Section 4, which made it
unlawful " to conspire, combine, agree, or arrange with any
other person (a) to limit the facilities for transporting, producing, harvesting, manufacturing, supplying, storing, or
dealing in any necessaries, (b) to restrict the supply of any
necessaries, (c) to restrict the distribution of any necessaries, (d) to prevent, limit, or lessen the manufacture or
production of any necessaries in order to enhance the price
thereof." [1]

On October 24, after the second conference with the
Secretary of Labor had come to an unsuccessful conclusion,
President Wilson issued a public statement from which
the following excerpts are given:

The strike is one of the gravest steps ever proposed in this
country, affecting the economic welfare and the domestic comfort and health of the people.

It is proposed to abrogate an agreement as to wages which
was made with the sanction of the United States Fuel Administration,[2] and which was to run during the continuance
of the war, but not beyond April 1, 1920. This strike is proposed at a time when the Government is making the most earnest effort to reduce the cost of living and has appealed with
success to other classes of workers to postpone similar disputes
until a reasonable opportunity has been afforded for dealing
with the cost of living.

It is recognized that the strike would practically shut off
the country's supply of its principal fuel at a time when interference with that supply is calculated to create a disastrous
fuel famine. . . .

The country is confronted with the prospect at a time when
the war itself is still a fact, when the world is still in suspense
as to negotiations for peace, when our troops are still being

[1] Chap. 53, sec. 4, 40 Stat. 277.
[2] *Cf. supra.*, p. 129.

transported, and when their means of transport is in urgent need of fuel.

From whatever angle the subject may be viewed, it is apparent that such a strike in such circumstances would be the most far-reaching plan ever presented in this country to limit the facilities of production and distribution of a necessity of life and thus indirectly to restrict the production and distribution of all the necessaries of life. A strike under these circumstances is not only unjustifiable, it is unlawful.

The action proposed has apparently been taken without any vote upon the specific proposition by the individual members of the United Mine Workers of America, throughout the United States, an almost unprecedented proceeding. . . .

In these circumstances I solemnly request both the national and the local officers and also individual members of the United Mine Workers of America to recall all orders looking to a strike on November 1, and to take whatever steps may be necessary to prevent any stoppage of work. . . .

I can do nothing else than to say that the law will be enforced, and the means will be found to protect the interests of the nation in any emeregncy that may arise out of this unhappy business.

I express no opinion on the merits of the controversy. I have already suggested a plan by which a settlement may be reached, and I hold myself in readiness at the request of either or both sides to appoint at once a tribunal to investigate all the facts with a view to aiding in the earliest possible orderly settlement of the questions at issue between the coal operators and the coal miners, to the end that the just rights, not only of those interests, but also of the general public may be fully protected.[1]

On October 29 the Attorney General, who had been instructed by the President to take whatever steps were necessary to protect the public interest, issued a statement setting

[1] *Monthly Labor Review*, December, 1919, p. 1731.

forth the government's position. He maintained that the government had the right to prevent the strike because of its illegality, without impairing the general right to strike; that the armistice did not end the war and that the courts had in many cases held that the war-emergency statutes were still in force; that Congress had recognized the existence of a war emergency as late as October 22, 1919, in the passage of an act making the food and fuel control act more effective; that the proposed strike would be a concerted arrangement to restrict the production and distribution of the necessaries of life, which Congress, by the enactment of the Lever Act, had intended to prevent; that the government would give protection to any men desiring to work; and that the facts presented a situation which challenged the supremacy of the law, and every resource of the government would be brought to bear to prevent the national disaster which would inevitably result from the cessation of mining operations.[1]

The representatives of the miners met at Indianapolis on the same day to consider the situation, particularly the suggestion of the President that negotiations be resumed and that a board of arbitration be appointed. After voting not to rescind the strike order they gave out a statement of their position. They maintained that the order came from the regularly constituted convention of the miners, the highest authority in their organization; that their wages had not been increased for two years, while the cost of living had mounted rapidly; that their contract had legally expired, since the war had ended; and that they would meet the mine operators at any time for the purpose of resuming negotiations. " Such action alone," they stated, " will put the mines in operation and guarantee the nation an adequate supply of coal." [2]

[1] *Monthly Labor Review, op. cit.,* p. 1733.

[2] *Ibid.,* p. 1735.

Two days later Judge A. B. Anderson, of the federal court at Indianapolis, handed down a temporary restraining order presumably based on the Lever Act, and operative until November 8, when a hearing on a temporary injunction was scheduled to take place. The order commanded 84 national and district officers of the United Mine Workers and " all other persons whomsoever," not to issue any message that the strike was to be enforced as previously announced, " and to desist and refrain from doing any further act whatsoever to bring about or continue in effect the above described strike, . . . from issuing any further strike orders to local unions and members of local unions or to district unions for the purpose of supporting such strike by bringing about or maintaining any other strikes; from issuing any instructions, written or oral, covering or arranging for the details of enforcing such strike, . . . from issuing any messages of encouragement or exhortation to striking miners or mine workers or unions thereof to abstain from work or not to return to the mines, . . . and from issuing and distributing, or taking any steps to procure the issuance or distribution, to miners and mine workers striking and abstaining from work in pursuance of such strike, of so-called strike benefits, . . . and from conspiring, combining, agreeing, or arranging with each other or any other person to limit the facilities for the production of coal, or to restrict the supply or distribution of coal, or from aiding or abetting the doing of any such act or thing." [1]

On the same day the Attorney General said, " No strike can go on without being directed, and if this injunction is obeyed this strike of the coal miners cannot continue, for this restraining order acts to make it leaderless so far as the national scope of it is concerned." [2]

[1] *Monthly Labor Review*, p. 1737.
[2] *N. Y. Times*, November 1, 1919.

However, strike orders had gone out, strike preparations had already been made, and on November 1 approx-
imately 425,000 bituminous miners quit work, tying up
75 per cent of the bituminous industry. The walkout affected not only the central competitive field, consisting of
Illinois, Indiana, Ohio, and western Pennsylvania, but extended to seventeen other states.[1]

The hearing on the government's motion for a temporary
injunction took place on November 8. The miners' lawyers
being unsuccessful in their attempt to convince Judge Anderson that such action was unwarranted, the injunction was
granted. Since the restraining order had been up to that
time without apparent effect in preventing the strike, the
new order contained a mandate from the court ordering the
defendants to issue a withdrawal and cancellation of the
strike order, " and communicate the same to district or
local unions, committees and members of said . . . United
Mine Workers of America, as fully and completely as the
said strike order has been heretofore distributed and cir-
culated . . . and the said defendants are allowed until
six o'clock, P.M., on the 11th day of November, 1919,
within which to withdraw and cancel said strike order . . . ,
said notice of withdrawal and cancellation to be submitted
to the Court for his approval " by November 11.[2]

This order of the court was obeyed by the United Mine
Workers' officials, but no resumption of mining took place
in the affected areas, and the hardships resulting from the
strike became more severe. On November 18 the Secretary
of Labor once more invited the miners and operators to
meet him in Washington. The conference, representing all
the bituminous miners and operators, decided to take up
negotiations for the central competitive field first. On

[1] *Monthly Labor Review, op. cit.*, p. 1725.

[2] Sayre, *Cases on Labor Law*, Cambridge, 1922, p. 757.

November 20 the operators of that field offered to increase wages 15 cents per ton or 20 per cent for day work, on condition that Fuel Administrator Garfield, whom the President, on October 30, had recalled to his war-time duties of controlling the prices of fuel, would permit an increase in the selling price of coal. This offer the miners rejected, reasserting their original demands. The next day they modified the wage demands by offering to accept a 40 per cent increase, which the operators in turn rejected.

With conditions thus at a deadlock the Secretary of Labor submitted a proposal that a general increase of 31.61 per cent should be granted by the operators as a basis of settlement. This amount, which the Secretary had arrived at by determining the increase necessary to bring the wages of tonnage workers up to the increased cost of living, and extending that increase to day workers, was accepted by the miners, and approved by the operators on condition that the Fuel Administrator would permit an increase in prices high enough to yield them a profit.[1]

The conference thereupon adjourned and the proposition of Secretary Wilson was referred to Mr. Garfield. On November 26 the latter stated his conclusions to the operators and miners. He refused to approve the 31.61 per cent increase and instead offered his own proposal of a 14 per cent increase, based on the same Bureau of Labor figures used by the Secretary of Labor, but arrived at by determining the weighted average increase to all mine workers and adding to this an amount, 14 per cent, sufficient to bring the average wage of all miners up to the increase in the cost of living. This increase the miners rejected, again expressing their willingness to accept the offer of the Secretary of Labor. The operators, on the other hand, im-

---

[1] *Report of the Secretary of Labor, op. cit.*, pp. 105-106; *Final Report of the Fuel Adminstration, 1917-1919*, Washington, 1921, p. 18.

mediately accepted the Garfield proposition.[1] Upon this the conferences ended.

On December 3 government attorneys brought information against 84 representatives of the United Mine Workers, charging them with contempt of court for disobeying the injunction. Many of them were arrested and placed under bonds of $5,000 and $10,000 each.[2] Meanwhile the War Department had given orders that troops be sent at the request of the executives of the coal-mining states to protect all men who desired to work in the mines.[3] Federal troops were accordingly sent into West Virginia, Pennsylvania, Tennessee, Wyoming, Utah, New Mexico, Oklahoma, Kansas, and Washington.[4] The presence of the troops, the arrest of the union officials, and the inability of the latter to continue to pay strike benefits under the terms of the injunction, gradually weakened the strikers.[5]

On December 6 President Wilson issued a public statement again urging a settlement of the strike. He said:

I understand the operators have generally agreed to absorb an increase of 14 per cent in wages, so that the public would pay not to exceed the present price fixed by the Fuel Administrator, and thus a way is opened to secure the coal of which the people stand in need, if the miners will resume work on these terms pending a thorough investigation by an impartial commission, which may readjust both wages and prices.
By the acceptance of such a plan the miners are assured immediate steady employment at a substantial increase in

[1] *Rep. Sec. Labor, op. cit.,* p. 107; *Final Rep. Fuel Adm., op. cit.,* p. 18.

[2] *Report of President Lewis to the 28th Convention of the U. M. W. of A,* 1921, p. 23.

[3] *N. Y. Times,* Nov. 29, 1919.

[4] *Ibid.,* Nov. 1, 3, 4, 29, 30, 1919; *Report of the Secretary of War,* 1920, pp. 71-72.

[5] *Rep. of Lewis to Convention, op. cit.,* p. 23.

wages and are further assured prompt investigation and action upon questions which are not now settled to their satisfaction. I must believe that with a clear understanding of these points they will promptly return to work. If, nevertheless, they persist in remaining on strike, they will put themselves in an attitude of striking in order to force the Government to increase the price of coal to the public. . . . No group of our people can justify such a position. . . . Immediately upon a general resumption of mining I shall be glad to aid in the prompt formation of such a tribunal as I have indicated to make further inquiries into this whole matter, and to review not only the reasonableness of the wages at which the miners start to work, but also the reasonableness of the Government prices for coal.[1]

On the publication of this statement President Lewis and Secretary-Treasurer Green of the miners went to Washington and conferred with the Attorney General and the President's secretary, Mr. Tumulty. The miners' leaders being convinced that it was desirable to end the strike,[2] the following memorandum, which had been approved by the President, was accepted by Messrs. Lewis and Green, and on December 10 was approved by the representatives of the miners in meeting at Indianapolis:

In accordance with the request of the President, as contained in his statement of December 6, the miners will immediately return to work with the 14 per cent increase in wages. . . . Immediately upon a general resumption of operations . . . . the President will appoint a commission of three persons. . . . [to] consider further questions of wages and working con-

[1] *Award and Recommendations of the U. S. Bituminous Coal Commission*, Washington, 1920, pp. 9-10.

[2] Concerning this President Lewis, in his report to the 1921 convention, *op. cit.*, p. 24, said, "While protesting in our hearts against what we believed to be the unjust attitude of the government, we decided to submit to the inevitable."

ditions as well as profits of operators and proper prices for coal. . . . Its report will be made within 60 days, if possible, and will be accepted as the basis of a new wage agreement, the effective date and duration of which shall be determined by the commission.[1]

As a result of the agreement the government had the contempt charges against all but one of the miners' leaders dropped.[2]

On December 19, the miners having in the meantime returned to work, President Wilson appointed Henry M. Robinson, chairman, J. P. White, representing the miners, and Rembrandt Peale, representing the operators, as members of the United States Bituminous Coal Commission, and urged upon them the importance of reaching unanimous conclusions.[3] The commission spent most of the winter hearing testimony, and on March 10, 1920, it presented majority and minority awards to the President. The majority award granted increases of 31 per cent to tonnage miners, and 20 per cent to day workers, the average increases for all miners over 1919 rates being 27 per cent. It refused to grant the six-hour day, recommended the setting up of bipartite commissions in the various districts to make further study of disputed points and to adjust wages on the basis of the award, and decided that the contracts based on

---

[1] *Award of the Bit. Com., op. cit.,* p. 10. Mr. Garfield resigned as Fuel Administrator on the adoption of the agreement, being opposed to the plan of settlement as contrary to " sound principle ". See the *Final Rep. of the Fuel Adm., op. cit.,* p. 19.

[2] The exception was Alexander Howat, leader of the Kansas miners, who, in the opinion of Judge Anderson, had been too defiant in his continued direction of the strike after the injunction had been issued. The case against him was continued indefinitely on December 29, following the return of the Kansas miners to work. See *N. Y. Times,* Dec. 8, 17, 23, 24, and 30, 1919; *United Mine Workers Journal,* Dec. 15, 1919, and Jan. 1, 1920.

[3] *Award of the Bit. Com., op. cit.,* pp. 7-9.

the award should remain in effect for two years, beginning April 1, 1920. The minority report, signed by the miners' representative, dissented principally from the low increase given day workers.[1]

On March 19 President Wilson transmitted a copy of the report to the miners and operators, and suggested the convening of the necessary joint conferences for the purpose of drawing up agreements based on the award. " I regret," he wrote, " that the members of the commission were not unanimous on all points as I had expressed the hope they would be, but the report of the majority is none the less the report of the commission and binding as such." He announced also that on and after April 1, it no longer being expedient to continue the control of prices, no government maximum prices would be enforced.[2]

The officials of the United Mine Workers remained in Washington for some days longer, and held numerous conferences with the President, trying to get him to accept the minority report of the commission, but were unsuccessful.[3] Finally, on March 29, a joint conference of operators and miners representing the central competitive field met in New York. The operators having refused to grant wage increases larger than those awarded by the commission, a joint agreement embodying the terms of the award was signed on March 31. Shortly afterwards the outlying districts held joint conferences and signed agreements based on the New York one, as the commission had suggested.[4]

To what extent the responsibility for the administration's handling of the bituminous strike can be charged to the

[1] *Award of the Bit. Com., op. cit.,* pp. 38-65.

[2] *Ibid.,* p. v.

[3] *Rep. of Lewis to 1921 Convention, op. cit.,* p. 27.

[4] *Ibid.,* p. 38.

President is a question of considerable uncertainty. It will be remembered that in September, 1919, he suddenly returned from a trip through the West because of a serious failure of health. No cabinet meetings at which Mr. Wilson was present are known to have been held during the period when the administration was handling the strike. The acts of his cabinet officers are of course ultimately chargeable to him, and the public statements and letters sent out in his name during the period, in the absence of proof to the contrary, must be assumed to have come from him directly. Although President Wilson, in his letters of December 19, 1919, appointing the bituminous commission, and written when his health had improved somewhat, assumed responsibility for the injunction and the other activities of the administration,[1] one is led to believe, from a study of the administration's part in the strike, that the policies followed were determined and carried out by the cabinet, without the active direction of the President, and usually under the leadership of his secretary, Mr. Tumulty, Attorney General Palmer and Fuel Administrator Garfield. It does not seem possible that the President, were he directing the administration's policies, would have permitted the making of two such contradictory offers of settlement within five days of each other as the 31.61 per cent of Secretary Wilson and the 14 per cent offer of the Fuel Administrator. Further evidence that the cabinet, and not the President, handled the strike is shown by the general tenor of the letters exchanged between Director General Hines, of the Railway Administration, Mr. Garfield, and Mr. Tumulty, with regard to the need of government fuel control,[2] and by the nature of the despatches to the newspapers, especially to the *New York Times,* from Washington during the strike.

[1] *Award of the Bit. Coal Com., op. cit.* pp. 7-9.
[2] *Final Rep. of the Fuel Adm., op. cit.,* pp. 15, 16, 19.

Regardless of the question of immediate responsibility, however, certain phases of the government's treatment of the strike are deservng of thorough consideration. First, was the government justified in seeking to prevent the strike by obtaining an injunction, and, secondly, was it justified in using the provisions of the Lever Act for this purpose? Some criticism of the use of the injunctive method in dealing with strikes has been offered in the treatment of the Pullman Strike, and this matter will be further discussed in the following chapters, so that the question at issue here largely resolves itself into one of the government's right to seek an injunction based on the violation of the Lever Act.

The American Federation of Labor claimed, on November 9, 1919, that the administration had promised, when the Lever bill was in Congress, that it would not be used against strikers.[1] If this assertion is true the administration can properly be charged with a breach of faith. The matter is therefore worth investigating.

When the bill was under consideration in the United States Senate in the summer of 1917, Senator Hollis of New Hampshire introduced an amendment providing that nothing in the act should be construed to prohibit labor unions from carrying on their ordinary functions. The Senate conference committee, when it reported the bill back to the Senate, struck out the amendment. Some senators thought this should be done because strikes should be prohibited in war-time; others, because they thought the provisions of the act in question, particularly Section 4, were directed only against hoarding and monopolizing, and could not be used against strikers.[2]

On August 6, 1917, Senator Husting of Wisconsin made the following statement on the floor of the Senate:

[1] *N. Y. Times*, Nov. 10, 12, 1919.
[2] *Congressional Record*, vol. lv, pp. 5828-5837.

I was sufficiently interested . . . . in the argument made by
the Senator from New Hampshire, and by arguments already
made upon the legal effect· of striking out the Hollis amendment, to inquire from those who will have the administration
of this law in their hands as to what construction would be
placed upon it by them in case it became a law in its present
form.
I am authorized by the Secretary of Labor, Mr. Wilson, to
say that the administration does not construe this bill as prohibiting strikes and peaceful picketing, and will not so construe the bill, and that the Department of Justice does not so
construe the bill and will not so construe the bill. . . .
[The] Secretary of Labor advised me that this was the opinion
of the administration and the Department of Justice. He did
not give it merely as a matter of belief on his part, but said
that he was authorized to so state.[1]

Further evidence of the promise of the administration not
to use the Lever Act against labor was given by Samuel
Gompers in a speech delivered at Washington on November
22, 1919.[2] On August 7, 1917, Secretary of Labor Wilson
told Mr. Gompers that he talked over the matter with the
President, who promised that instructions would be forwarded to the U. S. District Attorneys directing them not
to bring cases against workmen in contravention of the
Clayton Act of 1914, which legalized strikes, unions, etc.
The Secretary further said that in the opinion of the President it would be wise to pass the Hollis amendment after
the Lever bill was passed. He further promised that the
President would assist in the passage of a bill embodying the
amendment.

At a conference held soon after between Mr. Gompers,
Secretary Morrison of the A. F. of L., and Attorney General

[1] *Congressional Record, op. cit.,* p. 5904.
[2] *N. Y. Times,* Nov. 23, 1919.

Gregory, the latter promised to instruct the U. S. District Attorneys not to construe Section 4 of the Lever Act as in any way interfering with the normal activities of labor.[1]

One cannot avoid the conclusion that the administration was not justified in using an act the purpose of which was to prevent hoarding and profiteering in war-time against striking miners almost a year after hostilities had ceased, especially after it had promised not to use it for such a purpose.

To go into the courts and obtain an injunction based on such a measure was still more unjustifiable. Judge Anderson, who issued the injunction, gave no opinion in support of his action, except to say, just before signing the order of November 8, " I think it [the strike] is about the most lawless thing in this country. If the strike conspiracy to reduce the coal output could be carried out it would be rebellion." [2]   There may be some citizens in the United States who believe that a strike in an essential industry constitutes rebellion, but it is fair to suppose that if such persons were in the majority laws forbidding such strikes would have been enacted by Congress. The failure of Congress to do so does not seem a sufficient excuse for the Attorney General's action in asking a federal judge to issue an order, having the power of the law, commanding "all . . . persons whomsoever " not to carry on a strike.

The principal ground for the injunction in the government's petition was the violation of the Lever Act. Yet that measure said specifically that violations of it were crimes, subject to criminal penalties. Nowhere did it make such violations a ground for relief in equity, by injunction. According to the general principles of law crimes are not

[1] *N. Y. Times*, Nov. 23, 1919.

[2] *Ibid.*, Nov. 9, 1919.

to be enjoined merely because they are crimes.[1]   Injunctions are granted presumably only to prevent irreparable injury to the property of the petitioner.   In this case the only property rights of the government affected by the strike were its rights in the railroads.   It seems a considerable expansion of the conception to assume such property rights were injured by failure to produce coal.   Furthermore, even if this had been a proper ground for injunctive relief, the restraining order should have applied only to the mining of coal for the use of government-controlled railways, not to all bituminous coal mining.[2]

A final objection, perhaps the most important to the practically minded, may be given against the 1919 injunction.   It really failed to accomplish its purpose.   The strike continued in spite of the court's order, and though the prohibition of the payment of strike benefits was beginning to be felt by the miners, the strike came to an end not through the use of the injunction, but principally as a result of more satisfactory and commendable efforts of the administration in conference with the miners' leaders.

5. THE RAILWAY LABOR TROUBLES OF 1920

It has already been mentioned that in the summer of 1919 the various unions of railway employees had presented demands for higher wages, and that the President and the Director General of the railways had refused any general increases on the ground that the government's campaign to reduce the cost of living would make them unnecessary.

[1] Lord Eldon, called by Professor Z. Chafee "the greatest of chancellors", said, "I have no jurisdiction to prevent the commission of crimes." *Gee v. Pritchard*, 2 Swans, 402, 1818. Mr. Chafee, in 34 *Harvard Law Review* 405, says, "Judge A. B. Anderson differs from him, but felt unable to give the reasons therefor."

[2] See discussion by Professor Chafee, 34 *Harvard Law Review* 401-407.

But prices had continued to rise in spite of the government's efforts.   As a result of this increase dissatisfaction among the railway employees became more and more serious.

In January and February of 1920 practically all the railway unions presented demands for increases in pay to Director General Hines.[1]   On January 23 W. G. Lee, president of the Brotherhood of Railway Trainmen, informed Mr. Hines that his union intended to invalidate its wage agreement in thirty days, unless some answer to the wage demands were received.   Later it developed that the maintenance of way men had ordered a strike for February 17.[2] With the situation threatening continued operation of the railways, the Director General, on February 3, began a series of conferences on wages with the representatives of the railway unions.   On February 11 he announced that he was unable to come to an agreement with the men.[3]

He thereupon wrote to the President, indicating the great cost involved in increasing wages, and the difficulty of granting such increases when the control of the roads was soon to be returned to the private owners.[4]   On the 13th the President met the representatives of the unions in conference and presented a plan of settlement to them.   He proposed: (1) in case a board were set up by the new transportation law, to use his influence to obtain prompt consideration by it of the wage demands; (2) in case no board were set up by law, to use his influence with the railway managers in having them join the men in setting up such a board; (3) to constitute at once a board of experts which would gather and consider all wage data in order to get the facts ready for a hearing.   He admitted that, though the govern-

[1] *Monthly Labor Review*, May, 1920, p. 1123.

[2] *N. Y. Times*, Feb. 11, 1920.

[3] *Ibid.*, Feb. 12, 1920.

[4] *Monthly Labor Review*, May, 1920, p. 1124.

ment's campaign to reduce the cost of living would have an increasingly beneficial effect, " preparation, consideration, and disposition of these important wage matters ought not, in my opinion, to be postponed for a further indefinite period, and I believe the matters involved ought to be taken up and disposed of on their merits at the earliest practicable time." Urging the acceptance of his proposal, he said, " I am sure that it will be apparent to all reasonable men and women in railroad service that these momentous matters must be handled by an agency which can continue to function after March 1, and, therefore, cannot at the present stage be handled to a conclusion by the Railroad Administration." On February 14 the union heads accepted the President's plan.[1]

On the same day the President and the Director General wired to the head of the maintenance of way employees' union, asking him to call off the strike set for February 17, and pointing out that the union had not even given the Railway Administration the required thirty day's notice of the proposed discontinuance of its contract. On the receipt of these messages the strike was called off.[2]

Meanwhile the Esch-Cummins bill, providing for the return of the railroads to their owners, was rapidly nearing enactment. It was passed by the House on February 21, and by the Senate two days later. The labor provisions of the act set up an arbitration board of nine members, three to represent railway labor, three to represent railway management, and three the public, all to be appointed by the President with the consent of the Senate.[3] In addition to creating this board, the act[4] provided that employers and

---

[1] *N. Y. Times,* Feb. 14 and 15, 1920.

[2] *Ibid.,* Feb. 15, 1920; *N. Y. Call,* Feb. 15, 1920.

[3] Section 304.

[4] Sections 301, 302, 303.

employees try to settle their disputes in conference without bringing them to the board unless settlement was impossible, and also made possible the setting-up of district "boards of labor adjustment" for the same purpose.

The heads of the railway unions, still filled with their old distrust for arbitration by "so-called impartial" arbitrators, protested against the passage of the act and wrote to the President asking him not to approve it. On February 28, however, Mr. Wilson attached his signature to the measure,[1] and wrote a letter in answer to the unions. He pointed out that the bill contemplated the setting up of bipartite boards by the employers and the employees:

I shall at once request the carriers and the employes to join in this action. I believe such a step will go far toward clarifying and maturing the subject for final disposition. In fact the sort of board thus contemplated . . . . appears to be an appropriate substitute for the committee of experts which I have heretofore suggested, and, indeed, such a board will be authorized to go further than such a committee could have gone. . . .

My hopes are that the putting into effect of [the labor] provisions with a carefully selected Labor Board, whose public representatives can be relied upon to be fair to labor and to appreciate the point of view of labor that it is no longer to be considered as a mere commodity, will mark the beginning of a new era of better understanding between the railroad managements and their employes and will furnish additional safeguards to the just interests of railroad labor.

. . . . [The] wage demands are entitled to the earliest possible consideration and disposition, and therefore I do not anticipate delay in the appointment and organization of the Labor Board or in the other necessary steps.[2]

[1] *U. S. Stat.* 66th Cong., 2nd Sess., Chap. 91, Title III.
[2] *N. Y. Times,* Feb. 29, 1920.

In accordance with the suggestions of the President, the wage requests previously made to the Director General were submitted to a joint conference of the managers and the men on March 10.[1] From that time negotiations continued until the conference broke up on April 1, the railway managers refusing to consider increases in wages unless the matter were handled by a tribunal on which the public was represented. The President, however, had not yet appointed the Railroad Labor Board provided by the Transportation Act, and on April 2 the railway unions appealed to him to do so.[2]

In the meantime unrest among the employees, whose demands had been hanging fire for months, became serious. This was especially true among the switchmen and other yardmen, who were members of the Brotherhood of Railway Trainmen. In January John Grunau had formed the Chicago Yardmen's Association, rallying to his organization many of the discontented Brotherhood members. Some time later he formed similar organizations breaking into the ranks of the other unions. Late in March he was discharged as yard foreman by the Chicago, Milwaukee, and St. Paul, at the behest of the trainmen's Brotherhood. The trouble arose over jurisdictional disputes between the organizations, but the discharge, coming as it did when dissatisfaction was rife among the men, aroused many of the yardmen in the Chicago district. On the night of April 1 about 700 switchmen left their work, demanding wage increases and the reinstatement of Grunau.[3] In a few days the strike had spread over many sections of the country from Los Angeles to New York. By April 9 every railroad in New York was effected, the strike involving not only yard-

---

[1] *Monthly Labor Review,* September, 1920, p. 504.

[2] *N. Y. Times,* April 13, 1920.

[3] *Ibid.,* April 3, 1920; *Survey,* April 24, 1920, p. 135.

men, but also other employees. On the same day the railway Brotherhoods denounced the strikers and threatened to punish their members for going out illegally.[1]

The seriousness of the situation evidently hastened the appointment of the Railroad Labor Board, which the President named on April 13.[2] On the next day he met the cabinet and it was decided to summon the new board to consider wage questions as soon as the Senate confirmed the appointment of its members. The strike now began to weaken, and though some strikers, especially in Chicago, stayed out for several weeks longer, transportation soon resumed its normal condition.

In the meantime government attorneys secured the arrest of strike leaders in various places, John Grunau having been arrested on April 15. The charges against the strikers varied in the different places, but the usual ones were interference with interstate commerce, interference with the mails, and violation of the Lever Act.[3] (Technically the war was not yet ended.)

On April 15 the Senate confirmed the appointment of all of the members of the Railroad Labor Board, which at once organized for business. Its first decision, rendered on April 20, was one announcing the board's refusal to hear the wage questions brought before it by the striking switchmen until the men returned to work. It thereupon went on to a consideration of the general wage demands of the unions, a consideration which took several months to finish. On June 23, labor unrest on the roads again having become serious, the President wrote to the board, asking it to hasten its decision on the wage question. Finally, on July 20, 1920, the board handed down an award granting wage in-

---

[1] *N. Y. Times,* April 9, 10, 11, 1920.

[2] *Ibid.,* April 14, 1920.

[3] *Ibid.,* April 15, 17, 19, 20, 21, and May 12, 1920.

creases retroactive to May 1, and affecting practically all railway employees. The increases, granted eighteen months after the first demands had been presented, though considered inadequate, were accepted by all but one of the sixteen railway unions.[1]

6. THE ANTHRACITE WAGE DISPUTE OF 1920

In May, 1916, representatives of the anthracite operators and miners had signed a four-year agreement, to terminate March 31, 1920, providing for wage increases, changes in working conditions, etc. Changes necessitated by war conditions were made in this agreement several times in 1917 and 1918. At a convention of the anthracite miners in August, 1919, demands were adopted for substantial wage increases and further changes in working conditions, particularly the recognition of the union.[2]   On March 9, 1920, these demands were presented to the operators at a joint conference, which referred them to the joint scale committee for consideration and report. For the next few weeks this committee attempted to reach an agreement. On March 24 it agreed, in order to avoid a strike, that work should continue under the existing terms until a new contract, retroactive to April 1, was made.[3]

Finally, on April 29, it having become evident that the miners and operators could not come to an agreement in joint conference, Secretary of Labor Wilson requested the scale committee to meet him in Washington.[4]   He held con-

---

[1] *Ibid.*, June 24, 1920; *Monthly Labor Review*, September, 1920, pp. 504-505; *Decisions of the U. S. Railroad Labor Board*, vol. i, 1920, pp. 13-25.

[2] *Report of the Secretary of Labor*, 1920, p. 111; *Award of the U. S. Anthracite Coal Commission*, Washington, 1920, pp. 9-11.

[3] *Rep. Sec. Labor, op. cit.*, p. 111.

[4] *United Mine Workers Journal*, Oct. 1, 1921.

ferences with the disputants for the next few weeks. Both sides agreed on a 65 per cent increase over 1916 rates for contract miners, but were deadlocked on the closed shop question and on the amount of increase to day men. The miners insisted on a 20 per cent increase, while the operators refused to give more than 17 per cent, a rate approved by Secretary Wilson.[1]

On May 19 the Secretary of Labor, convinced that it would be impossible to reach an agreement, referred the matter to the President. " If the miners persist in their position," he wrote, " I fear it will mean a strike of the entire anthracite field by June 1. I would like to know if I may say to the miners' scale committee that it is your desire that there should be no interruption of . . . . production and that the miners should either accept the terms that have been presented by me as a compromise and accepted by the operators, or submit the matters in dispute to a commission to be appointed by you and continue at work pending its decision." [2]

In answer to this letter President Wilson, on May 21, wrote to the joint scale committee, pointing out the importance of continued production of anthracite to the maintenance of our own economic standards and to the rehabilitation of Europe. His letter went on:

If for any reason you are unable to [effect an agreement] I shall insist that the matters in dispute be submitted to the determination of a commission to be appointed by me, [its] award . . . . to be retroactive to the 1st of April . . . . and that work be continued at the mines pending [its] decision. . . . I shall hold myself in readiness to appoint a commission similarly constituted to the one which I recently appointed in connection with the bituminous coal mining industry as soon

[1] *Anthracite Com. Award, op. cit.,* pp. 13-15.
[2] *Rep. Sec. Labor, op cit.,* p. 111.

as I learn that both sides have signified their willingness to continue at work and abide by its decision.[1]

This proposal was accepted by a convention of the miners on May 27, and by the operators five days later. On June 3 the President issued a proclamation appointing the U. S. Anthracite Coal Commission, consisting of W. O. Thompson, president of Ohio State University, chairman, W. L. Connell, representing the operators, and N. J. Ferry, representing the miners.[2] The commission considered the demands of the men during the summer, and submitted an award which the President approved on August 30, with the exception of one section in which the commission had exceeded the terms of submission.

This award, which was signed by the chairman and the operator member, provided among other things that a 65 per cent increase over May, 1916, rates be granted to contract miners, that a 17 per cent increase over the rates then in effect be granted to day men, that the United Mine Workers be recognized to the extent that agreements be made with the presidents of the district unions, and that the agreement extend for two years from April 1, 1920. Mr. Ferry, the miners' representative, presented a minority report dissenting from the 17 per cent increase for day men as entirely inadequate, and from the majority's refusal to grant full recognition to the union.[3]

The President at once forwarded the award of the majority to the miners and operators and suggested that it be written into an agreement as provided by the commission, requesting the joint scale committees to meet at Scranton on September 2 for that purpose. In accordance with this re-

[1] *Rep. Sec. Labor, op. cit.,* p. 112.
[2] *Anthracite Com. Award, op. cit.,* pp. 5-6.
[3] *Ibid.,* pp. 16-48.

quest the miners met the operators and signed an agreement embodying the award on September 3.

Strong opposition, however, had developed against the award, particularly on the part of the day workers. On the same day, therefore, the district presidents of the unions wrote to the President and asked that the wage question be reopened, asserting that the decision was inadequate, and that since the bituminous award had also recently come up for reconsideration, the same policy should be followed in the anthracite field. Meanwhile many of the anthracite miners, being dissatisfied with the award, decided " to take a vacation ", as they called it. In a few days the disaffection spread throughout the whole anthracite field until practically all the miners were idle.[1]

On September 9 the President replied to the request of the district presidents that the wage question be reopened. When the award was first published several miners had wired the President threatening a strike if he approved it. In answer he had telegraphed:

If your communication . . . . is intended as a threat, you can rest assured that your challenge will be accepted and that the people of the United States will find some substitute fuel to tide them over until the real sentiment of the anthracite mine workers can find expression and they are ready to abide by the obligation they have entered into.

After quoting this, the President, in his letter of September 9, continued:

Notwithstanding the plain warning contained in that telegram, which was given wide publicity, the majority of the anthracite coal miners, following the leadership of these men, have refrained from work under the guise of taking a vacation. . . .

[1] *Rep. Sec. Labor, op. cit.,* p. 113.

Our people have fought a great war and made untold sacrifices
to insure, among other things, that a solemn agreement shall
not be considered as a mere scrap of paper. . . .

. . . . [We] could not look the world in the face or justify
our action to our own people and our own conscience if we
yielded one iota to the men in the anthracite coal fields who
are violating the contract so recently entered into between
themselves, the coal operators, and the Government of the
United States.

I appreciate the earnestness of your efforts to get the men
to return to work and commend your stand in support of the
obligations in your contracts . . . , but for reasons stated
above I regret that I can not grant your request to reconvene
the joint scale committee of operators and miners.[1]

The President's letter was interpreted by the miners to
mean that he would not ask the joint commttee to reconvene until the men resumed work. Accordingly, on September 13, the officials of the union ordered all men back.[2]
On October 5 the Secretary of Labor met a committee of
miners, and on ascertaining that practically all the men had
returned to work, he communicated that fact to the President. The latter, on October 12, invited representatives of
the operators and miners to meet at Scranton three days
later.[3] In accordance with this request a conference was
held and subsequent meetings took place from time to time.
The operators, however, persistently maintained their refusal to make any changes in the terms of the agreement,[4]
and during the two years for which it provided none were
made.

[1] United Mine Workers Journal, Sept. 15, 1920.
[2] Ibid., Oct. 1, 1920.
[3] Ibid., Oct. 15, 1920.
[4] Ibid., Jan. 1, Feb. 1, 1921.

7. THE ILLINOIS BITUMINOUS STRIKE OF 1920

It will be recalled that the award of the U. S. Bituminous Coal Commission, which was handed down on March 10, 1920, and provided but a 20 per cent increase in the wages of day miners, was accepted by the men only after considerable protest. The dissatisfaction with the increase continued, and much unrest developed among the men, especially in Illinois, Indiana, and Ohio. At a joint conference between the miners and operators of Illinois, held at Chicago in July, 1920, the former presented demands for a $2 per day increase for the day men. The operators refused to yield to these demands, and their refusal was followed by strikes in many Illinois mines.[1]

On July 21 representatives of the Illinois operators came to Washington and asked the President to take action towards checking the strike. They expressed a fear that the strike might spread over the entire central competitive field, and pointed out that they did not feel able to depart from the existing wage scale, which was based on the commission's award, "except through some governmental action." The President referred the matter to the Secretary of Labor, who, on July 23, appointed three conciliators to go to Illinois to attempt to end the strike. Three days later they reported to the Secretary that the miners refused to return to work unless they first had some assurance from the government that the question of wages for day men would be reopened. On the next day they reported that 60,000 miners were idle and that meanwhile many had also gone out in Indiana and Ohio.[2]

On July 30 President Wilson issued a statement addressed to the members of the United Mine Workers of

---

[1] *Report of the Secretary of Labor*, 1920, p. 108.
[2] *Ibid.*, p. 109.

America. He expressed his regret at learning of the strike,
not only because the action might result in great suffering
and might interfere with industry, " but also, and what is
of far more importance to you, because the violation of the
terms of your solemn obligation impairs your own good
name, destroys the confidence which is the basis of all mutual
agreements, and threatens the very foundation of fair industrial relations." The statement continued:

In the consideration of the Nation-wide scale, involving many
different classes of labor, by the Bituminous Coal Commission
in the limited time at its disposal, some inequalities may have
developed in the award that ought to be corrected. I can not,
however, recommend any consideration of such inequalities
as long as the mine workers continue on strike in violation of
the terms of the award which they had accepted . . . . I must,
therefore, insist that the striking mine workers return to work,
thereby demonstrating their good faith in keeping their contract. When I have learned that they have thus returned to
work, I will invite the scale committees of the operators and
miners to reconvene for the purpose of adjusting any such
inequalities as they may mutually agree should be adjusted.[1]

Immediately on receipt of this statement the officers of
the union ordered the men to return to work at once.[2] By
August 3, 50 per cent of the Illinois mines were in operation,
and six days later practically all those in Illinois and Indiana
had resumed.[3] On August 10 the President asked the joint
scale committees of the operators and miners to meet in
Cleveland three days later for the purpose of adjusting inequalities arising out of the award of the Bituminous Commission.

[1] *United Mine Workers Journal*, Aug. 15, 1920.
[2] *Ibid.*
[3] *Rep. Sec. Labor, op. cit.*, p. 110.

The conferences took place as the President had requested, but the two sides found themselves unable to come to an agreement with the whole field as a unit. Accordingly the conference adjourned on August 18. Thereupon the miners' representatives were authorized to make separate district agreements. The miners and operators of Indiana soon agreed on an increase of $1.50 per day for day workers, and additional settlements on a similar basis, though with some modifications, were made in the other three states in the central competitive field.[1]

[1] *Report of President J. L. Lewis to the 28th Convention of the U. M. W. of A.*, 1921, pp. 43-46.

APPENDIX

As has been pointed out, the usual peacetime procedure under which federal troops are used to quell domestic disturbances involves a request from the governor or the state legislature to the President, indicating that a condition of insurrection against the state has arisen with which the state authorities are powerless to cope. The President, even though no request for troops is made by state authorities, may send them if he thinks it impossible to enforce federal laws or the orders of the federal courts by means of the usual judicial proceedings.[1]

Early in the war with Germany the National Guard of the various states was made a part of the regular army of the United States, and the state authorities were thus, in many cases, left without state military forces to aid in preventing disturbances. Accordingly the War Department, in order to prevent delays in case of emergency, relaxed the usual rules which required that a request for troops be first forwarded to the President, and troops were sent directly to the scene of disorder in numerous instances during the war although no prior request for their use had been sent to the President.

After hostilities ceased, in November, 1918, the emergency which had occasioned a relaxation of the rules was still in effect, for on the discharge of the members of the former militia from the United States Army they did not automatically become part of the National Guard again, and the states required time to reorganize their forces. In consequence, no attempt was made to enforce peace time regulations until December 7, 1920, when the Secretary of War

---

[1] *Revised Statutes* 1989, 5297, 5298, 5299.

decided that the time had come to put them into effect again. Instructions directing that this be done were then sent to the corps commanders.[1]

During the war and for some time afterwards, therefore, President Wilson had little to do with the sending of troops to the scene of strike disorders. Nevertheless brief mention should be made of several important strikes in which they were employed, because the ultimate responsibility for their use rests on the President.

Probably the most significant of these instances was the Seattle General Strike, which lasted from February 6 to February 11, 1919, and involved about 60,000 workers, of whom about 40,000 struck in sympathy with shipyard workers who had been out for several weeks on a strike for higher wages. The Governor of Washington advised the Secretary of War of the proposed general strike, and the latter ordered troops to Seattle to be ready for an emergency. Though for several days the city was in practical control of the strike committee, no violence of any kind occurred, and the federal troops had nothing to do, remaining in camp their entire stay.[2]

Federal troops were also used in two strikes of copper miners in Butte, Montana, engineered by I. W. W. unions, and occurring in February, 1919, and in April, 1920. In the second instance the soldiers were stationed in the district from April, 1920, to January, 1921.[3]

On August 1, 1920, the street car workers in Denver, Col-

---

[1] *Report of the Chief of Staff*, 1921, p. 39; Wilson, *Federal Aid in Domestic Disturbances*, p. 317; Letter of June 8, 1922, to chiefs of branches, etc., of the War Department, entitled *Employment of Military Forces to Maintain Civil Order and Obedience to Law.*

[2] *N. Y. Times*, Feb. 7-11, 1919; *Survey*, vol. xxxxi, p. 281, vol. xxxxiii, p. 5; *The Unpartizan Review*, vol. xii, p. 35.

[3] *Report of the Adjutant General*, 1921, p. 58; *N. Y. Times*, Feb. 8, 9, 11, 18, 1919, and April 22, 1920; *Anaconda Standard*, April 19, 22, 23, 1920.

orado, went on strike for wage increases. The system was soon tied up, and the company's efforts to run cars with strikebreakers resulted in much violence. Accordingly the Governor asked for federal troops on August 7, and 700 men were sent. The officers in charge ordered the disarming of strikebreakers and posted soldiers on the top of each car. Order was quickly restored and the strike ended when the company deported the strikebreakers and re-employed the old men. The troops returned to camp on September 9.[1]

Federal troops were used in West Virginia during President Wilson's administration, although the more important use of troops in connection with the coal strike in that state occurred during the Harding administration. The hostilities between union miners and company guards and detectives in the non-union districts of the state came to such a pass in August, 1920, that the Governor appealed to the general commanding the Central Department for federal soldiers. About 450 men were accordingly sent to Williamson, and remained until matters appeared to be more peaceful, early in November. Their departure, however, seemed a signal for renewed hostilities, and a second request for their presence was made. On November 28 a battalion was again sent to Williamson. Colonel Hall, in charge of the troops, succeeded in having large quantities of arms and ammunition surrendered. When the operators attempted to run some of the mines with new men, he permitted peaceful picketing by the strikers, but forbade intimidation, and posted soldiers to protect the mines. The troops left the district in January and February, 1921.[2]

[1] Rep. Adj. Gen., op. cit., p. 58; N. Y. Times, Aug. 2, 4, 6, 7, 8, 9, 10, and 22, 1920; Rocky Mountain News, August 2-23, 1920.

[2] United Mine Workers Journal, June 1, July 15, Oct. 1, Oct. 15, Dec. 1, 1920, and Jan. 1, 1921; Rep. Adj. Gen., op. cit., p. 58: N. Y. Times, Aug. 29, 30, Sept. 2, 25, 29, Nov. 27, 28, 29, 30, Dec. 1, 3, 5, 1920, Jan. 15, 17, and Feb. 12, 1921.

CHAPTER VII

President Harding, 1921-1923

I. THE WEST VIRGINIA MINE DISTURBANCES OF 1921

THE non-union coal fields of West Virginia, centering in Mingo County, had been the scene of desperate attempts at organization on the part of the United Mine Workers for many years. The employment of Baldwin-Felts detectives by the operators, and the eviction of striking miners from houses owned by the companies, had particularly intensified hostilities between the miners and the companies in 1921.

On May 12 of that year a fusillade of shots was fired from the mountains in the direction of some of the mines in Mingo County. One person was killed and several wounded. The Governor of West Virginia thereupon asked the War Department for federal troops to restore order. A similar request was made by the Governor of Kentucky, the shots having been fired across the boundary of that state. For the next few days agents of the War Department investigated the situation, and though shooting continued and the governors renewed their requests for federal troops, none were sent. On May 17, the War Department having received a report on the situation, President Harding instructed his Secretary to write Governor Morgan of West Virginia that he did not feel justified in sending federal troops until he was assured that the state had exhausted its own resources, or until the situation men-

aced the federal government. Thus far he was not convinced that West Virginia had done all it could to bring
about order. He explained that the army could not be used
as a police force. Thereupon the state governors took further steps to end the disorder, and in a short time conditions
became relatively peaceful.[1]

Nevertheless the occasion for hostilities in the district
still existed in the continuance of the strike and the pres-
ence of detectives, and in June several men were killed.[2]
On August 1 Hatfield and Chambers, two of the leaders
among the miners, were killed in a quarrel with a Baldwin-
Felts detective.[3] Thereafter the feeling against the operators and the mine guards was even more intense. About
August 20 hundreds of union miners began to assemble at
Marmet, West Virginia, with the intention of marching on
Mingo County, eighty miles away across the mountains.
On August 23 the march commenced, other groups joining
in as it proceeded. On the 25th it was reported that 4000
men were approaching Mingo County, and that Sheriff
Chapin of Logan County, much hated by the miners, was
preparing to oppose their advance with hundreds of depu-
ties. On the same day Governor Morgan appealed to the
War Department for federal troops.

The administration at once sent General Bandholtz to
investigate the situation. On arriving in West Virginia
he interviewed District President Keeney and Secretary
Treasurer Mooney of the mine workers, and prevailed upon
them to try to stop the advance of the marchers. The two
leaders at once attempted to head off the miners, and prevailed on most of them to turn back on August 26. Gen-

[1] *N. Y. Times*, May 13-18, 21, 30, 1921.

[2] *Ibid.*, June 15, 29, 1921.

[3] *United Mine Workers Journal*, Aug. 15, 1921.

eral Bandholtz thereupon reported to the War Department that there was then no need for federal troops.

On August 28, however, a band of state troopers, claiming to have been fired upon by armed miners, shot into the town of Sharples. When the miners heard of this they started to reassemble and resumed their march on Mingo. On the next day the Governor sent in another request for troops. President Harding and Secretary of War Weeks, to whom General Bandholtz had reported in Washington that the state was making only a weak attempt to suppress the insurrection, decided not to accede to the request at once. On the 30th the President issued a proclamation commanding the insurgents to disperse, and ordered the general back to West Virginia to observe its effects. In the meantime another excited appeal for soldiers came from the Governor and was repeated the next day.

Early on the morning of September 2, General Bandholtz, satisfied that the men were not obeying the President's proclamation, advised the sending of troops. About 2000 of them arrived on the 2nd and the 3rd. Governor Morgan at once issued a proclamation putting the district under the control of the U. S. Army. During the next few days many of the miners, who were glad of the presence of the troops and later spoke of them as having " brought the Constitution back to West Virginia," surrendered their arms. The army authorities had 400 of them returned to their homes by train. Conditions soon quieted down to such an extent that on September 8 some of the troops were withdrawn. By December 6, 1921, all of them had left the strike zone. Thereafter, though many miners continued out on strike for months, violence was much less common.[1]

[1] *Report of the Secretary of War*, 1922, p. 204; *United Mine Workers Journal*, Sept. 1, Sept. 15, Nov. 1, Dec. 1, 1921; *N. Y. Times*, August 21-Sept. 6, 1921.

The care which President Harding exerted to make sure
of the facts, through an investigation, and to force the
state authorities to do as much as possible to put down the
disorders themselves, before he permitted federal troops to
be sent into West Virginia, is deserving of commendation.
The same may be said of the enlightened and impartial
policy of General Bandholtz in his attempts to get the miners
to return home and in his handling of the troops when they
finally arrived.   The situation was in all respects a difficult
one, and the manner in which the administration played its
part brought about a relatively early cessation of hostilities
without adding to the antagonism, which might easily have
led to prolonged industrial warfare in the disturbed areas.
Such an unfortunate result might well have followed had
the troops been sent in at once and carried out a high-handed
policy of suppressing the demonstrations of the miners.[1]

2. THE THREATENED RAILWAY STRIKE OF 1921

What was perhaps the first attempt on the part of President Harding to avert a strike occurred on October, 1921.
In June of that year the Railroad Labor Board announced
a wage cut averaging 12 per cent and applying to nearly all
railway employees, to take effect on July 1.[2]   In July, fearing that the railway managers were about to make requests

---

[1] It is not intended to leave the impression that real industrial peace
exists in West Virginia. As long as the operators continue their
bitter fight against the union, and the United Mine Workers continue
their attempts to organize, hostilities of a violent nature are likely
to arise without great provocation. For more complete information
about the labor troubles in the district see Suffern, *Conciliation and
Arbitration in the Coal Industry of America*, 1915, pp. 63-107; Lane,
Civil War in West Virginia, 1921; Hinrichs, *The United Mine Workers in West Virginia*, 1923; Senate Report 457, 67th Cong., 2nd Sess.,
being the *Report of the Senate Committee Investigating the West
Virginia Coal Fields*; and the published report of the hearings held
before the same committee, Washington, 1921.

[2] *Decisions of the U. S. Railroad Labor Board*, vol. ii, 1921, p. 136.

for further wage reductions, the railway unions met and directed that a strike vote be taken before September 1, ostensibly on the question of the acceptance of the board's decision, but in reality to determine whether the employees would strike should further reductions be made.[1]

Conferences between the managers and the men took place in August, but the railroads refused to promise that they would not request the board to make further wage reductions and changes in working rules. Instead they adopted a program calling for a reduction of 10 per cent, to be passed on to the public in the form of lower freight rates. Accordingly the unions ordered a strike vote to be taken at once. It showed that 94 per cent of the men were in favor of quitting.[2]

On October 15 the union heads set the strike date for the 30th of that month. On the same day President Harding, who had kept in touch with the situation through conferences, asked the public representatives on the Labor Board to take action to prevent a strike. Thereupon the board held meetings with the disputants. On October 25 it announced that it was then engaged in considering the question of working rules, a matter which was so involved and would take so long to decide, that no requests by the roads for further wage reductions could be handled by the board until a considerable period had elapsed. On being assured of this, the unions, on October 27, called off the proposed strike.[3]

3. THE COAL STRIKE OF 1922

The agreements between the anthracite and bituminous operators and miners, based on the awards of the coal com-

[1] *Monthly Labor Review,* December, 1921, pp. 1328-1329.
[2] *Ibid.,* pp. 1329-1330.
[3] *Ibid.,* pp. 1331-1340; *N. Y. Times,* Oct. 9, 16, 19, 21, 22, 26, 28, 1922.

missions of 1920, were scheduled to expire on March 31, 1922. In October of the previous year, President Harding, fearing the possibility of a suspension of work starting April 1, attempted to get President Lewis and other officers of the miners to arrange a conference with the operators in the bituminous fields at an early date, for the purpose of reaching an agreement to continue work after March 31 while a new contract was being drawn up. The miners refused to enter into any agreement to this effect, claiming that their recent convention had decided to defer action on the matter until it reconvened in February.[1]

On December 16, 1921, however, President Lewis invited the operators and miners in the central competitive field to attend a joint conference to be held in Pittsburgh early the next month. He referred to a clause in the bituminous agreement of 1920 which provided that such a conference meet some time prior to April 1, 1922, and asked that representatives be sent in accordance with the agreement. The operators of Indiana and Illinois accepted the invitation, but those of western Pennsylvania and some from Ohio refused to participate, asserting that they did not feel that anything could be accomplished by such a meeting. Because of the inadequate representation in a conference from which the Pennsylvania and Ohio operators were to be absent, President Lewis notified the parties that the meeting would not be held.[2]

During the week of January 16 the tri-district convention of the anthracite miners, meeting at Shamokin, Pennsylvania, adopted demands to be embodied in the new agreement, the most important being those for a 20 per cent increase in pay for contract miners, a $1 per day increase for day men, and the introduction of the check-off system. The

---

[1] *N. Y. Times*, Oct. 9, 1921; *Coal Age*, Oct. 13, 1921.

[2] *Coal Age*, Jan. 5, 1922; *United Mine Workers Journal*, Jan. 15, 1922.

convention also instructed its officers to arrange for the suspension of work on April 1 if no satisfactory agreement
were reached by that date. The keynote of the miners'
position was sounded in the speech of President Lewis before the convention, in which he took a firm stand against
any reductions in wages.[1]

Toward the end of January bituminous operators in
southern Ohio and in the Pittsburgh district posted announcements of wage reductions of from 35 to 40 per cent
and of the abolition of the check-off, to take effect on the
expiration of the existing contract. At the same time the
Indiana operators adopted a resolution favoring " radical
and sweeping reduction " in wages.[2]

In the middle of February the reconvened convention of
the miners met, and on the 18th it adopted a program opposing any reduction in wages and favoring a general suspension of work on April 1, subject to a referendum vote
of the members, unless a satisfactory agreement with operators in the central competitive field were reached before
that date. In accordance with the instructions of the convention Mr. Lewis, on February 21, sent another invitation to the bituminous operators to attend a joint conference to be held March 2 in Cleveland. In reply, some of the
operators promised to attend, as before, but others declined
to meet in a four-state conference and offered to meet the
miners in district conferences to draw up district agreements. Many of the operators maintained that they could
no longer make an agreement which placed them on a par
with the operators of better mines and forced them to pay
wages which such operators could afford. They felt that
the time had come to introduce agreements with the men
based on the conditions of their respective districts.

[1] *United Mine Workers Journal,* Feb. 1 and 15, 1922.

[2] *Ibid.,* Feb. 15, 1922; *Coal Age,* Feb. 2 and 9, 1922.

[3] *United Mine Workers Journal,* March 1, 1922; *Coal Age,* March 2,
1922.

Meanwhile, about February 24, President Harding had instructed Secretary of Labor Davis to use his efforts to bring about a conference between the bituminous operators and miners. In their answers to the Secretary's requests that they meet the miners the operators took positions similar to those taken in response to President Lewis' invitations. The Illinois and Indiana operators consented to attend, but most of the others refused to meet in a four-state conference and proposed district conferences instead. On March 9 the Department of Labor issued a statement referring to the Secretary's efforts to obtain a joint conference. The statement said, in part:

The Secretary's action is heartily approved by President Harding. None of the Government officials in touch with the threatened coal situation can see any objection to a council table gathering of those directly interested in the bituminous coal industry, and particularly in the present situation, when it is a part of the last agreement and in line with longtime practice in the coal industry. . . .
Secretary Davis cannot see why, in the interests of common sense, the two sides to the coal controversy cannot get together and adjust their differences and save the country from the costly results of a strike.

The answers of the operators having indicated the impossibility of a four-state agreement, the Secretary, in an interview on March 16, stated his position as follows: " I say to both of them, ' You made the agreement and you should stand by it.' " In answer to the assertion of some of the operators that they feared a four-state agreement would be in violation of the Sherman Act, in view of Judge Anderson's statement to that effect in November, 1921, Secretary Davis pointed out that the Attorney General had stated his opinion that a joint meeting to discuss a new scale was not unlawful.[1]

In the meantime, on March 15, the anthracite operators and miners met in joint conference to negotiate a new wage scale. Most of the bituminous operators, however, still persisted in their refusal to meet in a four-state conference, and the miners were equally firm against district agreements. The union officials, since the men had voted overwhelmingly in favor of suspension, issued directions to all miners to stop work on March 31 unless satisfactory agreements were made.[2]   In the meantime Secretary Davis continued his efforts with the bituminous operators, but to no avail. The anthracite joint conference, though still continuing its sessions, found it impossible to come to an agreement before April 1, and on that day about 600,000 miners, both anthracite and bituminous, suspended work.[3]

During the next few months the anthracite conferences continued, proposals and counter proposals for arbitration, for wage reductions, for investigation of prices, etc., being made, but without any agreement being reached.[4]

Early in April the Governor of New Mexico appealed to the Secretary of War for federal troops. He admitted that the strike had not as yet caused any violence, but he feared it if federal troops were not sent. On April 8, after conferring with President Harding, the Secretary wired the Governor that troops could not be sent " unless disorders [developed] to a point where the State authorities [were] unable to preserve order within the limits of the State." [5]

[1] *United Mine Workers Journal*, March 15, April 1, 1922.

[2] *Ibid.*, April 1, 1922.

[3] *Ibid.*, April 15, 1922; *N. Y. Times*, April 1, 1922; *Coal Age*, April 6, 1922.

[4] *United Mine Workers Journal*, May 1, June 1 and 15, 1922.

[5] *N. Y. Times*, April 9, 1922.

Meanwhile the strike, or, as the miners insisted on calling it, " the suspension," continued. Since comparatively little fuel was required in the spring, and since miners had prepared themselves in advance for a strike, little hardship was incurred. On June 21, however, the nation was roused by the report of the killing of a number of men in Herrin, Illinois, when an operator attempted to run a mine in a strong union district with imported strikebreakers.

The administration at once resumed its efforts to settle the strike. On June 23, Secretary Davis, referring to the Herrin affair, said, " Surely no better argument can be advanced for the settlement of these disputes around the conference table, than the dead bodies of a score or more of American workmen, who met a futile death in this outbreak." [1] During the next few days President Harding conferred with President Lewis, and with A. M. Ogle, of the National Coal Association. On June 28 he invited the representatives of all the miners and operators to meet him at the White House on July 1, for the purpose of arranging plans to end the strike.[2]

The President met the disputants on the date set, and addressed them, in part, as follows:

The government has no desire to intrude itself into the field of your activities. It does feel an obligation to see that the common American interest shall not be menaced by a protracted lack of fuel. It prefers that the two great and associated interests—mine workers and employers—should settle this matter in a frank recognition of the mutuality of their interests.

If you can not do that, then the larger public interest must be asserted in the name of the people, when the common good is the first and highest concern.

[1] *N. Y. Times*, June 24, 1922.

[2] *Ibid.*, June 29, 1922; *United Mine Workers Journal*, July 1, 1922.

You are admonished to arrive at such understanding with measurable promptness among yourselves. If the adjustment can not be reached by you alone, government aid will be available at your joint call. We wish you who best know the way to a solution to reach it among yourselves in a manner to command the sanction of American public opinion. Failing in that, the servants of the American people will be called to the task in the name of American safety, and for the greatest good of all the people.

Immediately after the address the anthracite and bituminous representatives of both sides held separate meetings, with members of the cabinet to aid them in arriving at an agreement. These joint conferences continued for a few days, but without reaching an understanding.[1]

Thereupon the President, on July 10, called the operators and miners to meet him again and proposed the following basis of settlement:

1. The miners shall return to work at the wages of March 31, this scale to be effective until August 10, 1922.

2. A coal commission shall be created at once, consisting of three representatives of the mine workers, three of the operators, and five members to be named by the President; all of the decisions of the commission to be accepted as final.

3. The commission shall determine, if possible within thirty days from July 10, a temporary basic wage scale, to be effective until March 1, 1923. In case the matter cannot be determined within that time, the commission shall have power to continue the 1922 scale until the new one is ready.

4. The commission shall investigate exhaustively every phase of the coal industry. The President shall ask Congress to confer the necessary authority and appropriations. The Commission shall make recommendations looking to

[1] *United Mine Workers Journal,* July 15, 1922; *Coal Age,* July 16, 1922.

the establishment and maintenance of industrial peace in the coal industry, the elimination of waste due to intermittency and instability, and suggest plans for a dependable fuel supply.

The President then urged the miners and operators to take his proposal to separate conferences for consideration. " With due regard for all concerned," he said, " it ought to be easy to find a way to resume activities and command the approval of the American public." [1]

The miners and operators soon replied to the President's proposal. The former indicated their willingness to accept the proposition for an investigation into the industry, but withheld their acceptance of arbitration.[2] The operators, not having been able to come to a uniform decision, answered by groups. The anthracite operators accepted the plan, but asked for a separate anthracite commission, which the President was willing to appoint. A majority of the bituminous operators accepted the proposal " without reservation and qualification." The Pittsburgh managers, however, suggested separate arbitration for the Pittsburgh district, with the wage scale of 1917 and elimination of the check-off to be in effect in the meantime.[3]

Having received answers from all concerned, the President met the operators and miners again, on July 17. After expressing his regret at the outcome he said to them:

I cannot permit you to depart without reminding you that coal is a national necessity, the ample supply of which is essential likewise to common welfare and interstate commerce. The freedom of action on the part of workers and on the part of employers does not measure in importance with that

[1] *United Mine Workers Journal,* July 13, 1922.

[2] *Ibid.,* Aug. 1, 1922.

[3] *Coal Age,* July 20, 1922.

of public welfare and national security. I, therefore, invite you to return to your mine properties and resume operation.[1]

It was understood that the President implied by this invitation that the government would afford military protection for all operators who would undertake to run their mines with strikebreakers. This was confirmed the next day, when Mr. Harding sent telegrams to the governors of twenty coal-producing states, asking them to second his invitation to the operators to resume activities. " I want to convey to you in this message," he said, " the assurance of the prompt and full support of the Federal Government whenever and wherever you find your own agencies of law and order inadequate to meet the situation. . . . To the task of lawful protection and the maintenance of order the Federal Government pledges you every assistance at its command." At the same time the War Department issued instructions to the corps commanders to be ready to move troops for strike duty at any moment.[2]

In response to the President's message all but two of the governors promised him their cooperation. Governor Ritchie of Maryland replied that he did not think it best to use troops as their presence might lead to serious trouble. Governor Morrison of North Carolina likewise refused to use troops, and indicated his general opposition to government interference in labor disputes.[3] The Pennsylvania operators attempted to run the mines, and the Governor immediately sent troops to the coal fields, but not enough workers could be obtained to resume operation. In other states no attempts were made.[4]

[1] *N. Y. Times*, July 18, 1922.
[2] *Ibid.*, July 19, 1922.
[3] *Ibid.*, July 20, 1922.
[4] *United Mine Workers Journal*, Aug. 1, 1922.

President Harding, describing the situation in an address before Congress on August 18, said, " But little or no new production followed the [message to the governors]. The simple but significant truth was revealed that, except for such coal as comes from the districts worked by non-organized miners, the country is at the mercy of the United Mine Workers." [1]

Finally, on August 1, President Lewis sent out another invitation to the bituminous operators of the central competitive field, asking them to meet the miners at Cleveland on August 7. The Illinois operators refused to attend the conference, insisting on the arbitration of the issues, a position which President Harding upheld in a letter sent to their secretary, in which he said, " I am frank to say I do not see how your workmen can refuse such a proposal. If terms cannot be settled on so liberal an offer it is manifest that the mining situation is very badly tied up, and the government must find for itself some way of extraction." In addition to the Illinois operators those in some other fields refused to send representatives. The conference, however, started as scheduled, though only a small proportion of the bituminous tonnage, most of it from Ohio, was represented.[2]

After a few meetings it was decided to admit into the conference operators from districts outside the central competitive field, thus breaking up the old alignment of districts. An agreement was finally signed on August 15, providing that on the execution of supplementary contracts with the various operators based on the agreement, work should be resumed under the terms of the old contracts until March 31, 1923. The conferees also agreed to send rep-

[1] *Congressional Record*, vol. lxii, p. 11537.
[2] *United Mine Workers Journal*, Aug. 15, 1922.

resentatives to a joint conference in Cleveland on October 2, 1922, which would formulate a method for negotiating a new agreement effective the following April. Finally, it was decided to select a committee of inquiry to investigate the coal industry, the personnel of the committee to be approved by the President.[1]

With the signing of the supplementary contracts bituminous mining was resumed in many districts. Gradually operators not represented at the joint conference accepted the terms of the Cleveland agreement. When the Pittsburgh Coal Company signed it on August 30 the operators' organ, " Coal Age ", admitted that the " last of the opposition to the union in this strike [had] crumbled." [2]

In the meantime the operators and miners of the anthracite field met on August 17 for the purpose of reaching an agreement. The conference was brought about through the efforts of Senator Pepper of Pennsylvania, in response to the request of President Harding that he act in the matter. On August 22, however, the conference adjourned, having been unable to come to an agreement.[3] But Senators Reed and Pepper of Pennsylvania, assisted by Secretary Davis, continued their efforts to bring about a settlement. They submitted a proposal to the disputants which had been approved by President Harding, and which provided that a contract be made between the three anthracite districts of the union and the operators, extending the wages and conditions of March 31, 1922, to August 31, 1923, and that both sides ask the President to appoint a fact-finding commission to investigate the coal industry.

On September 1 the President wrote to the operators and

[1] *United Mine Workers Journal,* Aug. 15, 1922.

[2] *Coal Age,* Sept. 7, 1922.

[3] *United Mine Workers Journal,* Sept. 1, 1922.

miners, " The public interest transcends any partisan advantage that you might gain by further resistance. I urge you in the name of public welfare to accede to the proposal that has been advanced by Senators Pepper and Reed." [1] On the next day the plan was accepted by the operators and the heads of the union, and a week later was ratified by a convention of the anthracite miners. [2]

During the strike it became more and more apparent that an essential preliminary to industrial peace in the coal industry was a thorough investigation of its basic difficulties and conditions. The necessity for such an inquiry was recognized by the operators and miners, as well as by the public at large. In his address to Congress on August 18 President Harding asked for the enactment of a law providing for a commission of investigation. [3] On September 22 he approved an act of Congress providing for such a commission, and on October 10 he named its members. About a week later the new commission organized with John Hays Hammond, famous mining engineeer, as chairman, and commenced its work. [4]

It is evident from the description of the events of the strike that President Harding played a very active part, first in attempting to avert the suspension of mining, and afterwards in seeking to end it. Perhaps in the case of no other strike, with the exception of President Wilson's attempts in the Colorado Strike of 1914, did a President play such a lively and persistent part in trying to settle a great strike. He displayed not only a creditable activity in striving to end the disagreement, but also excellent judgment in handling

[1] N. Y. Times, Sept. 3, 1922.
[2] United Mine Workers Journal, Sept. 15, 1922.
[3] Congressional Record, vol. lxii, p. 11537.
[4] N. Y. Times, Oct. 11, 19, 1922.

one other phase of it, i. e., in refusing to send troops to New Mexico in April when no real cause for their presence existed.

He cannot, however, be said to have shown the same good judgment when he invited the operators to resume operations in July under the protection of federal troops, if necessary. Had the operators really desired to accept the invitation, and had the miners been less strongly organized, so that resumption of mining would have been generally attempted, such a wholesale invitation to import strikebreakers might have resulted in serious consequences to domestic peace and industrial good-feeling. Fortunately attempts to break the strike with the aid of federal troops were not made. In reviewing the case, one is forced to the conclusion that hopeless as it seemed to rely on friendly intervention to bring the bituminous miners and operators to an agreement, this was the better course to pursue. A further effort through intermediaries might have proved as successful as in the case of the anthracite men. Even had this failed, the wisdom of attempting to break the strike by the use of troops may be seriously questioned.

4. THE RAILWAY SHOPMEN'S STRIKE OF 1922

While the administration was engaged in attempting to end the coal strike, it was at the same time faced with a problem even more serious, from the viewpoint of public welfare, the strike of the railway shopmen, which began on July 1. The Railroad Labor Board, which had just before announced an important reduction in the wages of maintenance of way employees, on the ground that the cost of living had decreased, rendered a decision on June 6, the labor members dissenting, cutting the pay of the shopmen 7 cents an hour. The cut, which averaged about 12 per cent,

was to go into effect on July 1.[1] The decision had the
result of still further arousing the shopmen, who had for
some time been complaining against the practice of important railroads, such as the Pennsylvania, in having their
shop work done by outside concerns employing non-union
men, which was contrary to the orders of the Labor Board.

At a convention of the Railway Employees' Department
of the American Federation of Labor, made up largely of
shop employees, the men had, in the previous April, directed
the issuance of a strike vote if no satisfactory settlement
of the difficulty were reached.   In compliance with this resolution the executive council of the shopcraft unions conferred with the Railroad Labor Board late in May, and informed it of the intention to issue a strike vote unless there
were some guarantee that the contracting-out practice would
be ended.   On June 7 the Board replied that it had no power
to enforce its decisions and could give no such guarantee.
This situation, made more serious still by the wage reduction, resulted in the taking of a strike vote on both issues,
which showed an overwhelming readiness to strike on the
part of the shopmen.[2]

On June 27, B. M. Jewell, leader of the shopcrafts, notified T. DeWitt Cuyler, chairman of the railway executives
committee, that a strike would commence on July 1 if the
railroads did not meet the following demands of the unions:
(1) that an immediate conference be held; (2) that the
roads ignore the wage-cut order of the board; (3) that the
roads restore certain working rules ordered changed by the
board; and (4) that the roads stop the practice of contracting-out.[3]   Two days later the executives flatly refused to
grant the demands and implied that a strike, if it took place,

[1] *Monthly Labor Review*, July, 1922, pp. 93-94.

[2] *Machinists' Monthly Journal*, Aug. 1922, pp. 563-566.

[3] *N. Y. Times*, June 28, 1922.

would not be against the railroads, but against the government.[1]

On being notified that the shopmen were planning to strike, the Labor Board, on June 29, ordered the representatives of the unions and the railways to appear before it the next day. The Board, however, found it impossible to get word to the union men, the latter having purposely disappeared to avoid just such a contingency, and its attempt to prevent the strike therefore proved of no avail.[2]

When July 1 came nearly 400,000 shopmen obeyed the strike order. Chairman Hooper, of the Labor Board, issued a statement pointing out that the new men who took the places of the strikers could not justly be called " scabs " and " strikebreakers ", and that they would be " merely accepting what is equivalent to an open position, the wages and working conditions of which have been established by a government tribunal." " Under these circumstances," he said, " it is a foregone conclusion that both public sentiment and governmental power will protect the men who remain in the service of the carriers and the new men who take the service." [3]

The Board, on July 3, adopted a resolution to the effect that the shopmen, by striking, had placed themselves outside its jurisdiction, and invited the recruits taking the places of the strikers to organize into unions at once and come in under the shelter of the Transportation Act.[4] At the same time a conference of the roads entering New York decided that all strikers would be dropped from the payrolls and would lose their seniority rights.[5] These announcements

[1] *N. Y. Times,* June 30, 1922.
[2] *Machinists' Monthly Journal,* August, 1922, p. 566.
[3] *N. Y. Times,* July 2, 1922.
[4] *Monthly Labor Review,* Dec., 1922, p. 1173.
[5] *N. Y. Times,* July 4, 1922.

laid down a policy which was so readily adopted by nearly all of the roads that before long the sole issue of the strike was whether the strikers, on returning to work, would have their seniority rights restored.[1]

In a few days reports came to the Postoffice Department from several points in the South that the strikers were interfering with the mails. On the 8th Attorney General Daugherty authorized the district attorney and the U. S. Marshal to use force if necessary in order to prevent any interruption of interstate commerce and the movement of the mails. Two days later he announced that he had authorized the appointment of a number of deputy marshals in various sections of the country. " This policy will be continued," he said, " wherever justified and required. Law and order must be preserved and property and life protected. Transportation of the mails must not be interfered with and interstate commerce must not be interrupted. The President has been fully advised and has the situation fully in hand." [2]

The President, on July 11, issued a proclamation in which, after referring to the decisions of the Board, he continued:

Whereas, The shopcraft employees have elected to discontinue their work, rather than abide by the decision rendered, and certain operators have ignored the decision ordering the abandonment of the contract shop practice; and
Whereas, The maintained operation of the railways in interstate commerce and the transportation of the United States mails have necessitated the employment of men who choose to accept employment under the terms of the decision, and

[1] The seniority rights, which are highly prized by railway men, have to do with pension privileges and preferences concerning type of work, tenure of jobs, etc., which accrue to the men in order of length of service.

[2] N. Y. Times, July 8, 9, 11, 1922.

who have the same indisputable right to work as others have to decline to work; and

Whereas, The peaceful settlement of controversies in accordance with law and due respect for the established agencies of such settlement are essential to the security and well being of our people;

Now, Therefore, I, Warren G. Harding, President of the United States, do hereby make proclamation, directing all persons to refrain from all interference with the lawful efforts to maintain interstate transportation and the carrying of the United States mails. These activities and the maintenance of the supremacy of the law are the first obligations of the Government and all the citizenship of our country. Therefore I invite the cooperation of all good citizens to uphold the laws and to preserve the public peace, and to facilitate [the operation of the railroads]. . . .[1]

The War Department, which had received a message from the receiver of the Missouri, Kansas, and Texas lines reporting violence and the capture of a train by strikers, and requesting federal troops, answered the request by directing the receiver to apply first to the Governor of Texas for militia. In case the state authorities did not act the Department was willing to afford the necessary protection. The Governor, to whom application was then made, refused to send state troops on the ground that they were not needed. Thereupon the Secretary of War sent an inspector-general to investigate conditions and to determine the need for troops. As far as is known the investigator decided they were unnecessary, for there does not seem to be any record of troops having been sent to the district. On July 20 Postmaster General Work announced that any menace endangering the delivery of mails arising out of the strike had passed.[2]

[1] *Monthly Labor Review*, December, 1922, p. 1174.
[2] *N. Y. Times*, July 14, 15, 21, 1922.

Meanwhile Chairman Hooper of the Labor Board succeeded in bringing the strike leaders and some of the railway executives into a conference on July 14. Though most of the roads agreed to drop the practice of contracting-out, they refused to restore the strikers to their seniority rights, and the men being firm on this point, the conference came to an unsuccessful conclusion. On the 19th Mr. Hooper announced that since there did not seem to be any possibility of reconciling the men and the executives, the Labor Board had ceased its efforts to end the strike.[1]

During the next few days President Harding conferred with Mr. Hooper concerning a settlement. On the 26th and the 27th of July he had separate conferences with Messrs. Cuyler and Atterbury, of the railway executives, and with Mr. Jewell, of the shopcrafts. On the 29th he sent a plan of settlement to both sides for their consideration.[2]

The President's proposal, as given in his letter to Mr. Cuyler, was as follows:

First—Railway managers and workmen are to agree to recognize the validity of all decisions of the Railroad Labor Board, and to faithfully carry out such decisions as contemplated by law.

Second—The carriers will withdraw all lawsuits growing out of the strike, and Railroad Labor Board decisions which have been involved in the strike may be taken, in the exercise of recognized rights by either party, to the Railroad Labor Board for rehearing.

Third—All employes now on strike to be returned to work and to their former positions with seniority and other rights unimpaired. The representatives of the carriers and the representatives of the organizations especially agree that there will be no discrimination by either party against the employees who did or did not strike.

[1] *N. Y. Times*, July 15, 20, 1922.
[2] *Ibid.*, July 28, 29, 30, 1922.

After urging the advantages of such a settlement, especially because it upheld the Labor Board, the President concluded his letter: " I need hardly add that I have reason to believe that these terms will be accepted by the workers. If there is good reason why the managers cannot accept, they will be obligated to open direct negotiations or assume full responsibility for the situation."

Secretary of Commerce Hoover was sent by the President to act as his personal representative at a meeting of the executives held in New York on August 1 to consider the proposal.[1] The executives, however, rejected the seniority proposal, though willing to accept the first two parts of the plan. They called attention to Chairman Hooper's statement early in the month to the effect that the rights of the new men could not be ignored by the Board. They asserted that they could not fail those to whom they had promised protection " without doing violence to every principle of right and justice involved in this matter and without the grossest breach of faith on the part of the railroads to the men at present in their service."[2] The shopmen accepted the President's plan of settlement on the next day.[3]

Meanwhile considerable complaint was being made to the leaders of the railway Brotherhoods that the men operating the roads were subjected to much danger because of the defective condition of the rolling stock due to the strike. They complained also that the danger was increased by the presence of armed guards on railroad property. The Brother-

[1] A week later it was reported that Mr. Hoover had met a group of New York bankers in the headquarters of the Federal Reserve Bank and had urged them to use their influence with the executives to get the latter to accept the proposal of the President. *N. Y. Times,* August 8, 1922.

[2] *N. Y. Times,* Aug. 1, 2, 1922.

[3] *Ibid.,* Aug. 3, 1922.

hoods, on August 5, presented the situation to the President and expressed fear that their members might go out on strike if the conditions were not remedied.[1]

On August 7 the President made a new proposal for the settlement of the strike. After pointing out that the only remaining issue between the railroads and the shopmen was the question of seniority, he asked the men to return to work, the carriers to assign them to work, and both to take the question in dispute to the Railroad Labor Board for decision. At the same time the Board announced its readiness to hear the seniority question.[2]

In the meantime the presence of armed guards and the poor condition of the rolling stock had caused a strike of members of the Brotherhoods at Joliet, Illinois. On August 10 the Brotherhood men on the Santa Fé notified the management that they would refuse to run trains through any points where armed guards were employed. Within a short time trains were tied up at several places in Arizona and California, and the strikes soon spread to other points.[3]

The executives replied to the second proposal of President Harding on August 12, most of them accepting it, but a number of others, representing about one quarter of the mileage concerned, reserved the right to carry the decisions of the Board to the courts if they affected the agreements already in existence between the roads and their employees. On the same day the shopmen informed the President of their rejection of his proposal.[4]

Thereafter, for a few weeks, the strike continued without further attempts at settlement by the administration. The Brotherhoods tried to get the President to make further ef-

[1] *N. Y. Times*, Aug. 5, 6, 1922.
[2] *Monthly Labor Review*, December, 1922, p. 1177.
[3] *N. Y. Times*, Aug. 10, 11, 12, 1922.
[4] *Ibid.*, Aug. 14, 1922.

forts to mediate, but he declined to do so. Chairman Mc-
Chord, of the Interstate Commerce Commission, reported
to him that railway equipment was failing, that motive
power was progressively deteriorating, and that safety legislation was being violated. Mr. Harding, in reply, recommended that the Commission insist on the full enforcement
of the safety laws; a matter much easier to recommend than
to carry out, with many thousands of shopmen continuing
the strike.[1]   The Brotherhood chiefs and the railway executives conferred a number of times on a settlement of the
shopmen's strike, but on August 25 their meetings ended
without an agreement being reached.[2]

Meanwhile, on August 18, the President addressed Congress on the coal and railroad strikes. He defended his
proposals for settlement, pointed out the necessity of en-
abling the Railroad Labor Board to enforce its decisions,
denounced the lawlessness and violence of the strikers, upheld the rights of workers to remain at work or to take
employment if they wished, accused the strikers of a conspiracy to paralyze transportation by deserting transcon-
tinental trains in the desert regions of the Southwest, and
concluded his discussion of the shopmen's strike thus:

It is not my thought to ask Congress to deal with these fundamental problems at this time. No hasty action would con-
tribute to the solution of the present critical situation. There
is an existing law by which to settle the prevailing disputes.
There are statutes forbidding conspiracy to hinder interstate
commerce. There are laws to assure the highest possible
safety in railway service. It is my purpose to invoke these
laws, civil and criminal, against all offenders alike.[3]

[1] *N. Y. Times*, Aug. 15, 16, 1922.
[2] *Ibid.*, Aug. 26, 1922.
[3] *Congressional Record*, vol. lxii, p. 11537.

During the last week of August numerous cabinet meetings were held, and the reports of violence and interference with interstate commerce were discussed at length. Probably as a result of these meetings Attorney General Daugherty appeared before Judge Wilkerson, of the U. S. District Court in Chicago, on September 1, and obtained what was perhaps the most sweeping and thoroughgoing restraining order ever issued. In the government's bill asking for the order attention of the court was called to alleged acts of destruction, violence, assaults on those remaining at work, and interference with interstate commerce and the passage of the mails. The government further maintained that the issue of the strike orders, as well of the orders arranging for pickets and counselling against violence, was evidence of an illegal conspiracy in violation of the Sherman Act and the Transportation Act of 1920, the seriousness of which violation was intensified by the deterioration of rolling stock, the lack of cars to carry coal, the consequent hardships to the public and industry, etc. The bill for the injunction further charged that the defendants, the Railway Employees' Department of the A. F. of L., " conspired, combined and confederated together and agreed with each other and among themselves to repudiate, ignore, violate, disobey and refuse to accept the decision of the [Railroad Labor Board] and to quit in a body and abandon the service of the railway companies at one and the same time, all as an objection to or protest against and as contempt for Decision 1036 [the shopmen's wage decision] and as a protest against and as contempt for the Railroad Labor Board and as contempt for the United States and the Government thereof." [1]

In his request for the restraining order the Attorney General said to the court:

[1] *Government's Bill of Complaint in U. S.* v. *Rwy. Employees' Dept. of the A. F. of L.,* Sept. 1, 1922, Washington.

No labor leader or capitalistic leader, nor organization or association of any kind or kinds, or combination of the same, will be permitted by the Government of the United States to laugh in the frozen faces of a famishing people without prompt prosecution and proper punishment. . . . I will use the powers of the Government to prevent the labor unions of the country from destroying the open shop. . . .

By refusing to comply with the decisions of the Railroad Labor Board in the matter of shopmen's wages the unions held the Government of the United States in contempt. When a man in this country is not permitted to engage in lawful toil, whether he belongs to a union or not, the death knell to liberty will be sounded and anarchy will supersede organized Government. . . .

The Government of the United States is not opposed to labor unions if they perform such functions as can be performed in lawful America. . . .

The underlying principle involved in this action is the survival and the supremacy of the Government of the United States.[1]

The restraining order, which was at once issued by the court, restrained all the officers of the unions, their employees, or anyone acting in aid or in conjunction with them, from doing any of the following acts:

(a) in any manner interfering with the railway companies engaged in interstate commerce and the transportation of the mails, or with their employees, or from preventing or attempting to prevent the latter from entering or continuing employment;

(b) in any manner conspiring to do any of the above things; or to injure, interfere with, hinder, or annoy any of the employees in connection with their work or in going to or from it, " or at any time or place, by display of force or

[1] *N. Y. Times,* Sept. 2, 1922.

numbers, the making of threats, intimidation, acts of violence, opprobious epithets, jeers, suggestion of danger, taunts, entreaties, or other unlawful acts or conduct towards any employee or employees or officers of said railway companies, or any of them, or towards persons desirous of or contemplating entering into such employment;"

(c) or loitering or being unnecessarily in the vicinity of places of egress or ingress of railroad property;" or aiding, abetting, directing, or encouraging any person or persons, organizations, or associations, by letters, telegrams, telephone, word of mouth, or otherwise to do any of the acts aforesaid;" or trespassing on the premises of the companies;

(d) or "inducing or attempting to induce by the use of threats, violent or abusive language, opprobrious epithets, physical violence or threats thereof, intimidation, display of numbers or force, jeers, entreaties, argument, persuasion, rewards, or otherwise, any person or persons to abandon the employment of said railway companies, or any of them, or to refrain from entering such employment;"

(e) or engaging, directing, or encouraging others to picket;

(f) or congregating about railway property to picket;

(g) or doing or causing any employee any injury or bodily harm, or going to his home to prevent him, by violence, threats, "or otherwise" to induce him not to work or not to seek work;

(h) or in any way hindering the operation of trains in interstate commerce or in carrying of the mails, or encouraging anyone to do so;

(i) or "in any manner by letters, printed or other circulars, telegrams, word of mouth, oral persuasion, or suggestion, or through interviews to be published in newspapers or otherwise in any manner whatsoever, encourage, direct, or command any person whether a member of any or either of said labor organizations or associations defendants herein, or otherwise, to abandon the employment of said railway companies, or any of them, or to refrain from entering the service of said railway companies."

In addition the officers of the Federated Shop Crafts were enjoined (a) from issuing any instructions, requests, public statements or suggestions in any way to any defendant or to any officials or members of the shop crafts unions as to what they were to do after quitting employment, or calculated to get anyone to leave the employment of the roads or to refrain from entering it; and (b) from " using, causing, or consenting to the use of any of the funds or monies of said labor organizations in aid of or to promote or encourage the doing of any of the matter or things hereinbefore complained of." [1]

One of the first steps in the enforcement of the order was the arrest of a striker in Chicago alleged to have jeered at railroad employees bound for work, who was later released because he was drunk when arrested. [2]

The first and perhaps the only important consequence of the order was a tremendous protest from citizens of all kinds, and from conservative as well as liberal newspapers, against the restriction of liberties involved in it. This complaint was so great that Mr. Daugherty, on September 5, asserted that " the Government [had no] intention of abridging personal liberty or the constitutional rights of free speech and lawful assembly," and that its only intention was to prevent violence and interference with interstate commerce. At the same time a statement of a like nature, adding that the order was sought by the government in

---

[1] *Restraining Order in U. S. v. Rwy. Employees' Dept. of the A. F. of L.*, Sept. 1, 1922, Washington.

[2] *N. Y. Times,* Sept. 4, 1922.

order to protect the travelling public, was issued at the White House.[1]

On September 11 D. R. Richberg, counsel for the strikers, appeared before Judge Wilkerson, who had issued the order, and moved that it be dismissed on the following grounds: (1) that the government had erroneously assumed that the strikers violated the law when they declined to accept the Labor Board's decision; (2) that the open shop issue, cited as an important reason for seeking the injunction, was not one to be dealt with by the Department of Justice; (3) that federal courts had held that strikers have a right to attempt to recruit their ranks from non-union men; and (4) that the government failed to establish an unlawful conspiracy on the part of the strikers, as alleged in the injunction bill. The court, however, continued the order until the application of the Attorney General for a temporary injunction might be heard.[2]

In the meantime conferences looking towards a settlement of the strike were going on between the shopmen's leaders and a number of railway executives, led by President Willard of the Baltimore and Ohio and President A. H. Smith of the New York Central. The conferees finally drew up the following terms of settlement, later known as the Baltimore agreement, which the Shop Crafts General Conference Committee accepted on September 13: All men to return to work to positions of the class they held prior to the strike, and at the same point; as many men as possible to be put to work at present pay at once, and all strikers except those guilty of proven violence to be put to work or under pay within 30 days; any dispute arising as to the relative standing of employees, or any other controversy arising from the

---

[1] *N. Y. Times,* Sept. 6, 1922.
[2] *Ibid.,* Sept. 12, 1922.

strike that cannot be adjusted locally, to be referred for final decision to a bipartite commission of 12, a majority vote to be sufficient to decide; both parties to pledge no intimidation or oppression against strikers or non-strikers; all suits at law brought as a result of the strike to be withdrawn.[1]

On September 15 the Baltimore and Ohio, the Chicago and Northwestern, and the Chicago, Milwaukee, and St. Paul signed the agreement. Four days later the New York Central did likewise. By September 27 it was reported that 78 roads had settled with the strikers. Gradually more and more roads came in, until by October 30 over one hundred roads, 50 of them in Class I had signed up. Meanwhile the strike continued on the other roads, though it gradually weakened even on them. On March 6, 1923, government agencies reported that 120,000 men were still out.[2] As late as August, 1923, the *Locomotive Engineer's Journal* reported that the strike was still continuing on those roads which had not yet signed the Baltimore agreement.

To return to the injunction proceedings, the government attorneys, during the middle of September, 1922, presented further evidence of violence and alleged conspiracy. On September 23 Judge Wilkerson handed down his decision supporting the government's suit, and on the 25th he issued a temporary injunction the terms of which were practically the same of those of the restraining order of September 1.[3]

In his decision the judge said:

The law is clear, in my opinion, that if the dominating, primary purpose of the combination is to restrain trade or to

[1] *Monthly Labor Review*, December, 1922, p. 1181.

[2] *N. Y. Times*, Sept. 14, 16, 20, Oct. 12, 31, 1922, March 7, 1923.

[3] *Injunction Writ in U. S. v. Rwy. Employees' Dept. of the A. F. of L.*, Sept. 25, 1922, Washington.

do things unlawful in themselves, and which by reason of their inherent nature operate to restrain trade, the purpose of the combination is unlawful, and that purpose may not be carried out even by means that otherwise would be legal. . . . These unlawful acts are shown to have been on such a large scale and in point of time and place so connected with the admitted conduct of the strike that it is impossible on the record here to view them in any other light than as done in furtherance of a common purpose and part of a common plan. . . .

These defendants will not be permitted, upon the record here, to deny responsibility for these unlawful acts. They will not be permitted to continue acts which, even though they may be peaceable and lawful in themselves, it has been demonstrated are only part of a program of unlawful conduct and are done for the accomplishment of an unlawful purpose. . . .

It is asserted by the defendants that to prohibit some of the acts against which the complainant seeks an injunction is to deprive them of fundamental rights guaranteed by the Constitution. This contention has been answered by what has been said with reference to the unlawful purpose of the conspiracy. . . .[1]

The record in this case shows that the so-called peaceable and lawful acts are so interwoven with the whole plan of intimidation and obstruction that to go through the formality of enjoining the commission of assaults and other acts of violence and leave the defendants free to pursue the open and ostensibly peaceful part of their program would be an idle ceremony.[2]

On September 11 Representative Keller of Minnesota presented impeachment charges against the Attorney Gen-

---

[1] It is evidently the thought of the court that the Constitution does not legalize acts illegal under the common law.

[2] *Statement and Opinion of the Court, in U. S. v. Rwy. Employees' Dept. of the A. F. of L.,* Sept. 23, 1922, Washington.

eral in the House, asserting that Mr. Daugherty had used his office to violate the Constitution. A week later the House Judiciary Committee, to whom the matter had been referred, decided to postpone hearings on the impeachment charges until Congress reconvened in December. Nothing ever came of this matter. In a speech at Canton, Ohio, delivered on October 21, the Attorney General said that the strike had put the nation in the grip of civil war, and asserted that if he had not taken the action he did take he could have been and should have been impeached.[1]

Later on the government sought to have the injunction made permanent, and proceedings for that purpose continued for many months. Finally, in June, 1923, Judge Wilkerson granted the government's plea, the shop crafts having withdrawn from the case some time earlier when the U. S. Supreme Court had rendered a decision maintaining the right to disobey the orders of the Railroad Labor Board.[2] Attorney General Daugherty, commenting on the action of Judge Wilkerson, said, " No extensive strike tying up interstate commerce will ever again take place in this country." Nevertheless, as the *Locomotive Engineer's Journal* pointed out, the shopmen were still on strike on some roads.[3]

There are two phases of the President's handling of this strike on which it is worth while centering discussion. The first involves the justice of his proposals for a settlement, and the other one the question of the injunction. The shopmen, it will be recalled, struck on July 1 for two principal reasons: (1) against the contracting-out policy of some roads in violation of the Board's decision, and (2) against

N. Y. Times, Sept. 12, 20, Oct. 22, 1922.

[2] 43 Sup. Ct. 278.

[3] *Locomotive Engineer's Journal,* August, 1923.

the wage reduction ordered by the Board. It was not long before the strikers evidently realized that the strike had been a hasty and ill-judged one. The public stand against them for violating the Board's decision practically doomed them to defeat from the beginning. They found themselves in the position of being unable to disobey the decisions with the same impunity as some roads had been able to do in contracting out their shop work. Disobedience on their part meant public inconvenience. Disobedience on the part of the roads harmed only the unions and the Labor Board. The situation was perhaps unjust to them, but it existed nevertheless.

The strike had scarcely begun, however, when the issue became, because of the stand of the Board and of the railway executives, not that of the shopmen's original demands, but that of seniority, a much more fundamental matter as far as they were concerned. President Harding, in his proposal of July 29, made an offer which was apparently just to both sides. The men were asked to give up their most important demand, that concerning wages, for there was little likelihood that the Board would rescind the wage decision when the question came up before it under the President's plan. The roads were asked to give up the contracting-out practice, which, since only a few of them had a part in it, was no sacrifice for most of them. Seniority, it is believed, should of right have been restored to the men, as President Harding first asked. If such an issue were to arise in strikes generally no strike could be fought on its merits. If strikers, in addition to failing to obtain that for which they strike, are also to lose their places and be treated as newcomers when they seek to return to work, the right to strike itself is impaired, for under such circumstances no strike could be undertaken unless the chances of winning it were overwhelmingly in favor of the strikers. Not until the right to strike is generally denied by public opinion, should the denial of seniority have a right of its own to be considered in such cases.

When President Harding, on the executives' refusal to accept his first plan, proposed that the seniority question should be decided by the Railroad Labor Board, he was asking something which was unjust to the men. The Board, in its announcements following the commencement of the strike, had practically placed itself in the position of protecting the men who took the places of the strikers. It seems justifiable, under the circumstances, for the shopmen not to have permitted a body which had taken such a position to decide on so fundamental a question as seniority. The President's second offer is a further illustration of what appears to be the *leitmotif* of executive activity in labor disputes, the principle of expediency, or, to put it differently, to get a settlement in any way possible.

The restraining order obtained by the Attorney General, presumably with the approval of the President, may be characterized as unjustifiable, unfair, and ineffective for the following reasons:

1. One of the grounds on which it was obtained was that the strike violated the anti-trust laws, prohibiting conspiracies in restraint of trade and commerce among the states. It has elsewhere been pointed that those laws were not intended to prevent labor unions from carrying out their ordinary activities. A strike is such an activity. Though lawyers may find loopholes in the anti-trust laws making labor unions unlawful conspiracies, ordinary citizens are aware that such laws were enacted for an entirely different reason.

2. Another ground on which the order was obtained was that the strike violated the provisions of the Transportation Act of 1920, and that thereby the strikers showed " con-

tempt for the United States and the Government thereof."
Anyone who has read the act knows that it compels no one
to accept the decisions of the Railroad Labor Board. Such
decisions may be accepted or rejected, as the parties concerned desire. It is difficult to comprehend how the refusal to accept a decision when the laws of the United
States plainly permit its rejection can be construed as " contempt for the United States and the Government thereof."

3. Another basis for the order was the general doctrine
of conspiracy, which, as applied to this case, may be put as
follows: Acts, which, though lawful and peaceful in themselves, are done in pursuance of an unlawful purpose, are
in themselves unlawful, and those responsible for such
acts are guilty of an unlawful conspiracy. Courts have,
under this rather expansive principle, prohibited nearly
everything which a labor union can possibly do, as is evident
from the terms of the 1922 injunction. But if, as is indicated in the last two paragraphs, the purpose of the strike
was not really unlawful, the doctrine of conspiracy does
not seem to fit the case. It would excuse the restraining
only of acts of violence, which are distinctly unlawful.
There is no intention here of defending such acts.

4. The injunction was unjustifiable because it declared
the calling of a strike an unlawful act. No state except
Kansas has ever taken such a position. Congress has never
been willing to accept it. The people of the country do
not believe a strike is an unlawful act. For the Attorney
General, under such conditions, to obtain an order making it unlawful and for a federal court to grant such an
order was an abuse of authority.

5. The Attorney General, in asking for the restraining
order, said, " I will use the powers of the Government to
prevent the labor unions of the country from destroying
the open shop." The order was presumably granted with

that as one of its grounds. But the question of the open shop is one with which the Attorney General properly has nothing to do. It is a question to be decided in fair struggle between labor and capital. The Attorney General had no more right to try to prevent labor unions from trying to destroy the open shop, even had that been their purpose in the strike, than he had to attempt to force employers to accept the closed shop. His position in this instance was woefully biased in favor of labor's opponents.

6. The injunction was unjustifiable because, on the plea of the conspiracy doctrine, it tried to prohibit acts which always have been thoroughly recognized as within the constitutional rights of freedom of speech, of press, and of assembly. An injunction which makes illegal such things as jeers, taunts, entreaties, argument, persuasion, reward, encouragement, letters, telegrams, requests, instructions, public interviews, public statements, and suggestions the purpose of which is to get men to go on strike, or to keep them on strike, or to prevail on others not to take the striker's places—such an injunction is so obviously extreme that to say it does not violate constitutional rights is like denying that there is a Constitution.

7. The injunction was furthermore harmful in that, through the excess of its prohibitions, it tended to make both the office of the Attorney General and the federal courts appear ridiculous, biased, and unreasonable.

8. Perhaps the most important argument of all against the injunction was that it was not of any great use in ending the strike. When the strike ended on certain of the roads the cause was not the restraining order, but the more normal method of peaceful, voluntary conference. The strike continued on some roads for many months, despite the injunction. It served no purpose in the apprehension of those guilty of violence which could not as well have been served by ordinary arrest and indictment.

When one considers all the valid objections to the 1922
injunction in particular, and the injunctive method of ending strikes in general, and then is faced with the realization that such an instrument has proved of little value in
effecting its principal purpose, one wonders how much
longer Presidents of the United States will seek to exercise
their influence towards a settlement of labor disputes by
a resort to such means.

CHAPTER VIII

Conclusion

A study of presidential intervention in labor disputes during the past thirty years makes it apparent that the reason above all others which has caused the executive to exert his influence has been the pressure of public opinion. In the earlier troubles, such as the Pullman and the Coeur d'Alene cases, he was, of course, impelled by the desire to perform his duty as the head of the nation by helping to keep order and by protecting the interests of the public. But, since the establishment of the precedent by President Roosevelt in 1902, whenever a great industrial crisis threatens, the people turn naturally to the White House for help. However little encouragement the President may receive from the parties to the dispute, public opinion alone virtually forces him to intervene.

The public considers that its national executive is the one to represent its interests in such a case, and it has added this to the numberless other tasks it places upon its chosen leader. Failure to save the country from the misfortune of industrial conflict is visited upon his head as surely as failure to prevent any other thing which affects the prosperity of the nation. His party realizes the truth of this statement in the next election if he has no worthy record to show.

Despite the ever-increasing pressure on the President to intervene in labor disputes, he has usually been somewhat slow to act, and wisely so. Numerous agencies exist whose principal purpose it is to settle industrial disagreements. By immediate action the President would not only needlessly add to his already heavy burdens, but he would also be infringing on the rightful province of such bodies as the Department of Labor and the Railroad Labor Board.

By reserving his influence to be used as a last resort, he adds greatly to the effectiveness of his efforts when action is finally taken. If the President made attempts to end strikes frequently, and with only slight cause, it would be easier for the disputants to reject his proposals. The public, grown accustomed to his pleas, would not be so ready to become indignant at a refusal to heed them. The great prestige of the executive office would be lessened and the chances of averting serious strikes would be jeopardized.

When Presidents have finally determined on action in labor disputes the records show that they have used many different methods to carry out their purpose. The variety of activities has been nearly as great as the variety of situations which gave rise to them. A presentation of these activities in outline form, excluding those peculiar to wartime, shows the extent of this diversity.[1]

PRESIDENTIAL ACTIVITIES IN CONNECTION WITH LABOR
DISPUTES IN TIME OF PEACE

1. Activities the purpose of which is to avert or end a strike.

   A. Friendly intervention:

      1. Investigation of strike issues.

      2. Letters to either or both sides urging settlement.

[1] Consideration of war-time activities has been omitted from this conclusion because they are taken up as far as is thought necessary in chapter v.

    3. Letters to federal officials, mediators, or arbitrators urging settlement.

    4. Requesting or appointing federal or state officials to act as mediators.

    5. Meeting contestants in conference.

       a. Acting as mediator or conciliator.

       b. Securing agreement to submit to arbitration.

       c. Making definite proposals for settlement.

    6. Securing changes in arbitration law to obtain arbitration agreement.

B. Publicity:[1]

    1. Publication of results of investigation made under President's direction, in order to influence public opinion and thus hasten a settlement.

    2. Publication of President's efforts at mediation and their results, in order to influence public opinion and thus hasten a settlement.

C. Coercion:

    1. Securing the passage of a law making possible the end of a strike by enacting some of the demands of a contestant.

    2. Threatening investigation of one of the contestants with regard to prices and profits.

    3. Securing an injunction for the purpose of averting or ending a strike.

    4. Instituting other court processes for the purpose of averting or ending a strike by making possible the arrest of strike leaders and strikers.

    5. Using federal troops to end a strike.

---

[1] Publicity would logically come under the heading, " Coercion," but is so different in its nature, and usually in its results, from the other measures enumerated under that heading that it seems to deserve a place of its own.

II. Activities the purpose of which is not to avert or end a strike:

A. Investigations made for the purpose of deciding whether to take action.

B. Use of troops to prevent domestic violence and execute federal laws during a strike.

C. Securing the arrest and indictment of strikers and strike leaders on charges of violating the laws.

The number of methods employed seems ample to provide some definite procedure for every condition which may arise, but when it is asked, " Have the executives had a well defined program to follow when a great strike threatened?" the answer must be in the negative. There is no evidence of the existence of strike programs, except in the case of President Wilson during the war. A brief inquiry into the facts will show the truth of this assertion. In practically no instance other than in wartime, does an executive appear to have decided in advance of a given strike, threatened or actual, what ought to be done in such a case. The policy, as far as any has existed, has been one of waiting, and in many instances not even one of watchful waiting. The executive has as a rule permitted a strike to occur, unless it came at a time when serious danger to the public interest was likely to result immediately. When public opinion has become sufficiently aroused to clamor for the prevention or the end of a strike, when state and local officials have asked that something be done, or when one of the contestants has appealed to the President to take a hand in the matter, then the President, if he has thought it desirable, has acted. There have, of course, been cases in which an executive has been foresighted and has acted a considerable period before danger to the public was at hand, but generally a waiting policy has been the practice.

When action has finally been decided upon, the course followed has as a rule been guided by a single principle, that of expediency. As far as one can judge, the question the executive has usually asked himself or his advisers has been, " What is the most effective way to prevent (or to end) the strike? " Some method, usually the invitation to a conference, has then been tried. If it has proved unsuccessful other methods have followed, until, in some instances, drastic means have been adopted, usually without success. It is true that the President, in proposing a certain plan of settlement, has been guided by considerations of fairness to both sides. But that the principal purpose has been to end the strike, regardless of fairness, is evident from those instances when a second plan, radically different from the first one and apparently unfair to one of the parties, has been proposed because settlement under the first method was impossible. An example of this is the case of the two proposals for settlement made by President Harding in the Shopmen's Strike of 1922. Another proof of the conclusion that expediency is the prime consideration lies in the fact that in several instances a course of action which has been fair in the beginning, has, on the failure to settle the dispute, developed into one of coercion with apparently little concern for justice, as in the 1919 and 1922 injunctions.

Expediency has commonly determined the nature of the President's activity, and to some degree the frequency and extent of his interference, but undoubtedly his own character and his theory of presidential powers have often played a part in shaping his program. It is interesting to consider how different the course of industrial disputes might have been in the last twenty years had not President Roosevelt been aggressive enough to establish a precedent by calling the anthracite men to a conference in 1902. President

Taft, with his more restricted theory of executive action, would probably not have set such a precedent even had the occasion arisen.[1] It is also to be doubted if Mr. Harding would have done so. In the case of President Wilson we have another example of the aggressive executive with broad views of his powers. He thought that a President could make his office what he wished, and his administration, in relation to strikes as well as otherwise, was evidence of the truth of his theory.[2] Mr. Harding found precedents already made for him, and he merely followed an already well established method in calling conferences, and went only a few steps beyond his predecessors in obtaining the most sweeping injunction ever recorded.

Another factor which undoubtedly helps determine the nature and extent of the President's activity is the character of his cabinet, particularly of his Secretary of Labor and of his Attorney General. It is to be doubted whether President Wilson would have taken such an active part in the settlement of labor disputes had his Secretary of Labor, William B. Wilson, been himself less active in calling the President's attention to such matters. There is also a question whether President Harding would have sought for an injunction in 1922 had Mr. Daugherty not been his Attorney General. Again, there seems little ground for doubting that it was the direct influence of Attorney General Palmer, rather than of President Wilson, who was at the time seriously ill, which was responsible for the 1919 injunction.

However much the President's own character, his theory of executive power, and the character of his advisers may effect the frequency as well as the nature of his intervention

[1] For some idea of Mr. Taft's theory of executive action see Taft, *The Presidency*, 1916, pp. 128-129.

[2] Wilson, *The President of the United States*, 1916, p. 42.

in labor disputes, the factor which, at least since 1902, has largely decided how often he shall use his influence has been the condition of the industrial world. Of the recent Presidents, Mr. Wilson has the record for intervening most frequently, but his activity was largely due to the unusual number of great strikes that occurred during his eight years in office. From 1913 to 1920 was a period of rapidly rising prices, when labor was fighting strenuously to get wages that would keep pace with the mounting cost of living. From May, 1920, to the end of the Wilson administration, in March, 1921, labor fought just as hard, though not as successfully, to prevent wage reductions. It carried its struggle into President Harding's administration, and Mr. Harding, a man with a reputation for comparative mildness and lack of assertiveness, was forced to play as active a part in 1922 as the aggressive Mr. Wilson was ever called on to take. One may conclude that the aggressive qualities and theories of the executive and his advisers are largely responsible for the setting of precedents, but once the precedents are created the degree of executive activity depends to a large extent on the frequency of labor disputes and their menace to public welfare.

The experience of the Presidents who have made use of the many different methods of dealing with labor disputes inclines one to believe, if a broad generalization be permitted, that those activities which may be classed under the head of friendly intervention and publicity are generally to be preferred, from the viewpoint of justice, efficacy, and public welfare, to those classed under the head of coercion. It may be said to the credit of the Presidents that they have rarely tried coercive methods first, though President Cleveland did so in the Pullman Strike. It is believed that even when friendly methods have failed, the adoption of coercive ones has as a rule been either ineffective, or has been accompanied by so many disadvantages as to make it most undesirable. Except in the case of an extremely serious strike, as that threatened by the railway Brotherhoods in 1916, less damage is likely to be done by actual suspension of work than by attempting to end the strike by some compulsory method. As a rule the disputants, who have usually been brought to a more complete understanding of each other's position and of their own relation to the public welfare through the President's efforts, will soon come to a voluntary settlement on their own account, even if his efforts have proved unsuccessful at the time they were made.

In general coercive methods are objectionable because they rouse antagonism toward the government, its officers, and its laws; they increase the ill-feeling between employer and employee; and, at best, they provide only a temporary solution of the difficulty.

Of these coercive methods the use of the injunction has undoubtedly given rise to the most bitterness in the ranks of labor. Its effect in 1894, in 1919, and in 1922 has already been mentioned. There remain only several more general points to consider. They are concerned with the need for the injunctive process in labor disputes, regardless of the particular act which the writ is intended to prohibit.[1] If an act is unlawful under the statutes it is difficult to see what the ends of justice gain by having it enjoined. Presumably the violators of the law can always be arrested as readily on the ground of disobeying the law as of disobeying an injunction. There is no reason to suppose that the authorities will arrest more readily in one case than in another. If the injunctive method has an advantage in

[1] The injunction according to the recognized principles of law, may not be issued to restrain the commission of a crime. It may only be issued to prevent acts which, if not restrained, would cause irreparable injury to property rights.

this respect it is that the performance of the act forbidden by it will be punished by the judge for contempt of court, without opportunity for trial by jury, and without chance for appeal on the facts to a higher tribunal.[1] In other words, the restraining by a court of an act already unlawful under the statutes does away with the safeguards for the accused which Anglo-Saxon law has set up only after centuries of struggle, and subjects the alleged violator to the whim of a single judge. Such procedure may be quicker, and more effective in rendering punishment, but is not likely to be as productive of justice as the process of indictment, arrest, and trial.

If an act is not unlawful under the statutes, but may be so construed under the common law, the injunction is of value in that it makes possible the punishment of acts which might otherwise remain unpunished. To the lawyer the necessity for the injunction in this connection may be unquestionable, but to the layman the matter is not so clear. The common law is so very inclusive, its principles may be so easily expanded in accordance with the honest though biased beliefs of the court, that there hardly remains a trade-union activity which some judge may not attempt to prohibit by injunction. It seems reasonable to suppose, as has been pointed out elsewhere, that if the people, who are generally given credit with being ultimately responsible for the making of the laws, had wished to prohibit a certain act as contrary to public policy, they would have done so through the passage of a law. For a judge, who in most cases has no future responsibility to the electorate, to be permitted to issue edicts which may be entirely opposed to

---

[1] Though courts will not hear an appeal on the facts concerning disobedience of an injunction, an appeal may be taken on the question of the right of the court to issue the injunction in a particular case. See the decision in the Debs case, 15 Sup. Ct. Rep. 900.

what the electorate considers desirable, is a situation which it is difficult for a believer in democratic government to reconcile with democratic principles. With the injunctive process so liable to criticism and abuse a President of the United States should certainly consider long and carefully whether it ought to be used.

Any conclusion with regard to the wisdom of sending federal troops into a strike area must be based on the use made of those troops. To use or to allow them to be used for the purpose of ending a strike or of assisting either disputant to win its case must be regarded as distinctly unjust. Troops were put to such a use in the Pullman Strike, when they helped to enforce an injunction designed to end the strike, and in the Coeur d'Alenes in 1899, when, through the negligence of the President, the employers used them to break up a union. When a strike has brought violence in its wake the use of federal troops to restore and preserve order is unquestionably justified. There is perceptible, ever since President Roosevelt's administration, a serious effort on the part of the executives to permit the use of troops only as a last resort, and then to take care that they are not being used to defeat the strikers, or to deny liberties to which citizens are entitled. Though there have been a few unimportant exceptions to the rule since 1900, in general the Presidents have used excellent judgment. This fact has even been recognized by the unionists, who have in most cases been bitterly opposed to the presence of state militia at the scene of a strike. In Colorado in 1914, and in West Virginia in 1921, the strikers and their leaders favored the presence of United States soldiers, because the state troops had proved so hostile to labor. Coeur d'Alenes seems to have been the "horrible example" which the later Presidents have been anxious not to follow.

Up to this time a President has never had to decide

whether troops should be employed to run an essential industry taken over temporarily by the government during a strike. In view of the fact that most of the railway labor and much of that employed in the mines must be skilled, such use seems hardly feasible.

Such a method of coercion as was embodied in the passage of the Adamson Act, the method of bringing to terms either party to a dispute by persuading Congress to pass coercive legislation, is not likely to prove a dangerous one. Rarely would a President find sufficient support in Congress to enable him to force through legislation which was not demanded by the country as a whole. Majority opinion does not often favor coercive legislation, and without public approval the President would be unlikely to ask for it.

One of the milder measures which might be called coercive is the use of publicity to force an agreement. When this applies merely to publicity of all facts underlying the dispute, it is a just as well as a most effective weapon in the hands of the President. Moreover, since neither party can feel that the government has discriminated against it, it does not arouse the same resentment as the more aggressive coercive measures. It does, however, give the public a basis for a fair decision as to the merits of the controversy.

When, in addition to making public the facts of the dispute, the executive makes known the proposals which have been made by him for a settlement, or his appeals to the contestants for a peaceful determination of the question at issue and the responses of the disputants to such proposals and appeals, he marshals behind him the immense support of public opinion. It is a hardy and determined partisan who long dares to withstand such a force. The Colorado Fuel and Iron Company and other groups of employers have done it, as have the strongly organized miners and railroad workers. But nevertheless the support of the public is perhaps the most powerful means the President has to effect a settlement. Such a support should be called forth only after the executive has assured himself beyond doubt that his proposal is just since the public is likely to support any proposal he makes, regardless of its fairness.

There have been times when it has been desirable to keep the public uninformed. In some delicate cases of mediation by the executive, publicity given to the situation would have done much to lessen the chance for settlement. As a general rule, however, publicity has been wholesome and desirable. In this connection there is another possibility against which the President must guard. If there is to be any publicity at all it should be shed on both sides. To permit a hurried request to a union not to strike to get into the newspapers, thus bringing about the opposition of the public if the union refuses to accede to the request, and not to publish the refusal of the employer to meet the unions for the purpose of preventing the strike, is to cause much injustice. This occurred just before the Steel Strike of 1919.

The experience of the past would suggest the following principles as a guide for executive action in labor disputes :

1. The President should have his advisers keep in close touch with impending or existing disputes, with orders to keep him informed when the controversy is likely to develop into a severe strike. The officials under him should have such information as to enable him to obtain a quick grasp of the essential points of the dispute and more detailed information to which he may have reference when necessary. In case such information is not at hand the President should appoint a representative to make a thorough and impartial investigation for his own use.

2. The President should make a personal attempt to prevent a strike, either by sending letters urging a settlement, or by inviting the contestants to a conference, only when it is apparent that all other agencies of settlement have been unsuccessful or are likely to be unsuccessful, and when the strike would be likely to cause much suffering and inconvenience to the public. If a strike is already in effect he should attempt to settle it only under the same conditions. His influence should not be used in the case of relatively unimportant strikes, for to do so is to minimize its effect in important ones. In the case of unimportant strikes he should instruct whatever agencies exist for the purpose, preferably through the Department of Labor, to use their efforts to bring about a settlement, if they are not already engaged in such efforts.

3. When the President has determined to make a proposal of settlement he should exercise all the care possible in order that his proposal, whether of arbitration or direct settlement, may be fair and just to all sides, and that there may be a reasonable expectation of its acceptance. To this end he should be sure to acquire as complete an understanding as possible of the issues at hand and the points of view of the disputants, by means of conferences with each side, and through the advice of impartial experts.

4. Except in those cases where it would minimize the chances of settlement, the President should make public full accounts of his attempts to obtain a settlement, of his proposals, and of the replies to them. In case his plan is not accepted he should be careful to give, in their own words, all the reasons offered by both sides for their action. In those cases in which the refusal of one side to concede anything toward a settlement seems to him unwarranted he should give publicity to the opinions of his advisers and to the reports of his investigators, if any have been appointed.

5. If the President's plan of settlement is not accepted he should endeavor to make further efforts, taking care not to suggest proposals unfair to either side. If he is convinced that his first plan is the only just basis of settlement he should make no others. If, however, it is possible to offer a second plan as fair as the first, and there is reason to hope that it may be accepted, the President should not hesitate to urge it. In many cases it is better for the strike to continue than that proposals be made which have no other excuse than that the earlier ones were refused and the continuance of the strike is harmful. In any case full and complete publicity should be given to continued refusals to accept the President's proposals.

6. The President should permit federal troops to be sent to the scene of a strike only when federal laws are being openly violated and ordinary judicial proceedings are unavailing; or when there exists within a state serious disorder and violence which local authorities cannot suppress and for the suppression of which the legislature or the governor asks the help of federal troops. Before sending the troops the President should make certain, by sending an impartial and judicious observer to the scene of alleged disorder, that there really exists a situation requiring the presence of federal troops, and that the state authorities have exhausted all their efforts to suppress the disorders. He should ascertain, before sending troops, that they have not been called merely to aid the employers in breaking a strike. On directing that troops be sent the President should have them carefully instructed so that they will not be used to favor either side. They should be continually under the direction of the federal government and at no time under the control of the local authorities, and they should be instructed not to restrict in any way the ordinary rights of citizens save as such restriction is absolutely indispensable

to suppress disorder. The President should keep continually informed of the activities of the troops in the strike zone, and of the situation with regard to the existence of disorder, so that there shall at no time be an abuse of their presence, and that they may be withdrawn as quickly as possible when there is no longer a need for them. If the request for troops has come from the governor of a state, because the legislature is not in session and cannot be convened in time, the President should insist that the legislature be convened as soon as possible, in order that the people of the state, through their representatives, may have an opportunity to express their will with regard to the presence of federal troops. If the legislature fails, on bring convened, to request that the federal troops remain, they should be at once withdrawn, unless the President is assured that the enforcement of federal laws would be impossible without them.[1] As long as strikes are not forbidden by law, federal troops should never be used by the government to end a strike.

7. The President should at no time seek to end a strike by having his assistants obtain an injunction.

8. The President should at no time seek to end a strike by having strikers and strike leaders arrested and imprisoned. Such arrests should be made only when they have been guilty of an actual violation of criminal law. They should not be made under laws which at the time of their passage were never intended to be used for such a purpose.

One more matter in connection with the President's activity in labor disputes which requires attention is the question of devising more efficient machinery for lightening the heavy burden which is imposed on him with the com-

---

[1] See article 4, section 4, of the *Federal Constitution*.

ing of nation-wide strikes in essential industries. Even a brief study of the past thirty years convinces one of the increasing frequency with which the executive has been compelled to intervene in order to avert suspension of production in such industries. It has often been said that the tremendous burden which the nation places upon its executive is more than even a strong man can bear. The breakdown of President Wilson and the fatal illness of President Harding bear out such an assertion.

The only possible method of lightening this task lies in the improvement of the machinery of administration so that the need for personal attention to details in dealing with a problem shall be reduced to a minimum. For dealing with industrial disputes of lesser importance or those not connected with the so-called essential industries machinery for mediation already exists in the Department of Labor. The disputes in the highly unionized industries in which a suspension involves national hardship are the ones which force the President to take on himself the responsibility for a settlement. It is for the adjustment of these that more efficient machinery is demanded.

Reference has already been made to the successive acts of Congress passed for the purpose of handling railway labor disputes. The Erdman and Newlands Acts undoubtedly performed a great service in relieving the President of the need of giving his personal attention to the settlement of many railway controversies. The strength of both these laws was to a large extent in the provision which they made for the mediation of industrial disputes by experienced government officials. Their principal defect was in those sections providing for arbitration in case mediation failed. As one case after another was decided in a manner which they considered unfair to them, the railroad employees acquired a distrust of arbitration. By the summer

of 1916 this distrust had become so great that they preferred to involve the whole country in a disastrous strike
rather than arbitrate their demands.

Their principal objection to arbitration in general was that
under the law the decision was in the hands of third parties,
supposedly neutral, who made up the boards along with the
representatives of the men and the roads.   They claimed
that these so-called " impartial " arbitrators were not impartial, and that they were usually owners of property who
had class interests which inclined them to the side of capital
in a dispute.   They did not accuse the " neutral " arbitrators of dishonesty, but pointed out that the bias and ways
of thinking of such individuals would naturally lead them
to favor the railways.   In an endeavor to prove their contentions they pointed to the decisions in a succession of railway arbitration cases in which they considered themselves
treated unfairly.   This criticism of arbitration virtually
resolves itself into an assertion that there are as a rule no
representatives of the public who are so entirely unin-
fluenced by their training and interests that they will cast
their votes in an arbitration case with strict scientific im-
partiality.   Moreover, employees, and often employers, objected to the system of neutral arbitrators on the ground
that the decision was thus left in the hands of persons with
no experience in the railroad industry, who found it impossible to understand fully the complicated and intricate working rules and wage schedules in effect on the roads.   Another important objection to arbitration which railroad
labor expressed was that the decisions were always interpreted by the railway managers, often in such a way that
in the end the employees received even less than it was the
intention of the arbitrators to give them.[1]

[1] Fisher, *Use of Federal Power in Railway Labor Disputes, passim.*

Soon after the government took over control of the railroads for the war period the Railway Administration set
up a Board of Railroad Wages and Working Conditions
to decide matters of labor policy and inequalities in pay.
In addition a number of boards of adjustment, consisting
of an equal number of representatives of the railroads and
the employees, were organized for the purpose of handling
controversies growing out of the interpretation of wage
schedules. As has already been pointed out, this machinery
maintained peace in the railroad industry during the war
and for some time afterwards. The two sides, without the
interference of supposedly impartial outsiders, succeeded in
settling their controversies with a minimum of friction.
Undoubtedly the success of the system was to a large extent
due to the war-time spirit of cooperation and to the favorable attitude of the Railway Administration toward labor,
but it showed the possibilities inherent in bipartisan machinery for adjustment.

With the return of the railroads to the private owners a
new system of adjustment was put into operation. The
Transportation Act of 1920 provided for a Railroad Labor
Board of nine members, three representing the roads, three
the men, and three the public, all of them appointed by the
President with the approval of the Senate. Provision was
also made for the setting up of regional boards of adjustment, made up only of representatives of the railroads and the
men. It was hoped that the roads would join the men in
organizing such boards, thus settling disputes at their source,
and limiting the work of the Railroad Labor Board to the
very important cases. As a matter of fact only a few adjustment boards were constituted, and even those functioned
to an inconsiderable extent. The burden was placed almost entirely on the Railroad Labor Board.

The Board has been of great importance. It has settled

many disputes, which, if ignored, might have developed into serious strikes. It has accordingly relieved the President of burdensome tasks. Its continuous existence, its powers of obtaining information, and its ability to keep the public informed of disputes have proved of great value. Despite its accomplishments, however, the board and the law establishing it have been severely criticized, until now large classes of the population consider it a failure.

Many persons believe that a board of arbitration with no power of enforcing its decisions must of necessity fail. This brings up the question of compulsory arbitration. Should there not be a law compelling the acceptance of arbitration decisions and prohibiting railway strikes by the imposition of adequate penalties in case of violation? Suggestions to this effect have been made from time to time. It is obvious that such a law, if enforced, would relieve the President of the great share of his burdens in preventing interruption of transportation. It would add greatly to the prestige of the Railroad Labor Board. If it were enforced it would relieve the public from any danger of the hardships which railway strikes involve. Such a solution was suggested by President Harding in his message to Congress on December 8, 1922.[1] It deserves discussion.

In the first place it would be extremely difficult to obtain the passage of national legislation of this kind, as is evidenced by the removal of the compulsory clause of the Transportation Bill of 1920 before it was made a law.[2] Labor unions and many employers are ever ready to fight any attempt to use legal coercion in the settlement of industrial disputes.

To enforce such legislation would be even more difficult than to enact it. The experience of Great Britain in war-

[1] *Monthly Labor Review,* January, 1923, p. 22.
[2] Fisher, *The Use of Federal Power in Railway Labor Disputes.*

time, of Australia and New Zealand during the past few
years, of Kansas, and of Canada merely in the matter of
compulsory investigation, show how often men strike in defiance of the law.[1] They likewise illustrate how difficult it
is to enforce a penalty for disobedience of the statute, especially in the case of labor. Even where it is possible to
pass an arbitration law carrying with it a penalty clause providing for imprisonment, its enforcement is found impracticable either against a mass of strikers or against their
leaders. Neither has the imposition of a fine proved more
satisfactory in the case of labor. Placing the burden of the
fine on the union which calls the strike is likely to develop
the technique of " outlaw strikes ", seemingly against the
orders of union officials, to a high degree of perfection.
If the fines were imposed on the individual workers the
great number of those without property would go unpun-
ised. Experience with the Canadian law shows that officials rarely attempt to collect fines from the workers. The
consensus of opinion seems to be that the compulsory fea-
tures of the act are of little use. Its real value lies in its
provisions for investigation and settlement.[2]

Is the social advantage to be gained from a prohibition of
railway strikes, assuming such a prohibition could be enforced, as great as the social disadvantage arising there-
from? If the right to strike is taken away from railway
workers there does not appear to be an adequate guarantee
that their interests will be properly protected. The workers

[1] Moses, *Journal of Political Economy*, November, 1918, p. 882; *Re-
search Report No. 23*, National Industrial Conference Board; Beebe,
The Survey, June 7, 1919, p. 339; Squires, *Operation of the Industrial
Disputes Investigation Act of Canada*, Bulletin 233, U. S. Bureau of
Labor Statistics, 1918.

[2] Squires, *op. cit.*, p. 139; MacIver, Arbitration and Conciliation in
Canada, *Annals of the American Academy of Political and Social
Science*, May, 1923, p. 297.

would have no other means of improving their condition than to ask that their demands be arbitrated. If arbitration could be made absolutely scientific and impartial strikes might with justice be prohibited. But the people who have attained sufficient prominence to be appointed representatives of the public on a board of arbitration are very often led by hardly perceptible but none the less effective bias and prejudice to favor, in many instances, the side of capital. It has been pointed out, moreover, that a dispute is often decided in accordance with the economic power of the disputants, rather than strictly on its merits. The great power of the employees is the strike threat. To take that away is to leave them virtually at the mercy of the stronger party. The public, with railway strikes permitted, is without doubt subject to possible hardships, but it is believed that less social harm is involved in occasional strikes than in the difficulty which the prohibition of strikes would place in the way of a continued maintenance of the railway worker's standard of living or in its gradual improvement.

Another criticism to which the Transportation Act has been subject is that it puts the determination of railway rates and of railway wages in the hands of two separate bodies. It is asserted that wages should be correlated with rates, and that therefore wages should be fixed by the Interstate Commerce Commission, rather than by an independent board. In his message of December 8, 1922, President Harding voiced this idea by suggesting that the Interstate Commerce Commission be enlarged by the addition of four members, representing each of the rate-making territories, and constituting a labor division of the Commission in charge of wage determination. An objection to this scheme is that the Commission is already kept so busy that it hardly has time to perform its present duties. Even were new members added the burden on each member of the board would probably be increased if the Commission were given authority over wages. What appears to be the greatest difficulty, however, would be that the Interstate Commerce Commission represents the public alone. To give it control over wages would practically make it a court hearing the arguments of employers and employees. The disadvantages of the determination of wages by public representatives would be intensified.

The most serious criticism to which the Railroad Labor Board has been subject is the usual one made by the employees, that the public representatives are not impartial. A long series of decisions reducing wages or opposing wage increases has strengthened this feeling. Though there are to the credit of the board numerous decisions favoring employees, those concerning wages have not as a rule done so. Even if this feeling of the employees were without foundation in fact, it is manifest that a board which depends on the voluntary cooperation of both parties for its sucess can hardly continue to function effectively with railroad labor strongly opposed to it, and many railroads likewise unwilling to cooperate. Such conditions call for the establishment of a more satisfactory method of handling railway labor disputes. Before discussing such a method it will be well to consider the machinery for the settlement of disputes in the coal industry.

Congress early took advantage of the interstate commerce clause of the Constitution to enact laws providing for the settlement of railway disputes. That clause has so far never been used to support the enactment of such laws for the coal industry. Whatever machinery has existed has been in the form of bipartisan boards representing the employers and employees equally. In the anthracite industry permanent boards of conciliation and joint scale committees, and in the bituminous industry different joint committees have settled many questions effectively. But at the time when national agreements expire and important changes are demanded disputes arise which have often required the intervention of the President. Undoubtedly the steadying influence of someone who represents the nation at large is needed at such a time, but as far as possible the President should be spared this duty.

It has been suggested that a Coal Labor Board, similar in composition and powers to the Railway Labor Board, be established as a solution of the problem. The objections to the latter board, however, would apply with equal validity to the former. The objections to compulsory arbitration and the prohibition of strikes in the railroad industry would also apply with equal force in the coal industry.

In a report made in July, 1923, the U. S. Coal Commission suggested that when all other attempts to prevent a strike fail and suspension seems certain, the President should have the power to declare the existence of a national emergency and to take over the mines, fix wages, prices, conpensation to owners, etc.[1] Such a proposal has often been mentioned as a means of dealing with a nation-wide strike in the coal or transportation industries. If Congress should authorize the President to take such action, it would give him an additional prestige among the disputants. Yet it may be said with confidence that a President would hesitate to use such a weapon unless virtually forced to do so. It would impose on him a tremendous burden, even if the administration were prepared to carry it out, and if commissions of trained men were at hand to lighten his task.

It has been generally assumed that such a method would prevent suspension of work on the ground that labor would not strike against the government. But if the government

[1] *Monthly Labor Review*, August, 1923, p. 318.

asked men to work for it under the same conditions against which they were prepared to strike previous to government control, it is to be doubted whether a strike would be prevented. In European countries employees of government railways have often gone on strike. In 1919 several minor strikes occurred on the government-controlled railways in this country, and serious ones were only narrowly averted. Temporary government control of an industry to prevent or end a strike would probably accomplish its purpose only if it were put into operation rarely. or if the government made some concessions to the men. Whatever the effect on the suspension of service it is obvious that temporary nationalization would increase rather than lessen the cares of the executive.

American experience with regard to coal and labor disputes indicates that (1) compulsory arbitration and prohibition of strikes seem undesirable; (2) joint conferences of employers and employees have, in the great majority of cases, been sufficient to bring about amicable agreements; (3) permanent joint conferences, such as adjustment boards, have been more effective than temporary conferences whose membership has changed with each dispute; (4) an active public opinion has been of great value in preventing and ending strikes; (5) a proposal from the President for arbitration or direct settlement, supported by public opinion, has usually been effective; (6) some method of protecting the public interest in important adjustments is necessary; (7) arbitration by boards with public representatives having the power to vote has not met with the approval of labor.

The evidence is clearly in favor of some form of permanent national joint conference in which the public interest is represented, but in which the public representatives have no power to determine the issue; and of complete publicity in any controversy which may arise.

Several proposals of the Coal Commission may well be incorporated in a constructive plan of adjustment. These are that regular reports of mine accounts on a prescribed form be made to some government agency; that a " continuing umpire " with the necessary assistants sit at all conciliation meetings but have no vote; that contracts be automatically renewed unless either party gives notice at least ninety days before the renewal date; that if such notice is given and no agreement is reached sixty days before the renewal date, a report shall be made to the President specifying clearly the points at issue; that the President shall thereupon appoint a person or persons to inquire into and make public a report upon all the relevant facts in the controversy before the date of renewal.[1] These suggestions of the Coal Commission would apply as well to the transportation industry.

The same general type of machinery may be suggested for the railroad, anthracite, and bituminous industries. In many cases existing local boards could be incorporated almost without change. These local and regional boards should represent the employers and the employees equally. They should be permanent in character and should settle all possible grievances before referring them to the national board in the industry, which should be largely free to consider matters pertaining to the industry as a whole, particularly the wage scales.

Each national board—there should be three, one for the railroads, one for the anthracite, and one for the bituminous industry—should, like the local ones, have a permanent existence, and should consist of an equal number of representatives chosen by the employers and the employees. It should also include an additional member appointed by the

[1] *Monthly Labor Review,* August, 1923, p. 318.

President to represent the interests of the public. This public representative should have no vote, but should sit in all the meetings of the national board, should keep a complete record of all proceedings, and should at any time be ready to report on the status of the disputes before the board. He should be thoroughly familiar with the industry and should at any time have complete access to all available information with regard to its management. Such an official would not arouse the antagonism of either side; but, if capable, he would nevertheless become a factor whose influence would make itself felt. His knowledge, and, in time, his experience would command respect, and the realization that he was a representative of the President might serve to facilitate the settlement of disputes.

Regular reports on prescribed forms such as are now made by the railroads to the Interstate Commerce Commission should be made by the anthracite and bituminous operators to the public representative on the appropriate board, and he, with the necessary assistance, should keep such records on file. The public representative on the railway board should have access to the reports in the hands of the Interstate Commerce Commission.

If either employers or employees should desire to obtain a change in working conditions notice should be sent to the national board at least ninety days before the date of the proposed change.

If no agreement has been reached by sixty days before the date of the proposed change the public representative should so report to the President, who should thereupon appoint as his direct representative a trained special investigator, familiar with the industry, to inquire into all the facts relevant to the dispute. This investigator should confer with the public representative on the national board, attend the board's meetings, and have access to all the information in the hands of the public representative. In the case of a railway dispute he should also have access to the necessary information in the possession of the Interstate Commerce Commission.

If the dispute is still unsettled thirty days before the date of the proposed change the investigator should report to the President on the facts of the controversy, and as far as possibile make an estimate of the result of the proposed changes on prices or rates. The President should at once make the report public.

After such publicity the weight of public opinion would in most cases tend to force an agreement. If it should not do so the President has all necessary information long enough in advance to insure intelligent intervention on his part, should he consider it necessary. Thus adequately prepared, and with the support of a well-informed public behind him, his efforts would have every promise of success. If such a plan, with its adjustment machinery, its protection of the public interest, and its provisions for keeping the public thoroughly informed, were enacted by Congress, it would do much to minimize the number of coal and railroad strikes and to lighten the burden of the President.

BIBLIOGRAPHY

Books

Beard, *Contemporary American History*. New York, 1914.

Bing, *War-Time Strikes and Their Adjustment*. New York, 1921.

Bishop, *Theodore Roosevelt and his Times*. New York, 1920.

Book of Chicagoans. Chicago, 1905.

Cleveland, *The Government in the Chicago Strike of 1894*. Princeton, 1913.

Croly, *Marcus Alonzo Hanna, His Life and Work*. New York, 1912.

Davis, *A Treatise on the Military Law of the United States*. New York, 1913.

Dewey, *National Problems*. New York, 1907.

Fairlee, *The National Administration*. New York, 1905.

Foster, *The Great Steel Strike and its Lessons*. New York, 1920.

Hale, *Rooseveltian Fact and Fable*. New York, 1910.

Interchurch World Movement, Commission on Inquiry, Report on the Steel Strike. New York, 1920.

Interchurch World Movement, Commission on Inquiry, Public Opinion and the Steel Strike. New York, 1921.

Lane, Franklin K., *Letters, Personal and Political*. Boston, 1922.

Lane, W. D., *Civil War in West Virginia*. New York, 1921.

Latane, *America as a World Power*. New York, 1907.

Mitchell, *Organized Labor*. Philadelphia, 1903.

Ogilvie, *Life and Speeches of William McKinley*. New York, 1896.

Olcott, *William McKinley*. 2 vols., Boston, 1916.

Peck, *Twenty Years of the Republic, 1885-1905*. New York, 1920.

Pierce, *Federal Usurpation*. New York, 1908.

Rastall, *The Labor History of the Cripple Creek District*. Madison, 1908.

Reinsch, *American Federal Government*. Boston, 1909.

Rhodes, *History of the United States from the Compromise of 1850*. 8 vols., New York, 1896-1919.

Roosevelt, *An Autobiography*. New York, 1921, (1913).

Roosevelt, *The New Nationalism*. New York, 1910.

Roy, *A History of the Coal Miners of the United States*. Columbus, 1907.

Shaw, *President Wilson's State Papers and Addresses.* New York. 1918.

Suffern, *Conciliation and Arbitration in the Coal Industry of America.* Boston, 1915.

Taft, *Ethics in Service.* New Haven, 1915.

Taft, *Present Day Problems.* New York, 1908.

Taft, *The Presidency.* New York, 1916.

Taft, *Presidential Addresses and State Papers.* New York, 1910.

Tumulty, *Woodrow Wilson as I Know Him.* New York, 1921.

Washburn, *Theodore Roosevelt.* Boston, 1916.

Watkins, *Labor Problems and Labor Administration in the United States during the World War.* Urbana, 1919.

West, *Federal Power: Its Growth and Necessity.* New York, 1918.

Who's Who. Chicago, 1910, 1911.

Wilson, *The New Freedom.* New York, 1914.

Wilson, *The President of the United States.* New York, 1916.

Woodburn and Moran, *The Citizen and the Republic.* New York, 1918.

Young, *The New American Government and Its Work.* New York, 1915.

GOVERNMENT DOCUMENTS

Adjutant General, Report of. 1921.

Activities of the War Department in the Field of Industrial Relations during the War, Report of. Washington, 1919.

Altgeld, John B., *Message of 1895.* Springfield.

Anthracite Coal Commission, Report to the President. Washington, 1903.

Appendix to the Report of the Attorney General, 1896. Correspondence in the Chicago Strike.

Attorney General, Report of. 1895.

Attorney General, Report of. 1920.

Board of Arbitration, Report of. Eastern Railways. Conductors and Trainmen. 3 vols., 1913.

Bisbee Deportations, Report on. President's Mediation Commission. Washington, 1918.

Board of Railroad Wages and Working Conditions, Report of. Washington, 1919.

Chief of Staff, Report of. 1921.

Coeur d'Alene Labor Troubles, Report of House Committee on Military Affairs. House Report 1999, 56th Cong., 1st Sess.

Coeur d Alene Labor Troubles, Statement by John L. Kennedy concerning. Senate Document 42, 56th Cong., 1st Sess.

Coeur d'Alene Labor Troubles, Statement by President of Western Federation of Miners concerning, Sen. Doc. 25, 56th Cong., 1st. Sess.

Colorado Coal Commission, Report of. Labor Difficulties in the Coal Fields of Colorado. House Doc. 859, 64th Cong., 1st Sess.

Colorado, Conditions in Coal Mines of. Testimony before Subcommittee of House Committee on Mines and Mining. Washington, 1914.

Colorado Strike Investigation, Report on. Subcommittee of House Committee on Mines and Mining. House Doc. 1630, 63rd Cong., 3rd Sess.

Commissioner of Mediation and Conciliation, Report of. 1914. House Document vol. 103, 63rd Congress, 3rd Sess.

Congressional Record.

Fisher, *Use of Federal Power in Railway Labor Disputes.* Bulletin 303, U. S. Bureau of Labor Statistics. Washington, 1922.

Hotchkiss and Seager, *History of the Shipbuilding Labor Adjustment Board, 1917-1919.* Bulletin 283, U. S. Bureau of Labor Statistics. Washington, 1921.

Industrial Commission, Report of. 1900-1902, 19 vols., Washington.

Internal Affairs of Pennsylvania, Report of the Secretary of. 1908.

Labor, Report of the Secretary of. 1914.

Labor, Report of the Secretary of. 1915.

Labor, Report of the Secretary of. 1918.

Labor, Report of the Secretary of. 1920.

Lauck, *Railway Labor Arbitrations.* Report of the U. S. Board of Mediation and Conciliation on the effects of arbitration proceedings upon rates of pay and working conditions of railroad employees. Washington, 1916, Sen. Doc. 493, 64th Cong., 1st Sess.

Merriam, *Report of Brigadier General H. C., on Miners' Riots in State of Idaho.* Sen. Doc. 24, 56th Cong., 1st Sess.

National War Labor Board. Bulletin 287, U. S. Bureau of Labor Statistics. Washington, 1921.

Neill, *Mediation and Arbitration of Railway Labor Disputes in the United States.* Bulletin 98, Bureau of Labor. Washington, 1912.

Palmer, *Labor Disturbances in Colorado, 1880-1904* Sen. Doc. 122, 58th Congress, 3rd Sess.

President's Mediation Commission, Report of. Jan. 9, 1918. Washington, 1918.

Railway Employees, Threatened Strike of. Hearings before Senate Committee on Interstate Commerce. Sen. Doc. 549, 64th Cong., 1st Sess.

Railways, Report of the Director General of. Washington, 1918.

Richardson, *Messages and Papers of the Presidents.* 10 vols., House Miscellaneous Documents, vol. 37, 53rd Cong., 2nd Sess.

Steel Industries, Investigation of Strike in. Report of the Senate Committee on Education and Labor. Sen. Rep. 289, 66th Congress, 1st Sess.

Steel Industries, Investigation of Strike in. Hearings before the Senate Committee on Education and Labor, Washington, 1919.

U. S. Anthracite Coal Commission, Report, Findings, and Award of. Washington, 1920.

U. S. Army Regulations. Revision of 1917.

U. S. Bituminous Coal Commission, Awards and Recommendations of. Washington, 1920.

U. S. Board of Mediation and Conciliation, Report of. 1913-1917, Washington, 1918.

U. S. Commission on Industrial Relations, Report of. 11 vols., Washington, 1916.

U. S. Fuel Administrator, Final Report of. 1917-1919, Washington, 1921.

U. S. Railway Labor Board, Decisions of. 2 vols., 1920, 1921.

U. S. Strike Commission, Report of. (Chicago Strike of 1894.) Sen. Exec. Doc. 7, vol. 2, 53rd Congress, 3rd Sess.

U. S. 8 Hour Commission, Report of. Washington, 1918.

War Department, General Orders of. Nov. 20, 1917.

War Department, Reports of. 1894, vol 1, House Exec. Doc. 53rd Cong., 2nd Sess.

War Department, Reports of. 1903, vol. 3.

War Department, Reports of. 1915, vol. 1.

War, Report of the Secretary of. 1920.

War, Report of the Secretary of. 1922.

West, *Report on the Colorado Strike for the U. S. Commission on Industrial Relations.* 1915.

West Virginia Coal Fields, Investigation of. Hearings before Senate Committee on Education and Labor, 67th Cong., 1st Sess., Washington, 1921.

West Virginia Coal Fields, Investigation of. Report of the Senate Committee on Education and Labor. Sen. Rep. 457, 67th Cong., 2nd Sess.

Wilson, *Federal Aid in Domestic Disturbances.* Sen. Doc. vol. 19, 67th Congress, 2nd Sess.

Wright, *Report to the President on the Anthracite Coal Strike.* June 20, 1902. Bulletin 43, U. S. Bureau of Labor, 1902.

PERIODICALS, INCLUDING SPECIFIC ARTICLES

Allen, *Injunction and Organized Labor. American Law Review*, vol. 28, p. 828.

American Federation of Labor, Weekly News Letter.

American Federationist.

Bing, *The Work of the Wage Adjustment Boards.* Journal of Political Economy, vol. 27, p. 421.

Chafee, *The Progress of the Law,* 1919-1920. Harvard Law Review, vol. 34, p. 401.

Coal Age.

Committee on Public Information, Official Bulletin.

Devine, *Winnipeg and Seattle.* Survey, vol. 43, p. 5.

Dunbar, *Government by Injunction.* Law Quarterly Review, vol. 13, p. 347.

Gadsby, *The Coal Strikes. Monthly Labor Review,* vol. 15, p. 931.

Gadsby, *The Strike of the Railroad Shopmen. Monthly Labor Review,* vol. 15, p 1171.

Gregory, *Government by Injunction. Harvard Law Review,* vol. 11, p. 487.

Groat, *The Injunction in Labor Disputes. Political Science Quarterly,* vol. 23, p. 408.

Hedrick, *The I.W.W. and Mayor Hanson. Unpartizan Review,* vol. 12, p. 35.

Hogaboom, *Trouble Between the Western Federation of Miners and Goldfield Mine Operators' Association. Overland,* vol. 51, p. 111.

Injunction in the Railway Strike. Yale Law Journal, vol. 32, p. 166.

Littlefield, *Use and Abuse of the Injunction in Trade Disputes. Annals of the American Academy of Political and Social Science,* vol. 36, p. 104.

Locomotive Engineers' Journal.

Love, *The Wreck on the B. R. & T. Survey,* vol. 44, p. 135.

MacDonald, *The Seattle Strike and Afterwards. Nation,* vol. 108, p. 469.

Machinists Monthly Journal.

Marshall, *A Missing Chapter in our War Labor Policy. Journal of Political Economy,* vol. 27, p. 397.

Marshall, *The War Labor Program and its Administration. Journal of Political Economy,* vol. 26, p. 425.

McMahon, *The Strike in Seattle. Survey,* vol. 41, p. 821.

Miners' Magazine.

Monthly Labor Review.

Nation, The.

Nelson, *Grover Cleveland. North American Review,* vol. 168, p. 161.

New Republic, The.

Outlook, The.

Pirnie, *Injunction: Coal Strike Enjoined as Violation of Lever Act. Cornell Law Quarterly,* vol. 5, p. 184.

Political Science Quarterly, Record of Political Events.

Railway Conductor, The.

Review of Reviews, The.

Soule, *Law and Necessity in Bisbee. Nation,* vol. 113, p. 225.

Soule, *The Railway Men Get Action. Nation,* vol. 110, p. 542.

Squires, *The Marine Workers' Affiliation of the Port of New York. Journal of Political Economy,* vol. 27, p. 840.

Squires, *New York Harbor Strike. Monthly Labor Review,* vol. 8, p. 330.

Squires, *New York Harbor Wage Adjustment. Monthly Labor Review,* vol. 7, p. 488.

Squires, *Readjustment of Wages and Working Conditions of New York Harbor Employees. Monthly Labor Review,* vol. 9, p. 475.

Stimson, *The Modern Use of Injunctions. Political Science Quarterly,* vol. 10, p. 189.

Stoddard, *The Bituminous Coal Strike. Monthly Labor Review,* vol. 9, p. 1725.

Survey, The.

United Mine Workers Journal.

Wehle, *Labor Problems in the United States during the War. Quarterly Journal of Economics,* vol. 32, p. 333.

Wehle, *War Labor Policies and their Outcome in Peace. Quarterly Journal of Economics,* vol. 33, p. 321.

Wellman, *The Award of the Anthracite Commission. Review of Reviews,* vol. 26, p. 552.

White, *Cleveland. McClure's Magazine,* vol. 18, p. 332.

INDEX

A

Act of 1888 (Arbitration), 26
Adamson Act, 113-116, 120-124, 258
Alger, Secretary of War, 41, 42
Altgeld, Governor, 21
American Federation of Labor, 126, 132, 138, 151, 162, 166, 190, 227
American Railway Union, 14, 15, 25
Ammons, Governor, 81-83, 87, 88, 93, 97
Anderson, Judge A. B., 182, 193, 217
Anti-trust Act of 1890, 17, 31, 52, 217, 235, 244
Anthracite Strike of 1902, 46-59; award, 55; demands of miners, 48; President's drastic plan, 58; strike commission, 54, 55
Anthracite Wage Dispute of 1920, 199-203

B

Baer, George F., 48
Baldwin-Felts detectives, 210, 211
Bandholtz, General, 211, 212, 213
Bisbee deportations, 126, 127
Bituminous Strike of 1919, 177-193; demands of miners, 177; injunction, 178, 182, 183, 190; offers of settlement, 184; President's statement of Oct. 24, 179; settlement plan, 185; troops, 185
Board of Railway Wages and Working Conditions, 155, 162, 265
Bowers, L. M., 80-84, 85
Bridgeport case, 146-148
Brotherhoods, Railway, 73, 74, 100, 103, 106, 110, 117, 131, 194, 232-234
Burleson, Postmaster General, 145
Butte miners' strike, 208

C

Carpenters' strike, Wartime, 134-137

Central Competitive Field, 183, 188, 206, 215, 216, 223
Chafee, Zechariah, 193
Chambers, Judge, 103
Chicago Yardmen's Association, 197
Cleveland, Grover, 21, 26, 28, 34, 58, 254
Coal strikes of 1906, 62-64
Coal strikes of 1922, 214-226; anthracite settlement, 224; bituminous settlement, 223; causes, 214-218; President's meetings with disputants, 219-221
Coeur d'Alene disturbance, 36-45; arrests, 38, 44; dynamiting, 37; holding prisoners, 41, 44; permit system, 39, 40, 44; troops, 38, 42, 43
Colorado Fuel & Iron Co., 70, 90, 95, 258
Colorado Strike of 1903-1904, 60-62
Colorado Strike of 1913-1914, 76-99; causes, 77, 78; House of Representatives investigating committee, 85; Ludlow massacre, 86, 87; mediation effort of Davies and Fairley, 93; mediation effort of Rep. Foster, 88, 89; mediation effort of E. M. Stewart, 79-81; mediation effort of President Wilson, 84-85; mediation effort of W. B. Wilson, 81-84; tentative basis of adjustment, 94, 96; troops, state, 81, 86; troops, federal, 88-92, 99
Colorado Strike Commission, 96-98
Columbian Exposition, 17
Compulsory arbitration, 266
Council of National Defense, 126, 137
Cuyler, T. De Witt, 227, 231

D

Daugherty, Attorney General, 220, 235, 238, 241, 242, 245, 246, 253

Davis, Secretary of Labor, 217-219, 224
Debs, Eugene V., 18, 24, 27
Denver street car strike, 208
Department of Justice, 176
Department of Labor, 79, 249, 263

E

Eastern Ohio coal strike, 105
Emergency Fleet Corporation, 132, 134
Erdman Act, 70, 73, 74, 263
Expediency, Principle of, 252

F

Federated Shop Crafts, 238, 239, 242
Fitzpatrick, John, 168, 170
Foster, Representative, 88, 89
Foster, W. Z., 166
Fuel Administration, 129

G

Garfield, H. A., 129, 184, 189
Garrison, Secretary of War, 90
Gary, E. H., 167-169, 176
General Managers Association, 15, 32
Gompers, Samuel, 126, 151, 166-170, 173, 191
Gregory, Attorney General, 192
Grunau, John, 197.

H

Hanna, Mark, 46, 48, 51
Harding, Warren G., 254, 263, 266, 268; coal strikes of 1922, 215, 217-226; railway shopmen's strike of 1922, 229, 231, 233, 234, 242-244, 252; threatened railway strike of 1921, 213, 214; West Virginia mine disturbances, 210, 212, 213
Hartford Valley Strike, 99
Herrin, 219
High cost of living, 154, 157, 159, 160
Hines, Director General of Railways, 155-157, 161, 165, 175, 194, 195
Hooper, Ben, 228, 231, 232
Hoover, Herbert, 232
Howatt, Alexander, 187
Hurley, Chairman of Shipping Board, 133, 134
Hutcheson, W. L., 134, 135

I

Illinois Bituminous Strike of 1920, 204-206
Industrial Commission, 40
Industrial Conference of 1919, 169, 173
Injunctions, 255, 256, 262; bituminous strike of 1919, 178, 182, 183, 190, 193; Pullman strike, 18, 32, 33; shopmen's strike of 1922, 235, 236, 239, 240, 244-246
Interchurch Commission on Inquiry, 172, 174
Interstate Commerce Commission, 107, 112, 234, 268, 273

J

Jewell, B. M., 157, 227, 231

K

Knapp, Judge, 72, 103

L

League of Nations Covenant, 175
Lewis, John L., 177, 186, 215, 216, 219, 223
Lever Act, 129, 178, 181, 182, 190, 191, 192, 198
Louisville and Nashville, 70-72

M

McAdoo, Wm. G., 132
McKinley, Wm., 40, 42, 45
Merriam, General, 38, 39-41
Milchrist, U. S. Attorney, 17
Miners' strike in Arizona, 59, 60
Miners' strike in Goldfield, 64-69
Miners' strike penalties, 129
Miners' war-time wages, 129
Mitchell, John, 47, 52, 63
Mooney case, 128
Morgan, Governor, 210
Morgan, J. Pierpont, 52, 53

N

Nagel, Charles, 103, 104
National Civic Federation, 49, 74
National Committee for Organizing Iron and Steel Workers, 166, 167, 170, 174
National Industrial Conference Board, 137, 138
National War Labor Board, 137-151, 152; Bridgeport case, 146-148; New York harbor strike, January, 1919, 150-151; prin-

ciples of, 140; proclamation creating, 139; record of, 141; Smith & Wesson case, 148-149; Western Union case, 142-145
Navy Department, 132
Neill, Commissioner, 72
New York Times, 189
Newlands Act, 74, 75, 101, 102, 263

O

Ogle, A. M., 219
Olney, Attorney General, 16, 17, 31
Ordnance Department, 146

P

Palmer, Attorney General, 178, 180, 182, 186, 189, 253
Peabody, Governor, 60, 61
President's Mediation Commission, 126-129
Public opinion, 248
Pullman Strike, 13-35, 248; attempted arbitration, 15, 25; boycott, 15; causes, 13; deputy marshals, 18, 30, 31; indictments, 24; injunction, 18; strike commission, 26; troops, 20-23; U. S. Supreme Court, 27

R

Railroad Administration, 165
Railroad Labor Board, 162, 195, 197, 198, 213, 214, 226-228, 231, 232, 234, 235, 243-245, 249, 265, 266, 269
Railroad Shopmen's Strike of 1919, 154-164
Railroad Shopmen's Strike of 1922, 226-247, 252; causes, 226, 227; injunction, 235; President's proposals, 231, 233; settlement, 239
Railroad Wage Commission, 132
Railway Employees' Department, A. F. of L., 227, 235
Railway labor disputes, War-time, 130
Railway labor troubles of 1920, 193-199
Railway Managers, National Conference Committee of, 106, 108
Rockefeller, John D., 88
Rockefeller, John D., Jr., 77, 79, 80, 81-85, 88-90
Roosevelt, Theodore, 248, 252, 257; anthracite strike, 50-56; coal

strikes of 1906, 62-64; Colorado strike of 1903-1904, 60-62; miners' strike in Arizona, 59, 60; miners' strike in Goldfield, 65-69; threatened railway wage reductions, 1908, 70-72
Root, Elihu, 42, 53, 60

S

Seattle General Strike, 208
Sinclair, State Auditor, 37, 38
Smith and Wesson case, 148-149
Sparks, Governor, 64-69
Steel Strike of 1919, 166-176, 259; demands of workers, 167; President's postponement request, 169; troops, 171, 172
Steunenberg, Governor, 37, 38, 42
Stewart, Ethelbert M., 79-81
Suggested adjustment machinery, 272-274
Suggested program of presidential activity, 259-262
Sympathetic railway strike in Southwest, 164-166

T

Taft, Wm. H., 72, 138, 143, 144, 253
Threatened Railway Strike of 1916, 106-124; counter proposals of managers, 111; demands of men, 106; mediation attempt by U. S. Board, 107; mediation of second dispute, 118; President's address to Congress, 113-115; President's proposal, 109
Threatened Railway Strike of 1921, 213, 214
Threatened Strike of Conductors and Trainmen, 1913, 73-76
Threatened Strike of Engineers and Firemen, 1914, 100-105
Transportation Act of 1920, 195, 228, 235, 244, 265, 268
Troops, 257, 261; bituminous strike of 1919, 185; coal strikes of 1922, 218, 222, 226; Coeur d'Alenes, 38, 42; Colorado strike of 1913-1914, 88-92, 99; laws concerning use of, 22, 43, 207; miners' strike in Arizona, 59, 60; miners' strike in Goldfield, 64-69; Pullman strike, 20-23; shopmen's strike of 1922, 230; steel strike of

1919, 171; war-time disputes, 207-209; West Virginia, 209, 210, 212

Tumulty, Secretary, 169, 186, 189

U

United Mine Workers of America, 46, 77, 97, 177, 178, 182, 183, 188, 204, 210, 213

U. S. Anthracite Coal Commission, 201

U. S. Bituminous Coal Commission, 187, 205

U. S. Board of Mediation and Conciliation, 100, 101, 103, 107, 130

U. S. Coal Commission, 225, 270, 272

U. S. Shipbuilding Labor Adjustment Board, 132-137

U. S. Shipping Board, 132

U. S. Supreme Court, 27, 117, 242

W

Walker, Edwin, 17, 20, 29, 31

Walsh, Frank P., 138, 143, 144

War Department, 146, 148, 149, 207, 210, 212, 230

War Labor Conference Board, 138, 139

War-time activities, 125-153

Weeks, Secretary of War, 212

Welborn, J. F., 91

West Virginia mine disturbances, 209, 210-213

Western Federation of Miners, 36, 40, 65, 69

Western Union case, 142-145

Wilkerson, Judge, 235, 239, 240, 242

Wilson, Wm. B., 81-84, 93, 105, 138, 145, 177-179, 184, 191, 199, 200, 203, 204, 253

Wilson, Woodrow, 225, 253, 254, 263; Adamson Act, 107, 108, 110-116, 118-124; anthracite wage dispute of 1920, 200-203; bituminous strike of 1919, 178, 179, 185, 187-189; Colorado strike of 1913-1914, 81, 84, 87, 90, 92, 93, 95, 96, 98; Illinois bituminous strike of 1920, 204, 205; railroad shopmen's strike of 1919, 156, 157, 159, 160, 161, 163, 164; railway labor troubles of 1920, 194-196, 198; steel strike of 1919, 168, 169, 174-176; sympathetic railway strike of 1919, 165; threatened strike of conductors and trainmen, 1913, 74-76; threatened strike of engineers and firemen, 1914, 101-103, 105; troops in war-time, 208; war-time activities, 126, 129, 130, 131, 133, 135-139, 142, 144, 147, 150, 151-153

Wood, General, 172

Wright, Carroll D., 26, 50, 52, 54